Angela Lindt
Law in Conflict

Social Movement and Protest | Volume 13

Angela Lindt (Dr.) is an associated researcher at the Institute of Social Anthropology, University of Bern in Switzerland, where she completed her PhD in 2020. Her research focuses on the judicialization of mining conflicts in Peru and on the use of law by transnational mining corporations, protest movements, and state actors.

Angela Lindt

Law in Conflict

The Judicialization of Mining Disputes in Peru

[transcript]

Dissertation submitted at the Faculty of Humanities at the University of Bern to obtain the degree of Doctor of Philosophy by Angela Lindt from Nidau, BE. Accepted by Prof. Dr. Julia Eckert and Prof. Dr. Stuart Kirsch on behalf of the Faculty of Humanities in Bern, 23.10.2020, Dean: Prof. Dr. Elena Mango.

The Open Access edition is published with the support of the Swiss National Science Foundation.

Bibliographic information published by the Deutsche Nationalbibliothek
The Deutsche Nationalbibliothek lists this publication in the Deutsche Nationalbibliografie; detailed bibliographic data are available in the Internet at https://dnb.dnb.de

First published in 2024 by transcript Verlag, Bielefeld

Cover layout: Maria Arndt, Bielefeld
Printed by: Majuskel Medienproduktion GmbH, Wetzlar
https://doi.org/10.14361/9783839469699
Print-ISBN: 978-3-8376-6969-5
PDF-ISBN: 978-3-8394-6969-9
ISSN of series: 2701-0473
eISSN of series: 2703-1667

Printed on permanent acid-free text paper.

To Rosita
and to all those who have shared
and who continue her struggle for
justice and human rights.

Contents

Acknowledgments

"You have data – we have friends."

In one of the first courses I attended as a doctoral student, a lively debate erupted between the political scientists and the social anthropologists present. Fully aware that this would trigger a controversy, political scientist Klaus Schlichte raised the accusation that social anthropology is "not based on a reliable database, but only on stories and narratives told by people in the field." Political sciences, by contrast, work with reliable, objective data, he claimed. Stuart Kirsch, one of the anthropologists participating in the discussion, just raised an eyebrow, smiled mildly and replied, "Well, Klaus, you may have data, but we have friends."

On the journey of writing this book, I made new friends; existing friendships were strengthened; and a whole series of old and new friends accompanied me along the way, for which I am very grateful. First of all, I would like to thank the lawyers and activists of the Peruvian human rights movement who have placed their trust in me, shared their stories with me, and thereby made this research possible. I would especially like to thank Rosita, Ingrid, and David, who opened the door to their daily work at *Fedepaz* and who gave me an insight into what it means to work for a human rights organization in Peru. Thank you for your friendship and for your great patience.

I would also like to thank from the bottom of my heart the *compañeros* and *compañeras* of the PIC in Celendín, whom I was able to accompany for several months. My special thanks go to Palujo, Milton, Homero, Ramiro, Clavitex, Leo, Ramón, and Livaque. In addition, I also thank all the other members of the grassroots movements, the *ronderos* and *ronderas*, NGO workers, activists, *campesinas*, and *campesinos* who form part of the social movements in the province of Celendín and in the Cajamarca region. These include, in particular, the group of *líderes* and *lideresas* from Sorochuco and Celendín, whom I was privileged to accompany for the duration of a trial and who shared their concerns and hopes with me. In Cajamarca, I am especially grateful to Paola, Karina, and Mirtha for making time to answer my questions. Furthermore, my deepest thanks go to Lucy and Homero, who offered me not only a place to stay, but an actual home in Celendín, and to Maruja, Coco, and María, who did the same in Lima.

In Lima, I owe a big thank you to all the lawyers and employees of the various NGOs who took the time for an interview or an informal talk with me. In this context, I would like to especially thank Mar, Juliana, Julio, Maritza, and Joel. They provided me not only with information but also with contacts and background reports, which was very helpful. In addition, I am also very grateful for the support I have received from various academics on site. In particular, I would like to thank Sergio Miguel Huarcaya and Carlos Quispe Dávila for the lively discussions we had and for the helpful advice I received from both of them. Finally, I would also like to thank my interview partners outside Peru, namely in the United States, the United Kingdom, and Germany.

This research was part of the project "Law in Protest: Transnational Struggles for Corporate Liability," which was funded by the Swiss National Science Foundation and initiated by Julia Eckert. I am deeply grateful to Julia for having accompanied me so closely on the path of this research. In addition, I also thank Stuart Kirsch for being my second supervisor and for all the helpful advice and feedback.

The writing process was long and, especially in the beginning, also quite nerve-wracking and exhausting. I was fortunate to be supported during this process by a writing group that included Andrea, Marion, Noah, and Roman. Our time in the seclusion of Calonico, Bratsch, and Prêles was incredibly important to me. Grazie mille!

Many thanks also to Danaé, Kiri, Rahel, and Sabrina and to Anna-Lena, Corinne, Johanna, and Laura for their feedback, their support, and our friendship. And finally, I thank Cumi, Zora, and Mats for being my source of energy and motivation.

Notes on names

This book is about emblematic court cases of human rights violations on the one hand and about social conflicts over transnational mining projects on the other. Both are processes that take place in the public space and that are often under the scrutiny of the media and the general public. The actors involved in these processes are thus heavily exposed; they either express themselves in public in order to make their own voices heard or are pushed by others into the spotlight without having wished to do so.

This also applies to the human rights lawyers, plaintiffs, and activists who have been involved in the mining conflicts and the resulting legal proceedings in Peru. For me as a researcher writing about the perceptions and positions of these actors, this means that in many cases it was not possible to anonymize my interlocutors. Many of them have become public figures as a result of the legal proceedings and social conflicts. In many cases, the names of the individuals concerned are only a Google search away, although some of them have made considerable efforts to keep a deep profile over the years.

Most of my interlocutors are aware of their public role and have therefore agreed that I may refer to them by name in this work. However, as I explain in detail in the text, both the social conflicts and the involvement in court cases pose a risk for the actors involved of being defamed, harassed, or publicly attacked. For security reasons and to protect their identities, I therefore also use pseudonyms for some of my interlocutors, especially for many ordinary members of the grassroots movements in the provinces.

Abbreviations

Coordinadora	*Coordinadora Nacional de Derechos Humanos*, National Coordinator for Human Rights
CLS	critical legal studies
CSR	corporate social responsibility
Fedepaz	*Fundación Ecuménica para el Desarrollo y la Paz*, Ecumenical Foundation for Development and Peace
Grufides	*Grupo de Formación e Intervención para el Desarrollo Sostenible*, Training and Intervention Group for Sustainable Development
IACHR	Inter-American Commission on Human Rights
IDL	*Instituto de Defensa Legal*, Legal Defense Institute
NGO	non-governmental organization
PIC	*Plataforma Interinstitucional Celendina*, Interinstitutional Platform from Celendín
PNP	*Policía Nacional del Perú*, Peru's National Police
TNC	transnational corporation

Introduction

Law and legality shape our everyday lives and our way of living together in society. Law is used to settle disputes, strengthen or weaken relationships, ascribe property rights, exercise power, define responsibilities, negotiate accountability, obtain justice, and order penalties and punishment. Whenever people come into contact with each other, law is often not far away. The use of law is a social practice and inherently important for the conduct of social relations.

At the same time, the law is also a means for collectives and social groups to carry out political struggles. In recent years, an increasing "*juridification* of social protests" (Eckert *et al.* 2012a, emphasis added) has occurred worldwide. Social movements invoke rights to justify their claims and enforce their demands. Therefore, law is not only a social practice, but also a discourse on the basis of which claims are made and power relations are questioned. Furthermore, courts have become an important arena for social conflicts in this context. This *judicialization* of social disputes is reflected in an increasing reliance on courts, lawsuits, and legal norms. The principles of legal liberalism play an important role in this context; reference is made to the fact that, by virtue of fundamental rights, everyone is equal before the law. The mechanisms of the law should guarantee this equality. Consequently, law is also said to serve marginalized groups to make their voices heard and to demand justice, thus being a counterhegemonic means for social change.

When I started doing research for this book, I traveled to Peru with the aim of analyzing processes of judicialization in the context of social conflicts. More specifically, I intended to examine the strategies of mobilizing the law *from below* by movements struggling against transnational mining projects. At the beginning of my fieldwork, I spent several weeks in Lima where I met lawyers working with national and international non-governmental organizations (NGOs). These lawyers were exactly in line with the theoretical framework I had read about before going to the field: They pursue the approach of strategic litigation, use criminal and constitutional complaints to discuss emblematic cases of human rights violations in courts, and rely on national legislation to ensure access to justice for people affected by human rights violations. They work with *campesinas* and *campesinos*, i.e. with peasants who lost access to land or water resources as a result of mining activities; they represent people in court who have been injured by state or private security forces during demonstrations against mining companies. In general, these lawyers provide legal assistance and access to the judicial system for marginalized groups. As one NGO lawyer put it, "We want to make the judicial system take responsibility." My expectations, which had arisen from engaging with literature on the juridification of social protests thus seemed to have been fulfilled.

However, after I left Lima and traveled to Cajamarca, a region in the country's Northern Highlands, and things immediately became more complex. Over the past twenty-five years, Cajamarca has become the scene of large-scale industrial mining. As a result, various social conflicts have broken out between parts of the local population and the mining companies operating in the area. I contacted a grassroots movement that formed part of the social movements against transnational mining projects and told them about my intentions to investigate the use of law as a strategic means for social movements. During the first meeting I had with representatives of the group to present my research project, the activists only smiled mildly. One of them expressed what everyone in the room was thinking and said, "I think the answer to your research question is very simple from our point of view. Judges and prosecutors in Peru are all corrupt and are on the side of the companies. If we, from the social movement, file a complaint, it is immediately dismissed. At the same time, we are criminalized by the state for our activities and commitment." Thus, the group of activists completely disagreed with the human rights lawyers I had met in Lima. "The law is on the side of the powerful," the activists told me, "not on the side of marginalized groups." At the same time, however, this grassroots organization, as many other protest movements in Peru's mining regions, was closely collaborating with national and international NGOs that pursue the approaches of strategic litigation and legal mobilization, among them the lawyers from Lima mentioned above. The group's attitude toward the use of the law was therefore not as clear-cut as the activists argued. Moreover, this example revealed the ambiguity of law and legality.

It is precisely these encounters with different positions toward the law and the patterns of law's ambiguity that I examine in this book. My research starts with the observation in the field of what activists and lawyers involved in Peru's human rights movement experience when they engage in debates about whether law serves as an instrument of counterhegemony or whether it is rather a hegemonic instrument used by elites to prevent social change.

An ethnography of Peru's judicialized mining conflicts

This book traces the process of juridification and the "patterns of judicialization" (Sieder *et al.* 2005, 11) of Peru's mining conflicts. By analyzing how social conflicts over transnational mining projects in Peru are dealt with in the legal field, it examines the functioning of law as a social process. In doing so, I aim to trace the social life of the law in Peru's mining conflicts.

Empirically, I focus on two social conflicts that emerged from large-scale mining projects in Peru's Northern Highlands: the Conga conflict in Cajamarca and the Río Blanco conflict in Piura. The mining projects that led to these conflicts were both initiated by transnational corporations (TNCs) and received much support from the Peruvian national government. A large part of the population in the two affected regions, however, fears the mines' negative impacts on the environment, on the water supply, on local agriculture, and on people's health. As a result, parts of the local population have opposed the projects and organized protests against the corporations' plans to build the mines. In both cases, these local protests led to the suspension of the projects; neither the Río Blanco nor the Conga mine could be built. At the same time, the social conflicts were marked by severe human rights violations. During the protests, several people were injured, and some were killed by state security forces.

This volume examines how the two social conflicts were dealt with by the Peruvian judicial system and beyond. I examine how the various parties in the conflict approached the judicial system to enforce their interests. To this end, I analyze a number of court cases that arose from the mining conflicts in Cajamarca and in Piura. On the one hand, local social movements have attempted to bring legal actions against those responsible for human rights violations, i.e. against state security forces and against the corporations and their employees. I examine how activists and human rights NGOs make (strategic) use of the existing legal system in order to gain access to justice. Since both social conflicts involve the participation of foreign corporations, the question of the involved TNCs' responsibility plays a significant role in this part of my analysis.

On the other hand, however, state and corporate actors also use the judicial system to impede social protests and to enforce their economic interests. They sought to criminalize the members of the social movements for their involvement in the protests. In consequence, law and legal processes do not only serve the social movements as an instrument for resistance, but also pose a threat to them. The courtrooms in Piura and Cajamarca have become important battlegrounds for mining disputes – a process I call the *judicialization of social conflicts*.

Conceptually, I rely on two different theoretical approaches: the juridification and judicialization of politics, on the one hand, and anthropological debates on law as a social process, on the other hand. The *judicialization of social conflicts* is not only a judicialization of politics and of conflicts which were earlier dealt with in the field of politics and which are now brought to courts. Rather, the judicialization of social conflicts also includes the "judicialization of social relations" (O'Donnell 2005, 293) and thus goes beyond judicial processes in courts. Therefore, I am not only investigating how these social conflicts are negotiated in court, but I am also interested in how these court cases come about, what prevents them, what underlying negotiation processes they involve, and what effects and consequences they entail. It is thus the social life of law that I am concerned with. Thereby, my research also includes the process of judicialization "beyond the courtroom" (Rodríguez-Garavito 2011a) and incorporates everyday disputes and non-judicial aspects of Peru's mining conflicts. In this sense, I follow Huneeus *et al.*, who wrote that "law is created and lived not just in the court and through litigation, but beyond, in the conversations of lawyers and their clients, in social movements, in academia, and in everyday life" (2010, 14). I am interested in how the judicialization of social conflicts shapes the involved actors' perception of the "force of law" (Bourdieu 1987).

As Felstiner *et al.* argued, "disputes are not things: they are social constructs" (1980, 631). Consequently, studying "the emergence and transformation of disputes means studying a social process as it occurs" (*ibid.*, 632). Starting from this approach, the book examines the social processes that are initiated when conflicts emerge between transnational mining companies, state actors, and social movements and which are transformed when these conflicts are carried out in the legal sphere. This book asks what people gain on their journeys to the courts and what they lose, leading to the question of whether law and legal processes may serve as an emancipatory means for groups that are otherwise politically, economically, and socially marginalized in a society. More broadly, this contribution analyzes what conclusions we can draw from the observation of the judicialization of social conflicts in Peru's mining regions with regard to the functioning of law as a social process.

Judicialization of politics and the ambiguity of law

From a theoretical point of view, I follow Sieder *et al.*, who wrote that "[i]n analyzing processes of legal mobilization and judicialization, we need to distinguish between *process* and *outcomes*" (2005, 16, emphasis in original). This book's focus is therefore on both the actual processes and the consequences of these processes when mining conflicts are dealt with in the legal sphere. To analyze these different aspects, I rely on two theoretical approaches, which are, however, closely linked.

In studying the law's *processes,* I mainly rely on legal anthropological approaches dealing with, what I call, the "ambiguity of law." With this approach, I follow the observation that law has both a hegemonic and a counterhegemonic character. Legal anthropological research has traditionally been less interested in the judicial outcomes of specific lawsuits, thus in the judgments given by the courts, but has rather focused on the processes induced or shaped by the juridification in general – whether these are social, political, or legal processes and whether they take place in only the courtrooms or also beyond. Legal anthropologists analyze the use of law as a social process to settle disputes, to attribute responsibility, and to negotiate social relations. Law holds a central role in the organization of societies, and consequently, the use of law should, from a legal anthropological point of view, be examined in the context of the prevailing social conditions. The book's analysis is based on this theoretical background.

However, as mentioned above, the *juridification*, and moreover the *judicialization* of social conflicts not only induces legal, political, and social *processes*, but also leads to very specific *outcomes*, i.e. social consequences for the actors involved, and also to legal outcomes such as judgments or judicial orders. It is not sufficient to examine only the social processes that accompany legal mobilization, but that an analysis of what happens in the specific lawsuits is also of fundamental importance. We must understand how law is applied, utilized, and implemented in the particular lawsuits and how different forms and bodies of law actually work. In this sense, I wish to go beyond the anthropological approach, which often lacks an analysis of what is actually done and achieved in litigation. Rather, I base this part of my analysis on the theoretical considerations of political scientists and legal scholars who worked on legal mobilization. As an important complement to the legal anthropological analysis, this approach helps provide an understanding of the ambiguous forces of law by focusing on the mechanisms and instruments it entails.

Law's ambiguity

Since the discipline's very beginning, social anthropology has been closely linked to the research of law and legality.[1] The study of law was as much an integral part of early social anthropological research as the study of religion, exchange relations, and social organization. In the first decades of the twentieth century, the sub-discipline of legal anthropology, which emerged from early social anthropologists' generalist research, focused primarily on comparative studies analyzing the differences between "ordinary" Western law and so-called "customary" or "traditional" law in the (former) colonies. After the discipline's "reflexive turn" (Conley and O'Barr 1993, 48) in the second half of the twentieth century, legal anthropological studies became involved in the analysis of power relations related to law. Contemporary legal anthropology was shaped by the increased importance of rights discourse, which manifests, in the great amount of ethnographic research on justice, resistance, and legal activism, as a form of political action in the current world order (Goodale 2017, 117).

In this context, law's ambiguity or the "Janus-faced" (Nader 2002, 207, Comaroff 2012, ix) character of law became a central issue in legal anthropological research. The ambiguity of law is manifested in the ambivalence that law serves, on the one hand, as a hegemonic instrument favoring the interests of elites and, on the other

1 For a historical overview of the development of legal anthropology and the anthropology of law, see, for example, Poole (2001), Nader (2002), Sieder (2010a), or Goodale (2017).

hand, as a potentially emancipatory mechanism for marginalized groups to strive for social change. Sally Engle Merry wrote that "law contains both elements of domination and the seeds of resistance" (Merry 1990, 8). Elsewhere, she claimed that "[l]aw empowers powerful groups to construct normative orders that enhance their control over resources and people, but also provides to less privileged people avenues for protest and resistance" (2006a, 109). In a similar manner, Mark Goodale described law's ambiguity by referring to "law-as-regulation" and "law-as-agency" (2017, 118), a contradiction which he explained with the paradox "that sets the outer limits to exclusion (but also to inclusion), inequality (but also equality), and injustice (but also justice)" (*ibid.*, 138). In the words of Laura Nader, law "may serve those who contest power as well as those who wield power" (2002, 207), and Susan F. Hirsch and Mindie Lazarus-Black wrote that "law is simultaneously a maker of hegemony and a means of resistance" (2012, 9). With regard to the situation in Peru, finally, Deborah Poole (2004) characterized the judicial system as both a "threat" and a "guarantee" for people living at the margin of the state.

Thus, while a certain consensus has been established within the discipline regarding this ambiguity or the Janus-faced character of law, two different currents emerged within legal anthropology, each of which focuses on one of the two specific characteristics of law. Stuart Kirsch (2018, 16–7, 229) summarized this as the debate between *hegemony* and *counterhegemony* theorists. As I outline in the following, these two theoretical positions do not necessarily have to be in opposition to each other, but should rather be seen as complementary, since they describe different forms of legal mobilization. Both approaches describe how positions of power, social norms, and aspirations for change are negotiated in the contested field of law. When considered in combination, these two positions provide a useful theoretical framework for examining the *processes* induced by the judicialization of social conflicts in Peru.

Law, lawfares, and hegemony

There is a large body of literature from the field of anthropology and beyond on how political or economic elites use law as a hegemonic instrument in order to maintain existing power relations or to silence those who speak up. The discourse of so-called *hegemony theorists* has been especially shaped by the work of Jean and John L. Comaroff, who coined the debate with terms such as "fetishism of constitutionality" (2006, 24), "fetishism of the law" (2006, 25, 2007, 134), "culture of legality" (2009, 33, 2012, 78), and "lawfare"[2] (2006, 30, 2009, 36–7). Based on research in the "postcolonies" in southern Africa, but also on examples from U.S. courts and politics, they

2 For a more detailed discussion and conceptualization of the term "lawfare" beyond the term's use by the Comaroffs see the work by political scientist Siri Gloppen (see, for example: Gloppen 2018).

criticize the increasing use of law and claim that because of the judicialization of politics, "litigation has become an autonomic reflex of political life" (2012, 34). According to the Comaroffs, this has not led to an empowerment of marginalized groups, but has rather served the interests of elites and thus consolidated existing power relations.

The spread of law-oriented NGOs and "the planetary explosion of human rights advocacy" (2009, 34) have, in the Comaroffs' view, contributed to the fact that former political conflicts are now being fought out in the legal sphere. They criticized this development since the turn to law has, in their opinion, led to a depoliticization of conflicts. They acknowledged the efforts of the "little people" (2012, 150) to gain access through litigation to justice, or at least to reparation, but at the same time, they stressed that these struggles cannot be successful because "ultimately, it is neither the weak nor the meek nor the marginal who predominate in such things. It is those equipped to play most potently inside the dialectic of law and disorder" (2006, 31). Thus, according to the Comaroffs, the "'haves' come out ahead" in lawfare, to use Marc Galanter's (1974) phrasing, because elites have the knowledge and the resources to resort to the law as a political instrument and to implement and enforce legal mechanisms in their interests. Thus, in lawfare it is the powerful who can maintain their hegemony through law.

This criticism of the law's hegemonic tendency has a longer tradition. As a movement bringing together left-wing legal theorists and other scholars, Critical Legal Studies (CLS) criticized the hegemonic character of law since the late seventies (see, for example: Trubek 1984, Hunt 1986, Fitzpatrick and Hunt 1987, for a detailed overview on CLS see Kelman 1987). The CLS movement emerged from approaches inspired by Marxism and critical social theory as well as post-structuralism and Foucault's and Derrida's concepts of deconstruction (Fitzpatrick and Hunt 1987, 2, Merino 2017, 240). Its representatives saw themselves as a counter to the liberal ideology that dominated the field of legal studies at the time. Diverse views were represented in the movement, but CLS scholars shared the "rejection of the dominant tradition of Anglo-American legal scholarship, the expository orthodoxy or, more crudely, the 'black-letter law' tradition" (Fitzpatrick and Hunt 1987, 1). With the aim of developing radical alternatives to existing legal education and legal doctrine, CLS theorists examined the practices of legal institutions and explored how these support a "pervasive system" characterized by "oppressive, inegalitarian relations" (Fitzpatrick and Hunt 1987, 1–2). They called for new approaches to overcome the hegemonic character of law, which gave rise to approaches such as the *critical race theory* and *critical legal feminism* (Merino 2017, 241).

Conceptually, CLS scholars criticized the "indeterminacy" of law, which in their view enables legal practitioners, such as judges, in particular, to apply the law in the interests of elites (Kress 1989, 286). According to this approach, the indeterminacy of law calls into question the legitimacy of adjudication. It is this concept that has continued to receive much support, even after the CLS movement lost importance in the late nineties. In more recent years, the criticism of law's indeterminacy was again raised by Marxist theorists, such as China Miéville (2005), for example, who focused on the, in his view, limited emancipatory character of international law. Miéville observed that "[f]or every claim there is a counter-claim" (*ibid.*, 281) in international law. Based on Karl Marx' phrase that "between equal rights, force decides," he concluded that its indeterminacy impedes law of contributing to progressive change (*ibid.*, 8). Miéville ends his book with the pessimistic conclusion that "[t]he chaotic and bloody world around us *is the rule of law*" (*ibid.*, 319, emphasis in original), meaning that international law is a fundamental part of imperialist domination (see also: Marks 2007, 204). He argued for "eradicat[ing] the legal forms" and demanded a "fundamental reformulation of the political-economic system of which they are expressions" (Miéville 2005, 318).

Compared with other theorists, Miéville is undeniably radical in his argument to "eradicate the legal forms." Some aspects of his criticism, however, have been shared by others and are relevant for my research. From the turn of the millennium onward, several authors have criticized the hegemonic character of law emerging from its connection with neoliberalism. In the view of political scientist Wendy Brown (2015), for example, the use of law and legal reasoning are part of neoliberal governance practices that allow for the control and the regulation of specific groups of a society (see also: Foucault 2004). According to this approach, the rule of law is a fundamental precondition of neoliberalism. The link between the spread of neoliberalism and the juridification of politics was also stressed by the Comaroffs who saw in the "growing salience of the law [...] an integral feature of the neoliberal moment" (2012, 88). In addition, Suzana Sawyer wrote that "law, legal rhetoric, and abstract liberal principles have often been the trump card of a privileged elite" (2004, 188). Her research on Ecuador revealed how the use of the existing legal framework and the enactment of new laws foster the hegemony of elitist interests, especially in the context of the extractive industries (*ibid.*, 14). In a similar way, legal scholar Ugo Mattei and anthropologist Laura Nader (2008) claimed that the "rule of law" is an imperial instrument to be used for the "plunder" of natural resources in the Global South. These considerations are particularly relevant to my research because Peru's national government has pursued a strict neoliberal policy, especially in the extractive industries, since the early nineties. Thus, these reflections on law and neoliberalism are crucial in understanding Peru's mining conflicts.

In addition, some legal scholars examined the way in which law is beneficial for "those who have," be it corporations or other economic elites. Katharina Pistor, for instance, analyzed how "law helps create both wealth and inequality" (2019, 3). In her book "Code of Capital," she described how law, in the form of property rights, but also bankruptcy law, for example, benefits the holders of capital assets (Pistor 2019). Pistor examined how capital holders influence legislators through lobbying and other forms of interference so that they enact laws that protect property. In this sense, she demonstrated how the law serves capital in a very direct way.

In view of this range of different research approaches and theoretical concepts, it is evident that the category of hegemony theorists is only a loose classification. What all these authors' approaches have in common, though, is that they perceive law as an elitist means of preserving existing power relations and maintaining the domination of subordinate population groups. The term "hegemony," as coined by Antonio Gramsci (1992), is particularly suitable in these debates for describing law as an instrument of elitist – be it political or economic – actors. Gramsci understood hegemony as the "predominance obtained by consent rather than force of one class or group over other classes" (Femia 1975, 31). In this sense, hegemony is not a "rule by force," but a "rule by consent" (Im 1991, 127), which builds on the "production, reproduction, and mobilization of popular consent" (Hunt 1990, 311) of a society's masses. Thus, hegemony is not necessarily forced upon the subordinate classes, but they themselves – directly or indirectly – reproduce it, since it forms part of a society's prevailing discourses and power relations. The elites' hegemony permeates all fields of society, including the legal field, and law thus contributes to the consolidation of domination. These are precisely the theoretical considerations of hegemony theorists that are relevant to the discussions in this book.

Counterhegemonic struggles and the emancipatory force of law

The theoretical claim that law and legal processes serve as hegemonic means of elites is thus a powerful claim, which has had a considerable impact on legal anthropology and beyond. In recent years, however, the hegemony theorists' approach has been increasingly questioned. Empirical research, notably by anthropologists and often conducted in the context of the global "human rights revolution" (Goodale 2017, 101), has given rise to these debates. *Counterhegemony theorists* studied the emergence of new rights discourses, especially among marginalized or subordinated groups, such as women's, peasants,' and indigenous peoples' movements in the Global South, that "recognized" that "the law is not omnipresent" (Ewick and Silbey 1998, 196).

Counterhegemony theorists' research has demonstrated that legal mobilization by organized and well-connected movements may lead to social change and that the hegemony of political and economic elites can thus be challenged through the use of law "from below" (Sieder *et al.* 2005, 5). Boaventura de Sousa Santos and César Rodríguez-Garavito (2005) speak in this context of "counter-hegemonic movements," which represent a counterweight to the neoliberal globalization driven by business actors. They observed an increasing tendency, particularly in Latin America, of social movements to make strategic use of national law (see: Santos 2002, 2005, Rodríguez-Garavito 2005, 2011a). These movements attempt to use precedents in court to demand rights that benefit not only the people directly affected but also broader population groups. Regarding the development of the counterhegemony theorists' approach, we can observe that there was a temporal correlation with the new rights discourses, which marked the beginning of a global human rights revolution after the end of the Cold War (Moyn 2010, 4, 213, Goodale 2017, 181, Merry 2017, x).

In contrast to the Comaroffs' criticism against "lawfares," the mobilization of law is positively connoted by counterhegemony authors. They claim that the strategy of using law and legality may lead to the empowerment of marginalized groups. In this context, the "right to have rights," as described by Hannah Arendt (1998 [1951], 614), plays an essential role (see also: Dagnino 2003, 213). Social movements and activists claim to have rights and actively demand these rights before courts, and this often leads to the judicialization of their struggles. According to Rodríguez-Garavito (2011b, 273), it is in "law's intrinsic procedural nature" to offer a "lingua franca" that allows for contact and negotiation between otherwise radically different ideas and perceptions, for example, between protest movements and state institutions. The law is thus ascribed an ordering power that provides the mechanisms for resolving disputes but also for formulating demands and for making political claims. Whereas the hegemony theorists claim that the turn to law silences the marginalized, counterhegemony theorists, on the contrary, claim that law provides these groups both with a channel to express their demands and with a language to formulate these claims.

To make their voices heard, however, the movements do not only resort to legal mechanisms. For many counterhegemony theorists, transnational networks play a key role in successful judicial activism from below. Santos described these transnational attempts to use legal means from below as "subaltern cosmopolitan legality" (2005, 54); Manuel Castells wrote about a "global social movement for global justice" (2005, 13); Kate Nash (2012) called them "subaltern cosmopolitans;" and Rodríguez-Garavito (2005) used the term "transnational advocacy networks," a concept which was originally coined by Margaret Elizabeth Keck and Kathryn Sikkink (1998). Thus, the recipe for success of judicial activism from below seems to lie in organizing people, whenever possible, on a transnational scale. According to many counterhegemony theorists, international NGOs play a major role in building transnational advocacy networks and in organizing activists beyond borders (Fortun 2001, 51, Castells 2005, 13, Rodríguez-Garavito 2005, 66, Kirsch 2006, 17, 2007, 2016, Nash 2012, 801). These networks help establish the flow of information between actors in different world regions, and they contribute to the transnational sharing of values and the creation of common discourses (Keck and Sikkink 1998, 2). The neoliberal globalization of corporations and political elites is, in this sense, opposed by a "counter-hegemonic globalization" (Santos 2002, 458–9, 2005, Rodríguez-Garavito and Arenas 2005, 242).

In a Gramscian sense, it is thus a matter of changing the discourses in the globalized world society. Counterhegemonic power becomes effective only through the emergence of such a counter public. This counter public introduces new discourses into international law or into domestic law in different world regions. Only when these discourses of a new "legalism from below" (Eckert 2006, 46) are established can the law become "emancipatory" (Santos 2002, 495, Nash 2012, 83–804). In this sense, the law becomes a "weapon of the weak" (Scott 1985). In her research on legal activism in Bombay's slums, Julia Eckert (2006, 2012, 152) described how ordinary citizens turn to courts to address their demands and to require a response of government institutions and state officials. Although the success of this judicial activism in individual cases may be small or only symbolic, these successes nevertheless "add up to a more profound transformation" and change "the ideas about the relation between citizen and the state" (Eckert 2006, 61–2). As Eckert concluded, the use of law enables marginalized groups to challenge elites and, in some instances, leads not only to normative but also social change (*ibid.*, 71). In this sense, her research also calls into question the hegemony theorists' concerns that the juridification of politics leads to a depoliticization of conflicts, because it, in turn, provides a powerful basis for making political demands.

In addition, counterhegemony theorists have also engaged in the debate on law's indeterminacy. In direct response to hegemony theorist Miéville's work, Susan Marks held that international law is not indeterminate per se and that the "emancipatory force" of international law is "not fixed, but context-dependent" (2007, 199). She argued that "[i]f force decides, it does not do so always and ever in the same way" (*ibid.*, 208), and thus, there is hope for people who mobilize law from below. Marks' observation that the emancipatory force of (international) law depends on the particular context may not come as a surprise for anthropologists. It underlines the importance of empirical studies on the ground which look at how law works in practice. In this way, we can assess the extent to which forces prevail and become effective in legal processes.

Context dependence also holds a decisive role for other counterhegemony theorists in assessing the emancipatory force of law. Many of them have also addressed the risks of judicial activism and of unforeseen processes that can be triggered by the mobilization of law. They have acknowledged that court cases tend to "individualize" social conflicts and that there is a risk of exposing individuals, leading to a possible demobilizing effect on social movements (Santos 2005, 50, Kirsch 2018, 38). Following this consideration, the strategy of legal mobilization prioritizes a specific form of knowledge, although social movements do not always have this legal expertise (Santos 2005, 56). Thus, a critical attitude toward law and its mechanisms is also an important part of counterhegemony theorists' considerations.

In addition, counterhegemony theorists stress law's ambiguous character. Kirsch, for example, observed how "indigenous peoples must present their claims in legal systems historically used to facilitate their dispossession" (2018, 16). International law has provided specific rights to indigenous peoples for some years.

At the same time, indigenous groups are often especially affected by large-scale development projects, such as dams, mines, or other extractive activities. In most cases, these activities are only made possible through (neoliberal) legislation and the hegemony of economic actors, such as TNCs, which has been consolidated by law. Bilateral or multilateral trade agreements facilitating such projects, for example, are an integral part of international law. Therefore, this kind of global legal pluralism again enhances the ambiguity of law as it provides the basis for resistance from below but also for maintaining dominant power relations.

In this context, Rachel Sieder described how the increasing role of international law concerning indigenous peoples has led to a "new rights consciousness" (2010b, 171), for example, among Mayan activists in Guatemala, who are, at the same time, affected by multilateral development projects. Sieder consequently wrote that although law "continues to be one of the principal tools of neo colonial power" under the current world order, the juridification processes "signal the counterhegemonic use of law" (*ibid.*, 178). This links back to the fact that most legal anthropologists have stressed the ambiguity of law – that is, the character of law to be *both* a hegemonic and a counterhegemonic instrument.

Legal mobilization and rights revolutions

This book examines specific lawsuits that were brought to court in the context of two mining conflicts in Peru. Accordingly, as mentioned above, I do not only examine the *juridification* of social conflicts – that is, actors invoking rights and legal discourses in disputes (Sieder 2010b, 162). Rather, I examine the *judicialization* of Peru's conflicts – that is, the strategy of litigation and of using courts as a "stage" for struggles over mining projects (Huneeus *et al.* 2010, 3). Court proceedings, litigation, and further activities taking place in law firms, offices of legal NGOs, and courtrooms are an important subject in this research. As outlined above, I examine not only the *processes* but also the lawsuits' *outcomes* and rely on the literature of the judicialization of politics in this part of my analysis.

More specifically, I follow Catalina Smulovitz's (2010, 235) definitional approach, which distinguishes between two different but interrelated aspects of the judicialization of politics. On the one hand, there is the core aspect of the judicialization of politics in the sense that courts – usually supreme or constitutional courts – decide on legal norms created by parliaments or governments and examine the potential unconstitutionality of a legal text. The courts thus pass a legal judgment on a norm created by political processes. This process of judicialization of politics can be initiated by the courts themselves, but often it is backed up by civil society organizations that file lawsuits in order to obtain a decision by a court on a socially or politically controversial legal norm. In the United States, these attempts were framed as a possible "Rights Revolution" (Rosenberg 1991, McCann 1994, Epp 1998); in Latin America they were discussed in relation to the concept of a "new constitutionalism" of social and economic rights (Brinks and Gauri 2014, Brinks *et al.* 2015).

In many Latin American countries, the institutional mechanism of constitutional complaints or injunctions (so-called *amparo* or *tutela* processes) assume a central role in this context. Such constitutional complaints deal with the violation of fundamental rights by private actors or by state officials or institutions (Smulovitz 2010, 242–3). This form of legal mobilization has been extensively discussed in relation to Latin America, for example, in Costa Rica by Bruce M. Wilson (2005), in Mexico by Pilar Domingo (2005), in Argentina by Smulovitz (2005, 2006, 2010), and in Colombia by Rodríguez-Garavito (2011a, 2013, 2019).

The second aspect of judicialization of politics, as described by Smulovitz, encompasses a much broader framework, which includes the development that politicians, state agents, (organized or loosely affiliated) social groups, and ordinary citizens increasingly turn to courts to resolve conflicts that were previously carried out either in private or political spheres but not in the judicial sphere (see also: Huneeus *et al.* 2010, 8). These court cases go beyond the use of constitutional law and also include civil and criminal proceedings. The purpose behind the lawsuits, however, remains the same: By bringing emblematic cases to court, the aim is to obtain a judgment that has a broader impact on the political and social circumstances that led to the violation of rights. A judgment should then not only benefit the plaintiffs directly involved but also other persons affected by the same rights violation. Such cases are often referred to under the concept of strategic litigation.

Various legal scholars and political scientists have examined the conditions under which these types of legal mobilization from below can lead to social change. As early as the seventies, legal scholar Mark Galanter (1974) explained "why the 'haves' come out ahead" in courts. He described the conditions that give the powerful an advantage in litigation and that limit "the possibilities of using the [legal] system as a means of redistributive (that is, systemically equalizing) change" (*ibid.*, 95). Galanter's finding was that the "haves" are much more experienced at using legal means because they are "repeat players" (*ibid.*, 97–8). This confers an advantage since they "develop expertise," have "access to specialists," and know the rules of the game and the processes of law in depth (*ibid.*, 98). Ordinary citizens or the so-called "have-nots," on the other hand, are, in his terminology, "one-shotters," since they often only come into contact with the legal system once (*ibid.*, 103). They lack experience in the legal field and depend heavily on lawyers who represent them. Lawyers, for their part, are repeat players who engage in litigation on a regular basis (*ibid.*, 114). According to Galanter, litigation has "a flavor of equality." By referring to the principle of being "equal before the law," he reminds us that "the rules of the game do not permit [actors] to deploy all of their resources in the conflict, but require that they proceed within the limiting forms of the trial" (*ibid.*, 135). In principle, therefore, the conditions are given to transform legal mobilization into a redistribution process. To utilize these conditions, however, institutional barriers for accessing the legal system must be reduced, and "one-shotters" need to organize themselves. In this way, Galanter concluded, the chances for social change through litigation may increase (*ibid.*, 150).

Galanter's contribution was later taken up by various authors discussing the notion of the *legal opportunity structure* for legal mobilization. To change the legal opportunity structure means, in the view of these authors, not only guaranteeing access to the legal system, but also strengthening the bargaining power of plaintiffs who would otherwise be in a rather powerless position (Brinks *et al.* 2015, 295, Gloppen 2018). According to Charles Epp (1998, 17–20), social organization, the support of "willing and able lawyers," the existence of "rights consciousness" among plaintiffs, sufficient material support and resources – often provided by rights-advocacy organizations – and a favorable legal framework are the basic prerequisites for successful legal mobilization. In addition, Siri Gloppen (2018) wrote that it is not enough to strengthen the position of the plaintiffs but that it is also necessary to change the political, legal, and normative opportunity structure of other actors involved, such as judges, for example, who decide on a particular case. She pointed out that litigation is multi-sited, dynamic, and highly political, which requires a diversified strategy (Gloppen 2018, 26). Since lawsuits are, as she demonstrated in her research, political struggles, it is a matter of changing the underlying discourses. This notion reminds us of the discussions of counterhegemony theorists and their claim to challenge legal discourses as implemented from above.

Peru's mining conflicts as a research field

The research field from which this book emerged has been shaped by two different but complementary dimensions: On the one hand, the investigated social conflicts and the resulting court cases are clearly determined by national circumstances. I examine how *domestic* law is applied by *local* actors within Peru in order to address human rights violations that have occurred *locally* and to bring about social change at the *national* level. Peru's political, historical, and social background marked the field in which this research was developed and thereby contributed to the particularity of the case study.

On the other hand, the field of judicialized social conflicts in Peru is also strongly influenced by transnational developments, discourses, and relations. I am investigating attempts to hold *transnational* mining companies liable. These corporations are – from a legal perspective – Peruvian companies, but at the same time, they are also subsidiaries of TNCs based in China and the United States. Thus, they are also part of *globally* operating corporations. From a local perspective they are often referred to as "foreign companies." In addition, the NGOs and social movements I worked with cooperate with *international* legal NGOs and form part of *transnational* advocacy networks. In their struggles against human rights violations, activists travel abroad to make their voices heard. They rely on *international* human rights norms and address *supranational* bodies such as the Inter-American Commission on Human Rights (IACHR), or even bring legal claims to foreign courts to hold the involved TNCs responsible. All this suggests that not only the TNCs' operations but also the social movements' struggles are thoroughly shaped by a transnational dimension. The research field is thus strongly influenced by the binaries between the national and the transnational, the local and the global, the domestic and the foreign. I outline these binaries in the following to provide insight into the research field.

The local dimension: a mining country

According to its Ministry of Energy and Mines, Peru is "*un país minero lleno de oportunidades*" (MINEM 2020), "a mining country full of opportunities." Since the former autocratic president Alberto Fujimori set the national economy on a tightly neoliberal course in the early nineties, the country has become one of the world's most important exporters of mining products such as copper, gold, zinc, and silver.[3] A large proportion of these minerals are extracted in industrial large-scale mines operated by TNCs, with artisanal and small-scale miners playing only a marginal role in production.

In the course of the sector's expansion, the mining industry has entered regions, which had previously been dominated by small-scale agriculture, especially in the Andean highlands (Li 2009, 218–9). The territory of indigenous and peasant communities has often been disproportionately affected by this expansion of extractivism (de Echave 2008, 19). Because of the mining activities' negative impacts on the environment and on peoples' livelihood, social conflicts between mining companies and parts of the local population have increased in the past twenty years (Working Group on Business and Human Rights 2018, 6). In many of these conflicts, the nation state and the central government in Lima were accused of actively siding with the corporations rather than acting as mediators in the disputes (Bebbington, Humphreys Bebbington, *et al.* 2008, 2900, Kamphuis 2012a, 574, Silva Santisteban 2013, 435). The governments that followed the transition in 2000 continued Fujimori's neoliberal economic policies and supported large-scale mining projects, arguing that they were "of national interest" (Bebbington 2008, 275, Arellano-Yanguas 2011a, 88). The

3 The development of the industrial mining sector in Peru has been extensively studied and is very well documented (see, for example: Bury 2005, Bebbington and Bebbington 2009, de Echave *et al.* 2009, Arellano-Yanguas 2011a, 2016, Bebbington 2012a, Gómez 2013, Hoetmer *et al.* 2013, Li 2015).

Conga mining project in Cajamarca and the Río Blanco project in Piura have emblematically illustrated this development.

I discuss the course of the social conflicts in Cajamarca and Piura in detail in the first chapter. In doing so, I provide an overview on the role of law in Peru's mining conflicts. The role that law plays in these conflicts is, for obvious reasons, closely tied the role of the nation state. Since the return to democracy in 2000, Peru is again officially considered a state under the rule of law, even though its institutions are still weak in many respects (Cotler *et al.* 2009, 117, Arellano-Yanguas 2011a, 619). Bribery scandals surrounding the Brazilian company Odebrecht revealed the high level of corruption within the former governments and the established political parties in the past years. Despite several attempts at decentralization, Peru is still an extremely centralized country, in which all the threads run together and all the major political decisions are made in the capital, Lima (Passuni and Chirinos 2013, 484–5, Pinker 2015, 97–8). In many of the rural areas of the Andean highlands and the Amazon lowlands, in contrast, the nation state and its institutions are still hardly present, as various authors have described (see, for example: Poole 2004, 36, 38, Yashar 2005, 6, Harvey and Knox 2015, 39). Consequently, the rural population in many regions feels forgotten or abandoned by the state and national governments (Nuijten and Lorenzo 2009, 101). The large gap between Lima and the provinces is further aggravated by pervasive racism in Peru's society (Drinot 2006, 19, Silva Santisteban 2013). The risk of being affected by poverty is considerably higher in the Andean region than in the coastal region. In this sense, the population of the rural area lives geographically, economically, and socially on the margins of the Peruvian state.

Despite these different aspects that cause or reinforce the marginalization of the highlands, however, the nation state and its system of justice are an important reference point for a large part of the rural population, especially in the context of recent mining conflicts. As I discussed elsewhere (Lindt 2015), citizenship rights play a pivotal role in Peru's protest movements opposing large-scale mining projects, especially in the Northern Highlands where people mostly do not consider themselves indigenous, but instead rely on their identity as *campesinos* or *campesinas*, thus as peasants (Thorp and Paredes 2010). As a political argument within these conflicts, people in the Cajamarca region, for example, invoke their "right to have rights" (Arendt 1998 [1951], 614) as citizens of the Peruvian state, although the nation state often does not guarantee these rights in practice. Invoking citizenship rights promises them a certain level of public accountability. Furthermore, it enables them to make their struggles heard on an international level and to exert pressure from abroad, which is linked to the worldwide spread of transnational rights movements and (human) rights discourses discussed above.

Moreover, protest movements in Peru's mining regions address their demands to the nation state and not, for example, to the corporations involved, because their rights as citizens provide them with certain legal guarantees. The relationship with the mining companies, in turn, is characterized by the concept of corporate social responsibility (CSR), which is based on soft law and legally non-binding regulations. After many years of experience with TNCs, people in Peru's mining regions have come to know the voluntary character of CSR programs. The role of the law for social movements as an important frame of reference within the mining conflicts thus results from the binding nature of the law (Lindt 2015, 94–5). In addition, since opportunities for political participation by the local population in large mining projects are limited, the law also provides a forum for making demands to the state. Within the social conflicts with the mining companies, social movements and local NGOs turn to the domestic justice system in order to make their voices heard. The social movements thus carry the conflicts into the courtrooms, thereby contributing to their judicialization.

On the other hand, the law is, by its very nature, also an important frame of reference for the nation state and its institutions. This is particularly evident in Peru's neoliberal economic policies, which were introduced by the adoption of new legal norms and by the enforcement of new legal provisions. The preconditions for Peru being a "mining country full of opportunities" for TNCs are laid down and encoded in law. In addition, state officials justify their action by referring to the law. They argue with the existing constitutional, legal, and normative framework, which allows for the state's interventions, for example, when police forces take action against protesters. Furthermore, as I describe in one of the chapters, state representatives also make active use of the existing legal framework in order to impede protest activities and to criminalize social movements. The research field's national dimension is thus characterized by this importance of law as a discourse for both state actors and social movements.

The transnational dimension: struggles against corporate impunity

My research field's second dimension goes beyond the national perspective in Peru and takes a closer look at the third important group of actors in these mining conflicts: the transnational mining corporations. As mentioned above, this part of the research field is not geographically bound, but rather includes transnationally circulating discourses and notions about the responsibility of TNCs. According to Kirsch (2014, 1), the corporation is "one of the most powerful institutions of our time." When these institutions act transnationally, their influence increases even further. TNCs are key actors in the contemporary globalized world order; they dominate global economy and influence our everyday life (Bury 2008, 308). In recent decades, TNCs have established a worldwide net of economic activities. This allows them to create value in even the remotest areas of the world. However, the influence of TNCs goes beyond the economic sphere and the everyday lives of people, and also has an impact on the field of law. As Juan Martinez-Alier (2002, 196) noted, in theory, corporations do not have political power but operate only in the economic sphere. In practice, however, their bargaining power *vis-à-vis* individual states is immense (Deva 2012, 26). The commercial power of some large TNCs now exceeds the economic output of individual states (Kremnitzer 2010, 909). This results in the fact that TNCs have considerable influence on national legislations (Pistor 2019, 68).

At the same time, we can observe a discrepancy between TNCs' political influence and their worldwide profits and the fact that corporate power does not result in global responsibility chains. The costs for remediating social and environmental damages caused by TNCs are, in large part, externalized to the *home* states, thus to the countries in which these corporations operate (Kirsch 2014, 4). Corporate impunity for human rights violations and environmental damages remains the norm not an exception, despite more than twenty years of self-regulating business standards and CSR programs.

The mining sector is a prime example of this global lack of transnational accountability. Firstly, there are environmental hazards caused by industrial mining activities – which occur in spite of the companies' commitment to so-called "sustainable mining" technologies (Benson and Kirsch 2010). Secondly, transnational mining corporations have repeatedly been involved in human rights violations – either committed by corporate employees or in complicity with state actors, such as military or police forces. This discrepancy between corporate profits and corporate impunity has been criticized for years by social movements from the Global South, but also by so-called solidarity groups in the Global North. The cooperation of these movements in the Global South and in the North gave rise to a transnational movement, whose aim is to "dismantle corporate power and stop impunity," as an international NGO campaign with the same name puts it.

Furthermore, pressure on TNCs has also increased over the years on the part of international organizations, such as the United Nations or the Organization for Economic Co-operation and Development (OECD). As a consequence of this multifaceted criticism, many companies have claimed to recognize the problem and have announced plans to overcome the "challenges" in their "global value chains." The efforts undertaken by TNCs are, however, almost exclusively limited to the area of CSR. Non-binding international frameworks such as the Global Compact, which is based on the companies' *self-responsibility*, were co-launched and implemented by various TNCs. Civil society organizations complained that these attempts are ineffective because they are based on voluntary and so-called soft law approaches.

Even the United Nations Guiding Principles on Business and Human Rights (UNGPs), an international framework unanimously adopted by the UN Human Rights Council in 2011, are now considered insufficient by many international NGOs because they are not legally binding. Within the United Nations' human rights system, this critique of voluntary frameworks was shared by some member states, and, in consequence, an "open-ended intergovernmental working group on transnational corporations and other business enterprises with respect to human rights" was established by the UN Human Rights Council in 2014. The intergovernmental working group has since attempted to elaborate an "international legally binding instrument on transnational corporations [...]" (UNHRC 2014, 1). Due to resistance from the business community and from a considerable number of states, this attempt is, however, making only slow progress. This example illustrates the difficulties involved in holding companies liable for human rights violations related to their activities.

However, the lack of an international legally binding instrument regarding the responsibility of TNCs has not discouraged transnational advocacy networks from seeking alternative routes to overcome corporate impunity. Bringing human rights violations to court is often especially difficult in the *host* states, i.e. in the countries in which the TNCs operate. Various NGOs and civil society organizations have therefore tried, in cooperation with lawyers from the Global North, to bring claims before courts in the *home* states – that is, in the countries where TNCs' parent companies are headquartered. I later discuss the challenges of bringing such transnational claims to court, but we can clearly see a tendency toward the judicialization of social conflicts in these processes as well.

The transnational field in which the responsibility of TNCs is debated, demanded, and negotiated is thus thoroughly shaped by legal discourses, as well. The demands that come from local social movements, such as those in Peru, for example, characterize these transnational discourses. At the same time, however, transnational discourses also shape social conflicts at the local level and influence the arguments, discourses, and rights used in local courts. This reveals how the judicialized social conflicts in Peru's mining regions are shaped by transnational and national discourses, international and local efforts, and different ideas about the law. This context serves as a field of research to explore the emancipatory potential of law in this book.

Chapter 1. Defending human rights in a mining country

Peru's Human Rights Movement

From the Internal Armed Conflict Until Today

The emergence of a national human rights movement in Peru is closely linked, on the one hand, to the internal armed conflict between 1980 and 2000 and, on the other hand, to President Alberto Fujimori's autocratic rule from 1990 to 2000.[1] Many of the civil society organizations and NGOs that fall into the heterogeneous category of Peru's human rights movement were founded during this time and were influenced by these two historical periods. Thus, compared to other Latin American countries, the human rights issue in Peru gained importance in public discussions relatively late (Kristenson 2009, 77). In global terms, however, the development coincides with the "human rights revolution" that took place in other countries of the Global South after the end of the Cold War (Sieder 2010a, 203, Goodale 2017, 101, 181, 184).

Peru's internal armed conflict began on the very day the country was to return to democracy after over ten years of military dictatorship. When presidential elections were held in May 1980, members of the Maoist guerrilla organization *Sendero Luminoso* carried out an attack on the polling station in a village in Ayacucho, in the central highlands, thereby initiating its armed struggle. After initial hesitation, the national government declared a state of emergency over large parts of the country, imposed restrictions on the population's civil and political rights, and sent the army to the affected areas. In the context of these counterinsurgency measures, there have been

1 In comparison to other Latin American countries, such as Chile or Argentina, for example, there has been relatively little research on the history of the Peruvian human rights movement until now. The overview in this chapter is primarily based on the work by Coletta Youngers (2003, 2006, 2007, Youngers and Peacock 2002), Rebecca Root (2009), Ezequiel A. Gonzáles-Ocantos (2016, 2017), and Lisa Laplante and Kimberly Theidon (Laplante and Theidon 2007, 2010, Theidon 2013), as well as on the conversations I had with members of the human rights organizations. For deeper insight into the history and the development of the movement, more structured research would have been necessary, including research into the archives of the organizations. This, however, would have gone beyond the focus of this book.

massive human rights violations and crimes against the civilian population, who got caught in the crossfire between the insurgents and the armed forces.[2] People disappeared and extrajudicial killings were reported. According to the official numbers of the Peruvian Commission for Truth and Reconciliation (*Comisión de la Verdad y Reconciliación*, CVR), almost 70,000 people died or disappeared as a result of the conflict, with around 30 percent being killed by state agents (CVR 2003a, 13, CVR 2003b, 315). The CVR's final report identified the *campesino* population, especially those of the central highlands, as the "main victim" (*la principal víctima*; CVR 2003b, 316): 79 percent of those killed or disappeared had lived in rural areas, 75 percent spoke Quechua or another native language. Furthermore, 56 percent had worked in agriculture (*ibid.*). Thus, the violence had a clear ethnic and socioeconomic dimension.

In response to the abuses committed by state agents and by members of the guerrilla, local groups organized themselves in the highland areas. In many cases, it was family members and relatives of those who had been killed or had disappeared who formed local associations and demanded an end to the violence. In addition, students, intellectuals, church members, and other engaged citizens became active in the coastal regions, especially in the capital, Lima. They formed groups to support the population in the areas under the state of emergency. These groups documented abuses committed by state forces and insurgent groups. Later, these groups also provided legal assistance to those who had been arbitrarily arrested under the pretext of counterinsurgency, as well as to the relatives of those who had been killed or had disappeared (Root 2009, 458).

In this context, the Peruvian section of Amnesty International was formed in Lima, as were independent national NGOs such as the *Instituto de Defensa Legal* (IDL), the *Asociación Pro Derechos Humanos* (APRODEH) and the *Comisión Andina de Juristas* (CAJ), three NGOs that were critical for the emergence of a national human rights movement in the following years (Youngers 2007, 14). Lawyers played a major role in the founding of most of these NGOs. This had a large impact on the development of these organizations. From the very beginning, the strategic use of judicial mechanisms constituted an important weapon for the movement.

Coordinadora Nacional de Derechos Humanos

In 1985, more than fifty NGOs and associations based in Lima and in the provinces joined together to form the national umbrella organization *Coordinadora Nacional de*

---

2 Theidon (2013) wrote a disturbing, but extremely impressive and engaging ethnography about the use of violence in the Ayacucho region and its consequences for the communities in that region during the *sasachakuy tiempo*, the "difficult time," as the local population calls the armed conflict.

Derechos Humanos (CNDDHH or, as hereafter, *Coordinadora*; Youngers 2007, 16, Bebbington, Scurrah, *et al.* 2008, 56, Gonzáles-Ocantos 2017, 145). The aim of the *Coordinadora* was to strengthen the human rights movement by coordinating the efforts of grassroots organizations and by improving national and international networking (Youngers and Peacock 2002, 9–10). A permanent secretariat based in Lima was created to organize the *Coordinadora*'s activities. Over the years, this office has been headed by an executive secretary, a position that has been held by leading figures from Peruvian civil society. To exchange information, the activists met in working groups on topics such as torture or indigenous peoples, for example. Over the years, the *grupo jurídico*, the Judicial Group, in which the movement's lawyers exchanged strategies for human rights litigation, has become the most influential of these working groups (*ibid.*, 20, 29, 34). In addition, in the nineties, the *Coordinadora* set up a network of professionals, such as dentists, psychologists, doctors, and social workers, who participated voluntarily in a working group for humanitarian aid (Youngers 2007, 33).

From the beginning, the *Coordinadora*'s member organizations were very heterogeneous. All of them, however, have committed themselves to following the organization's basic principles. These principles include the rejection of any kind of violence, independence from the state and from political parties, commitment to a democratic society, the unconditional defense of the right to life, and the rejection of the death penalty (CNDDHH 2019, 2, see also: Youngers and Peacock 2002, 29). Based on these principles, common strategies emerged, which the *Coordinadora* developed at the national level and which were spread to the provinces by its member organizations.

Over the years, the *Coordinadora* became one of the most powerful players in Peru's civil society, especially since other actors such as unions and political parties lost influence during the Fujimori era (Kristenson 2009, 77, Degregori 2012, Li 2015, 16). The *Coordinadora* became and still is "the unifying [...] element and acts as a voice of the [human rights] movement and of its concerns and demands" (Bebbington, Scurrah, *et al.* 2008, 43, own translation). Hence, when I write about "Peru's human rights movement" in this book, I am referring to the activists belonging to the *Coordinadora* and its member organizations, as well as to those individuals and associations that are independent of it but share its ideals and political goals. This also reflects the emic perspective from the field, for example when people affected by state and corporate abuses refer to the organization and its lawyers as "*derechos humanos*," as if the *Coordinadora* itself were equated with the principles it seeks to defend.

As mentioned above, the *Coordinadora*'s work in the late eighties focused primarily on providing legal assistance to people affected by state repression and on documenting human rights violations. This also included the defense of those who were falsely accused by the state of being supporters or members of guerrilla organizations. When Alberto Fujimori took office in 1990 and later, with his so-called *autogolpe* (self-coup) in 1992, the human rights situation was exacerbated. A new terrorism legislation was created, curtailing basic mechanisms of the rule of law and obstructing the work of defense lawyers (Gonzáles-Ocantos 2017, 145). The *Coordinadora* and its member organizations actively interfered in this field. In addition, the fight against torture, especially in prisons, was a further key concern of many NGOs in the nineties (Youngers and Peacock 2002, 23, Gonzáles-Ocantos 2017, 146).

Due to their commitment to non-violence, the human rights lawyers intervened on behalf of members of the guerrilla movements only when the accused were threatened with extrajudicial execution, disappearance, or torture, thus when their fundamental human rights and their lives were at risk (Youngers and Peacock 2002, 18, Youngers 2007, 26). However, they did not represent defendants who had publicly admitted to armed struggle or who had demonstrably supported the guerrillas. As I discuss in the course of the following chapters, this principle has been maintained by the legal NGOs until today. Only persons who have been unlawfully prosecuted or "criminalized" have received legal assistance. Despite this clear maxim, the lawyers were – and still are – accused by parts of the Peruvian society, Fujimori's followers in particular, of supporting "terrorists" in court (Gonzáles-Ocantos 2017, 146). These forms of discrediting human rights organizations began in the nineties when the movement became the target of the increasingly authoritarian state apparatus, which acted with a hard hand against any dissenting opinions in the public sphere (Root 2009, 461). As Youngers and Peacock (2002, 15) wrote, Fujimori referred to the human rights groups as "'useful fools' of terrorist groups" (see also: Youngers 2007, 12). Like other political opponents of the regime, the activists were intimidated, harassed and prevented from doing their work (*ibid.*, 21).

Despite the obstruction of its work, however, the human rights movement achieved some successes in the nineties. A major one was the establishment of the *Defensoría del Pueblo*, the Human Rights Ombudsperson's Office in 1996. As a body independent of other state institutions, the *Defensoría* became an important ally of the human rights movement in the nineties and in relation with the mining conflicts of the following years (Root 2009, 461). Finally, the human rights movement, and especially the *Coordinadora*, was instrumental in the campaign against the illicit re-election of Alberto Fujimori in 2000, which led to a massive protest movement. While this was not able to prevent Fujimori's re-election, shortly after, however, a huge system of corruption was uncovered. This system had been engineered by Fujimori's advisor and head of secret service Vladimiro Montesinos. Thereupon, the president fled to Japan and resigned by fax (Youngers 2003, 419–20, 427–8, Root 2009, 457–8).

The transition after Fujimori's fall provided a window of opportunity during which the human rights movement gained influence. In Valentín Paniagua's transitional government that followed Fujimori, several human rights activists were appointed to the cabinet and were thus able to carry the influence of the movement to the highest political level in the country (Youngers and Peacock 2002, 27, Root 2009, 465). The political influence of the *Coordinadora* and the NGOs based in Lima reached a peak at that time. These NGOs were able to play a significant role in Peru's return to democracy, which led to the transition often being described as an "NGO transition" (Gonzáles-Ocantos 2017, 160). The establishment of the Truth and Reconciliation Commission, which investigated the internal armed conflict, must also be seen in this context. Activists and NGO members, including several people with whom I worked during fieldwork in Lima, played an active role in the CVR's work (Youngers and Peacock, 2002, 27, Bebbington, Scurrah, *et al.*, 2008, 56). For many of the activists, this period was a formative and far-reaching experience, which, as several people told me, had a significant impact on their later work in the human rights movement.

Following the transition, and over the past twenty years, the human rights movement has become thematically more diverse. Recent campaigns by the *Coordinadora* and its member organizations have focused on the rights of indigenous groups, migrants, women, and the LGBTI community. In addition, since about 2003, the rights of population groups affected by extractive industries has been one of the movement's key focuses. Many legal NGOs from Lima have focused their work on capacity building workshops with peasant communities or indigenous groups. They have also provided legal assistance to people affected by human rights violations during protests and have attempted to take political action against the use of violence by state security forces during social conflicts. The case studies Río Blanco and Conga are excellent examples in this respect, as I will point out presently.

Fundación Ecuménica para el Desarrollo y la Paz – Fedepaz

One legal NGO whose emergence and development is exemplary for the historical background of the Peruvian human rights movement explained above is the *Fundación Ecuménica para el Desarrollo y la Paz* (*Fedepaz*[3]). *Fedepaz* is based in Lima and is one of the two organizations with which I have cooperated during fieldwork. The NGO was founded in April 1993, exactly one year after Fujimori's *autogolpe* – or as the NGO's director David Velazco called it, "*en plena dictadura* (at the height of the dictatorship)." *Fedepaz*' founding members were a group of lawyers. They had previously worked for the *Centro de Estudios y Acción para la Paz* (CEAPAZ[4]), an NGO close to

3 Ecumenical Foundation for Development and Peace. This name points to the Christian background of the NGO. Like many other Peruvian human rights activists, some of *Fedepaz*' members consider themselves to be devout, and their faith plays an important role in their private lives. Its director told me that the NGO's goal is to promote human rights "from a Christian perspective but with an ecumenical approach."

4 Center of Studies and Action for Peace.

the Catholic Church that was founded in Lima in the mid-eighties (Youngers 2003, 471–2, 495). The two lawyers of *Fedepaz*, with whom I was in close contact during my field research, have been working with the NGO from the very beginning. Rosa Quedena was one of its founding members and its first director; David started as an intern and later worked as a lawyer after completing his studies.

In the early years, *Fedepaz* focused its work primarily on the legal defense of persons who were prosecuted under the new terrorism legislation, as well as on legal assistance for persons affected by human rights violations. Since its founding, the fight against impunity of state actors, universal access to the legal system and due process and the protection of fundamental rights have been at the center of *Fedepaz*' work (Sanca Vega 2017, 195). As I discuss in detail in Chapter 2, the NGO has pursued the strategy of mobilizing the law and using judicial mechanisms to protect and promote human rights.

At the time of my field research, *Fedepaz* employed two lawyers and a social anthropologist, as well as a part-time accountant and a secretary. The NGO operated in a modest office with sparse, dark rooms and noisy neighbors in the district of Jesús María, a busy, middle-class area of Lima. *Fedepaz*' work is financed by foreign NGOs, and at the time of my stay, it was mainly by the Luxembourg NGO *Action Solidarité Tiers Monde* (ASTM), *Terre des Hommes France* and foreign sections of Amnesty International (ASTM 2018, 9, Terre des Hommes France 2020). Since funding is project-based and always limited to a few years, the NGO's future prospects have been – and still are – characterized by great uncertainty. In the nineties, the organization had been much larger, as Rosa and David told me, but due to problems in obtaining external funding, the team was subsequently reduced.[5]

As an NGO founded by a group of lawyers, *Fedepaz* works in different thematic areas of law. Firstly, the field of civil and political rights includes the provision of legal assistance for persons affected by human rights violations or criminalization. In addition to this work in local courts, the area of law also includes the use of mechanisms of supranational organizations, especially the IACHR, in whose sessions *Fedepaz* has regularly participated. Together with other human rights NGOs and as part of the *Coordinadora*'s *Grupo Jurídico*, *Fedepaz* was involved in the so-called Fujimori trials, in which the former president Alberto Fujimori was prosecuted and convicted in 2009 for crimes against humanity. Lawyers from *Fedepaz* represented the families of victims murdered during the massacre in Barrios Altos, both before Peruvian courts and before the Inter-American Human Rights Court (González-Ocantos 2016, 452,

5 Many Peruvian NGOs had to reduce their staff during this time. As the country experienced an economic upturn after 2000, funding agencies from the Global North ended their projects and withdrew from the country, although Peru experienced, at the same time, an increase in social conflicts, and local NGOs had to intensify their efforts to defend human rights.

Sanca Vega 2017, 195).[6] Since the transition, *Fedepaz* has provided long-term legal assistance to communities affected by mining conflicts, such as the conflict over the Río Blanco project in Piura, for example.

Fedepaz' also works within the field of economic, social, cultural, and environmental rights. In addition to representing peasant and indigenous communities affected by the extractive industries in courts, *Fedepaz* has conducted capacity building workshops in these communities to strengthen their collective and individual rights. They have supported the communities in formalizing their institutions and territory rights and have conducted specific trainings with community leaders and women (Sanca Vega 2017, 196). During my stay in the field, *Fedepaz* worked with the *comunidades nativas* Supayaku and Naranjos, two Awajún communities from the northernmost part of the Cajamarca region, and with the *comunidades campesinas* from Ayabaca and Huancabamba, which are located in the area of influence of the planned mine Río Blanco. As I describe in the following, the NGO thereby became a central player in this mining conflict.

Mining conflict Río Blanco in Piura

Context and project description

Piura is a region in the northern part of Peru that extends from the arid coastal region to the Andean highlands. Thanks to irrigation projects, large-scale agriculture is practiced near the coast, with production for the domestic market and for exportation. By contrast, the highlands, especially the provinces of Ayabaca, Morropón and Huancabamba, are characterized by small-scale farming and represent the region's marginalized hinterland (Bebbington and Williams 2008, 192, Toledo Orozco and Veiga 2018, 328). In parts of Piura's highland region, the rural population is organized into peasant communities, so-called *comunidades campesinas*. These *comunidades* represent a specific form of social organization through which the Peruvian state grants subsistence farmers a certain degree of autonomy within their communities (Nuijten and Lorenzo 2009, 113).[7] The *comunidades* hold special rights and obligations, for example regarding the administration of natural resources, the sale of land, or the decision-making processes in their territories (Arellano-Yanguas 2011a, 100, Salazar 2012, 10). However, as a result of the country's neoliberal

---

6 Case *Barrios Altos vs. Perú*, Inter-American Court of Human Rights, Judgment of March 14, 2001, p. 6.

7 In contrast, indigenous communities in the Amazon lowlands are referred to as *comunidades nativas*.

turn, the rights of the *comunidades* have been curtailed by allowing the establishment of individual land titles and the possibility to alienate communal land (Kamphuis 2012b, 222–3). This has made the communities vulnerable to large investment projects. According to estimates, more than half of the approximately six thousand *comunidades campesinas* in Peru are affected by mining (Bebbington and Williams 2008, 190, Jaskoski 2014, 874).

Before the Río Blanco conflict emerged, a dispute with another mining company had already shaped the region. In the late nineties, Manhattan Minerals, a Canadian company, attempted to build a gold mine near the city of Tambogrande. This mine's construction was, however, stopped by the resistance of the local population. A local referendum, a so-called *consulta vecinal*, in which the local population voted on the project in 2002, played a major role in this conflict.[8] The local government had organized the referendum in collaboration with a technical committee consisting of various NGOs from Lima, including *Fedepaz* (Paredes 2008a, 293). Although it was not legally binding and not recognized by the national government, the referendum was decisive for the protest against the mine. The social movement's experience in Tambogrande later influenced the resistance against Río Blanco.

The Río Blanco project envisaged the construction of an open-pit copper and molybdenum mine; the project was wholly owned and initiated by the British junior company Monterrico Metals. Originally, it was led by a Peruvian subsidiary under the name Majaz, which later changed its name to Río Blanco. In 2003, the Peruvian government granted the concession to operate and the company built a mine camp (Skinner *et al.* 2013, 93). The planned mine is located in an area with an important watershed and with primary cloud forests (Bebbington *et al.* 2007, 15). It is situated on land belonging to the *comunidades campesinas* of Yanta and Segunda y Cajas, two communities in the provinces of Ayabaca and Huancabamba, respectively (Alayza Moncloa 2007, 97). The *comunidades* hold official land titles for the affected area (Arellano-Yanguas 2014, 66).

The acquisition of a mining concession and the associated land resources is clearly regulated under Peruvian law: The subsoil resources are owned by the state, which grants the mining concessions; the holder of a concession must then purchase the overlying land from the owner of that land, whereas special legal conditions apply if the land is collectively owned by a *comunidad campesina* (Szablowski 2008, 45–6). In such cases, the land can only be sold if a two-thirds majority of the communities' general assembly agrees to the sale (Coxshall 2010, 42, Velazco Rondón and Quedena Zambrano 2015, 25). In the case of the land required for the Río Blanco

8 The *consulta vecinal* in Tambogrande had a great signal effect: In the following years, the idea of organizing such a local consultation was adopted in other conflicts in Peru and in other Latin American countries as an instrument for exercising non-violent resistance to large-scale mining projects (Li 2015, 8, Kirsch 2016, 54).

mine, however, these legal preconditions were not met, according to the project's opponents. Community members complained that there had been irregularities in the company's purchase of land, which led to an initial conflict (Bebbington *et al.* 2007, 17, Hoetmer 2010, 187–8, Skinner *et al.* 2013, 93). Moreover, members of the *comunidades* feared that industrial mining would have a negative impact on the regional water supply and on local agriculture, on which a large part of the population depends. Therefore, they opposed the project by organizing protest marches.

Following the example of Tambogrande, the political mobilization against Río Blanco resulted in a *consulta vecinal* in September 2007. This *consulta* was again organized by the local municipalities in collaboration with a group of NGO members from Lima under the coordination of *Fedepaz* (Bebbington *et al.* 2010, 322, Velazco Rondón and Quedena Zambrano 2015, 34). The population's vote was unequivocal and clear with more than 94 percent of the participants rejecting the mine's construction (Velazco Rondón and Quedena Zambrano 2015, 27f.). The referendum was not legally binding, but it demonstrated the company's lack of a so-called "social license to operate" (Hoetmer 2010, 185).[9]

The mine's supporters, in turn, attempted to prosecute the referendum's organizers. A local association that acted as a supporter of Río Blanco filed a complaint against thirty-five members of the technical committee in 2008, among them NGO members from Lima, local activists and members of the local government. For organizing the *consulta vecinal*, the group was accused of severe crimes, such as terrorism and rebellion (Hoetmer 2010, 192, Velazco Rondón and Quedena Zambrano 2015, 46–7, 59–60). This was one of several cases in which state and corporate actors, as well as their local allies, sought to criminalize the resistance against Río Blanco. In its role as legal advisor to the *comunidades* in Ayabaca and Huancabamba, *Fedepaz* assumed the role of legal defense in many of these lawsuits.

Despite these attempts to criminalize its members, the protest movement was able to achieve some success. Due to its protest, the construction of the mine was suspended in 2011 (Velazco Rondón and Quedena Zambrano 2015, 29). However, the plan to build the mine has never been completely abandoned by the Peruvian government and by the corporation but was rather postponed in the hope that public opinion toward the project would change over time. The company has remained active in the region and attempted to obtain the "social license to operate" from the local population through CSR programs (Bebbington 2012b, 78). In 2007, the ownership structure of the company changed with Monterrico Metals' assets being taken over by the Chinese consortium Xiamen Zijin Tongguan Investment (Kamphuis 2011, 74).

9 As other authors have discussed, for some time now, mining companies in various regions of the world have been required to have a "social license to operate," in particular, but not only, when it will affect indigenous communities (see, for example: Kirsch 2007, 313, 2016, 54–5, Sawyer and Gomez 2012, 1, Jaskoski 2014, 873–4).

More recently, Peru's former government under Pedro Pablo Kuczynski promoted the Río Blanco project in the context of its attempts to deepen economic cooperation with China (Amancio 2016). Thus, the social conflict surrounding the construction of the mine has continued and has led to ongoing social tensions within the *comunidades*.

Protest march and acts of torture

As with other social conflicts over industrial mining projects in Peru, serious human rights violations occurred in the course of the Río Blanco conflict, especially from 2003 to 2006 when the protests reached a climax. When the population took to the streets against the mine, state security forces repeatedly used repression and violence against demonstrators. Several people were killed during the conflict (Coxshall 2010, 38).

In this book, I focus on one particular case of human rights violations that occurred in the context of this mining conflict. At the end of July 2005, a group of two to three thousand people participated in a protest march that led to the planned mine area where the company had built a mine camp (Skinner *et al.* 2013, 94). The protesters demanded a continuation of the dialogue with the state and called for a suspension of the mine's construction activities (Bebbington *et al.* 2007, 17–8, Coxshall 2010, 38). Since the planned mine is located in a remote area, the demonstrators had to walk for several days and spend the night outside in the field in the vicinity of the mine camp (Calderón Concha 2010, 402, Kamphuis 2011, 74–5). In the early morning on August 1, 2005, members of the DINOES[10], a special unit of Peru's National Police (PNP), attacked the protesters' camp, using tear gas and live ammunition to disperse the demonstrators. One protester was killed during these clashes, and several police officers and demonstrators were injured (Bebbington *et al.* 2007, 17–8, Jahncke 2011, 51, Kamphuis 2012a, 543).

In the context of these violent confrontations, twenty-eight protesters – among them two women and one teenager – were detained by the police and brought into the mine camp where they were held captive for more than 72 hours (Skinner *et al.* 2013, 94). Within the camp, the detainees suffered physical and psychological violence as well as acts of torture. They were beaten, subjected to tear gas; forced to eat rotten food; and threatened with death, violence, and rape. The two women were sexually abused. For several hours the detainees did not receive either water or food; plastic bags containing an irritating powder were placed over their heads, and they had to remain seated during a long time with their hands bound. During these events, members of the national police's special unit and members of Forza, a

10 *División Nacional de Operaciones Especiales*, National Special Operations Division.

private security firm contracted by the mining company, were present in the mining camp (Kamphuis 2012a, 544, Velazco Rondón and Quedena Zambrano 2015, 26–7).

A public prosecutor visited the site on the second day to interrogate the detained protesters. Although he could see that the detainees were being mistreated, he did not intervene on their behalf. On the third day, the protesters were brought by helicopter and bus to the city of Piura, where they were interrogated again and then finally released. A few days later, they were reported along with nearly eighty other demonstrators for participating in the protest march (Jahncke 2011, 51, Kamphuis 2011, 75). The twenty-eight persons were thus criminalized for their participation in the protests; at the same time, the authorities were very reluctant to investigate the abuses they had suffered and opened investigation only as a result of the persistent intervention of human rights lawyers from Lima, in particular the lawyers working with *Fedepaz*. The three-day detention had serious physical and psychological consequences for the demonstrators, many of whom suffered physical injuries and have continued to suffer from post-traumatic stress disorder for many years.

With regard to the Río Blanco conflict, I limit my analysis to this one single case of human rights violations. This case, which is referred to as "the torture case" by *Fedepaz* lawyers, is an emblematic case of police violence in connection with a transnational mining project. As I discuss in Chapter 3, the case illustrates the obstacles of human rights litigation in Peru. Additionally, this case also led to a transnational lawsuit against Río Blanco's parent company in the United Kingdom, which I analyze in Chapter 6.

Minera Yanacocha and the Conga mining conflict in Cajamarca

Operating among comunidades and rondas campesinas

The second case example in this research emerged from an expansion project of an existing gold mine. Peru's mining era under the new neoliberal framework began in 1993 in Cajamarca, a region neighboring Piura in the country's northern highlands, where the company Minera Yanacocha began extracting gold and other minerals by using the latest technologies in open-pit mining.[11] The mine was considered a prestige project of Alberto Fujimori's cooperation with foreign investors and the World Bank (Li 2015, 18). In the nearly twenty-five years that followed, Minera Yanacocha

11 For many years, most of the gold produced by Minera Yanacocha was exported abroad, with about two thirds of the export volume going to Switzerland. In Switzerland, this gold was processed and refined by the Valcambi gold refinery in Ticino, to be then traded on the world market (GfbV 2012, 23–4).

was operated as a joint venture company involving U.S. Newmont Mining Corporation, the Peruvian company Buenaventura and the International Finance Corporation (IFC), a member of the World Bank Group.[12] The initial mining area of Minera Yanacocha was located at between 3,500 and 4,000 meters above sea level and about thirty-five kilometers north of the city of Cajamarca, the capital of the region of the same name (Bury 2008, 312). Over the years, the mining area has been continuously expanded. By 2016, it had expanded to cover approximately 160 square kilometers (RESOLVE 2016, 10). For several years, the mine was among the most profitable and largest open-pit mines in the world (Langdon 2000, 1, Bury 2008, 311).

For the Cajamarca region, the mining project marked the beginning of a new economic era, as Minera Yanacocha was followed by other transnational companies building mines in the region. The presence of these companies had a considerable impact on the region and especially on its capital Cajamarca, a city with about two-hundred thousand inhabitants in 2017 (INEI 2018a, 27). In the course of the mines' expansion, the town grew into a regional center after years of being considered a relatively marginal town by national standards. Cajamarca's fate, however, had been linked to gold before the arrival of Minera Yanacocha. The course of the Spanish conquest was decided in this city when Francisco Pizarro captured Inca ruler Atahualpa in Cajamarca and had him killed, even though the Inca had filled one room with gold and two rooms with silver to buy his freedom (Paredes Peñafiel and Li 2017, 15). Until today, this historical anecdote has served as an important point of reference for the population to describe their city's difficult relationship with foreigners searching for gold.

In a national comparison, Cajamarca belongs to the poorest regions of the country, despite years of mining activities. According to national statistics, sixteen of Peru's twenty poorest districts were located in this region in 2018 (INEI 2020). Before Minera Yanacocha's arrival, Cajamarca's economy was mainly dependent on agriculture. There was only one small area, the province of Hualgayoc, where mining had been carried out since colonial times (Chacón Pagán 2005, 357, Herrera 2013, 266). Besides this, the region was – and still is – known for its livestock and dairy production. Local farmers grow crops and hold livestock primarily for their own subsistence and for the markets in the region. Some of them, however, also produce for the na-

12 In December 2017, IFC sold its stake to its former partners Newmont Mining and Buenaventura (International Finance Corporation n.d.). Some months later, Japanese Sumitomo Corporation acquired a 5 percent share in Minera Yanacocha (Newmont Mining Corporation 2018). Newmont Mining then controled the company with a 51 percent share, whereas Buenaventura held a 44 percent stake. In 2022, Newmont Corporation acquired all shares in Minera Yanacocha and became the sole owner of the mine (Newmont Corporation 2022). In recent years, the parent company has changed its name several times from Newmont Mining Corporation, to Newmont Goldcorp, and finally Newmont Corporation.

tional market and deliver milk and dairy products to transnational food companies such as Nestlé or Gloria (van den Berge 2011, 67, Sosa and Zwarteveen 2012, 362).

Agriculture and the peasant communities play an important role for the local populations' identity. According to the census of 2017, there were 112 *comunidades campesinas* in the region (INEI 2018b, 24).[13] In the context of the recent international discussions on the rights of indigenous peoples, these *comunidades* have often been compared with indigenous communities, especially by foreign NGOs. Peru's government, however, has been reluctant to legally recognize the *comunidades campesinas* as "indigenous" communities and to grant them the rights to which it committed itself by ratifying international agreements, such as the Convention 169 by the International Labor Organization, for example (Kamphuis 2012b, 218).

Moreover, Cajamarca's rural population rarely identifies as "indigenous," which is also related to historical aspects. Only a few communities in Cajamarca are Quechua-speaking because the Incas had only brought the region under their control shortly before the Spanish conquest (Grieco 2016, 134). The North was consequently much less influenced by Quechua culture than other regions, and – in contrast to the Southern highlands – the concept of "indigeneity" (Huarcaya 2019) barely plays a role in Cajamarca.[14] The majority of the local population identifies rather as *mestizos*[15], i.e. as "mixed" descendants of both Spaniards and indigenous people; or they identify themselves based on their class affiliation as *campesinos* and *campesinas*, i.e. as peasants (Chacón Pagán 2005, 363–4, Bebbington, Humphreys Bebbington, *et al.* 2008, 2903, Sulmont 2011). Furthermore, the *comunidad campesina* is an important identity-forming characteristic in rural Cajamarca. Many *cajamarquinos* and *cajamarquinas* are extremely proud of the agricultural culture and feel

---

13 The data collection at the census was based on the *comunidades*' self-declaration; not all of them hold formal land titles and are recognized by the nation state. According to NGO information, 88 *comunidades campesinas* in the region of Cajamarca have been recognized and hold formal titles by the state (SICCAM 2016, 11).

14 In comparison with its neighboring countries Ecuador and Bolivia, only a weakly organized indigenous movement has developed in Peru in recent years. The reasons for this are diverse. On the one hand, the agrarian reform was decisive. This was carried out under the military dictatorship of General Velasco Alvarado at the beginning of the seventies. This reform meant that the rural population was no longer categorized under the disrespectful term of the "indios" but under the class name *comunidades campesinas* (in the highlands) or the ethnic term *comunidades nativas* (in the Amazon lowlands). On the other hand, the persistence of racism has contributed to the fact that many inhabitants in the *sierra* do not identify themselves as indigenous, as this term is considered by parts of society to be synonymous with "backwardness" and "poverty" (for a detailed discussion of this topic see, for example: de la Cadena 1998, Van Cott 2005, 144, Paredes 2008b, Sulmont 2011, Huarcaya 2015, 808, 829).

15 For a more details on the concept of *mestizaje* in the South see the work of Marisol de la Cadena (1998, 2000).

strongly connected to the countryside, even if they live in the towns of Cajamarca or Celendín.

Another element of great importance – in terms of the formation of a local identity, but above all in terms of social organization – are the so-called *rondas campesinas*. The *rondas campesinas* are community-based self-help organizations, which have their origins in the peasant communities' fight against cattle rustling. In the late seventies, peasants in the province of Chota, in central Cajamarca, organized themselves to prevent their cattle from being stolen (Chacón Pagán 2005, 353, Gitlitz 2013, 16). They gathered in small groups and conducted night patrols, *rondas* in Spanish, to guard their communities. Suspected perpetrators caught by the *rondas* were brought before the communities' *asamblea*, the communal assembly, which then decided whether and in what form the apprehended individual should be punished. Various authors described the emergence of the *rondas* as a community reaction to the nation state and its institutions' absence in the rural areas (Faundez 2005, 203, Gitlitz 2013, 19, Hoetmer 2013, 268). Since the communities lacked any protection by public authorities, they themselves began policing against cattle rustling and other minor crimes. This awareness of taking the administration of justice into one's own hands, since the state does not take responsibility for it, continues to shape the relationship with the ordinary justice system for many people in the region.

Due to the *rondas*' success in administrating justice in their territories, the organization form spread throughout Cajamarca and the neighboring regions, such as Piura, for example.[16] However, the *rondas* have also been harshly criticized, especially because the sanctions in the *justicia ronderil* often include corporal punishment and because those sentenced have no possibility of defending themselves against the *asamblea*'s decision. Nevertheless, in the 1993 Constitution and in the *Law on Rondas Campesinas*, the Peruvian state recognized this form of legal pluralism. The legal frameworks stipulated that the *rondas* were entitled to support the *comunidades campesinas*' authorities in administrating local justice (Faundez 2005, 188, 206).[17] According to this legal framework, the *rondas* are obliged to cooperate with state judicial authorities, such as the justices of the peace, and to hand over serious

16 At the time of the internal armed conflict, the Peruvian army itself adopted the concept and applied it in the regions of Ayacucho, Junín and Puno to mobilize the rural population against the guerrilla groups. These so-called *comités de autodefensa*, or self-defense committees, were also named as *rondas campesinas*; however, unlike the *rondas* from the North, the committees in the central and southern highlands were armed and followed the orders of the military (Fumerton 2001, 485). Orin Starn (1993, 5–6) argued that the military used the positively charged name *rondas campesinas* for the self-defense committees in response to the emerging criticism that the army was forcing the rural population to participate in counterinsurgency.

17 Article 149, Peruvian Political Constitution of 1993; article 1, Law No. 27908, *Ley de Rondas Campesinas*.

criminal cases to these authorities.[18] To strengthen their political influence, the local *rondas* formed federations at the provincial level and beyond, thus establishing a widespread network, which today covers a wide area in the *sierra*. As I explain later, the *rondas campesinas* thereby became important political players in the mining conflicts in Cajamarca and Piura as well (see also: Hoetmer 2013, 268).

Minera Yanacocha's early conflicts

Minera Yanacocha thus began its operations in a social setting that has been characterized by difficult economic circumstances but in which communal organization has been very pronounced and in which a local form of administrating justice, legal pluralism, and collective ties to land resources have played a fundamental role in creating identity. Under these circumstances, the first social conflicts between the mining company and parts of the local population developed during the nineties. As in Piura, these initial conflicts resulted from disputes over land acquisition. Later, communities in the mine's vicinity, but also people from the city, complained about negative impacts on the environment, public health, and local water resources. At the same time, the economic prosperity, which the company had promised, had still not arrived.[19]

In 2000, the population's unrest reached a first climax when a lorry transporting mercury from the Yanacocha mine to the coast spilled over 150 kilograms of this highly toxic material in three municipalities (Defensoría del Pueblo 2001, 14, Li 2017a, 176). This incident, which is known as the mercury spill in Choropampa, severely damaged the mine's image (Sydow 2016, 235, Li 2017a). At first, the company tried to downplay the incident and later attempted to appease the affected population with compensation payments.[20] In retrospect, the mercury spill was decisive in fueling local resistance against the company's plans to expand its activities, and this considerably shaped the relationship between the mine and Cajamarca's population (Li 2013, 401, Sisniegas Rodríguez 2016, 30–1). While the company had previously

---

18 Article 8, Law No. 27908, *Ley de Rondas Campesinas*.

19 The history of Minera Yanacocha's initial social conflict in the late nineties has been thoroughly discussed, especially by a group geographers including Anthony Bebbington, Jeffrey Bury and others (see, for example: Bury and Kolff 2002, Bury 2004, 2005, 2007, Bebbington, Humphreys Bebbington, *et al.* 2008, Bebbington and Bury 2009, Sosa and Zwarteveen 2012, Li 2013, 2015).

20 The spill in Choropampa has also been dealt with by the justice system, both in Peru and in a transnational civil suit against the parent company Newmont Mining in the United States (for a detailed discussion, see, for example: Defensoría del Pueblo 2001, Concha Takeshita and Navarro Elguera 2016, Sisniegas Rodríguez 2016, Torres Pachas and Conza Salcedo 2016, Li 2017a). The company was, however, able to evade legal responsibility to the greatest possible extent both in domestic and foreign courts through compensation payments.

announced that it would apply "new methods" to carry out "sustainable mining," it had to counter fierce criticism after the spill (Arellano-Yanguas 2011a, 145).

In 2004, the first major social conflict broke out when Minera Yanacocha planned to expand its mining area to the Cerro Quilish, the mountain that provides drinking water for the city of Cajamarca.[21] Weeks of protests followed, which united the urban and rural population and which were carried out with strikes, demonstrations, and roadblocks, some of them being violently suppressed by the police (Bebbington, Humphreys Bebbington, *et al.* 2008, Arellano-Yanguas 2011a, 145–50, Li 2015). The social movement mobilizing against Minera Yanacocha included peasant organizations, such as local *rondas campesinas*, teacher unions and students' federations from the urban area, church associations, and other grassroots organizations, such as the so-called *frentes de defensa* (defense fronts), which were loosely organized groups (Arellano-Yanguas 2011a, 103, Hoetmer 2013, 269, Li 2013, 407–8). Due to the protests, the company announced the suspension of its plans. This was the first success of the movement against mining in the region.

In 2001, the *Grupo de Formación e Intervención para el Desarrollo Sostenible*[22] (*Grufides*), a local environmental NGO emerged in the city of Cajamarca (Rojas 2009, 113). *Grufides* was founded by Marco Arana, a priest who had worked in Porcón, a community located in the vicinity of the Yanacocha mine, where *campesinos* and *campesinas* increasingly complained about being defrauded by the mining company in land transfers (Maquet 2013, Li 2017b, 122–3). Besides Arana, *Grufides* was initially run by students of the National University in Cajamarca, who after their graduation helped to professionalize the NGO (Kamphuis 2012b, 232–3). An important goal of the NGO was to document social conflicts and environmental damage caused by mining. In addition, the NGO provided legal assistance to communities and individuals affected by human rights violations committed during the social conflicts. As such, *Grufides* joined the national human rights movement and became a member of the *Coordinadora*. In the following years, the NGO became one of the main forces in the judicialization of the social conflicts in Cajamarca.

Mining conflict Conga

With the protests against the Quilish project, the local population successfully frustrated Minera Yanacocha's expansion plans. However, given that the mine's mineral deposits would eventually be exhausted, the company sought to secure its activities

21 There has been extensive research on the initial disputes between the local communities and Minera Yanacocha and on the protests against the project at Mount Quilish (see, for example: Bebbington, Humphreys Bebbington, *et al.* 2008, de la Cadena 2010, 339–40, 356–7, Arellano-Yanguas 2011a, 145–50, 2011b, 629, Kamphuis 2012b, 233, Li 2013, 2015, 31).

22 Training and Intervention Group for Sustainable Development.

with another expansion project, the Conga mine. The project involved a planned investment of around US$4.8 billion in a new gold and copper open-pit mine in an area bordering the three provinces of Cajamarca, Bambamarca and Celendín (Arellano-Yanguas 2016, 67). Several people from Celendín, a small town about 100 kilometers northeast of the city of Cajamarca, told me that the project was initially advertised under the name Minas Congas and that Minera Yanacocha attempted to conceal its involvement in the project. However, by at least 2011 it was known who was behind this project. In 2010, the project's environmental impact assessment study had been approved by the national government; one year later, Minera Yanacocha's parent company officially launched the project (Grieco and Salazar-Soler 2013, 152).

Due to Minera Yanacocha's bad reputation, resistance against Conga grew quickly, even in regions like Celendín that had not been affected by mining activities until then. The project was met with particularly fierce criticism because it involved the destruction of various mountain lakes, which, critics said, endangered the local water supply (Paredes Peñafiel and Li 2017, 2). The Conga project was therefore *inviable,* "unfeasible," as the opponents argued. Similar to the Quilish project, the endangered water supply again united the urban and rural population. A movement against Conga emerged in all three affected provinces, mobilizing different sectors of the population.

From October 2011, the movement carried out its resistance using road blockades, strikes and protest marches to the larger cities (Jaskoski 2014, 876). In the city of Celendín, the protests were mainly coordinated by the grassroots organization *Plataforma Interinstitucional Celendina* (PIC), which I discuss below. In addition, protest activities also took place directly on the planned mine site, a remote area located at around four thousand meters above sea level and a several hours' drive from the cities of Celendín and Cajamarca. Around ten thousand people participated in these marches. In retrospect, these protests had a long-lasting impact on the social movement since they revealed its popular support. Moreover, violent clashes with police forces occurred during these marches and indicated how the national authorities would deal with the protest movement in the following months. During a march in November 2011, the police fired tear grenades and live ammunition at demonstrators, injuring several protesters.

The national government of President Ollanta Humala, who took office in July 2011, came under pressure as a result of the protests, especially because Humala had promised, during his campaign, to stop the Conga project should he be elected (Arellano-Yanguas 2016, 182). In light of the protest marches, Humala's government announced that it would again revise the environmental impact assessment of the project. Moreover, it established a *mesa de diálogo*, a negotiation meeting bringing together the conflict's main actors for a dialogue (Silva Santisteban 2013, 437). When these negotiations failed, Humala's cabinet broke for the first time, and ten ministers resigned (Jaskoski 2014, 877). The cabinet's end demonstrated the political force the protest movement had gained, not only within the Cajamarca region, but also on the national level. In November 2011, the movement called an indefinite regional strike and largely paralyzed public life in Cajamarca. At the beginning of December, the national government responded by declaring a state of emergency (Vásquez 2015, 92).

In February 2012, the movement against Conga carried out its resistance with a "national protest march in defense of the water" to Lima (Paredes Peñafiel and Li 2017, 10). In May 2012, there were additional large street protests in Cajamarca, and another regional strike was declared, demanding that the government definitively cancel the project. This time the national government sent the military to the region to stop the protests. The cities, especially Celendín, were invaded by the military, as several activists told me, and the state security forces took repressive action against protesters. In early July 2012, one person in Bambamarca and four people in Celendín were shot dead by state security forces. Among those killed in Celendín was a sixteen-year-old boy shot from a helicopter (Silva Santisteban 2013, 436). The following day, the government again declared a state of emergency, thus preventing any further public protests. This led to the protests in the streets calming down in the following months and years, although the social movement did not disappear completely.

For the mining project Conga, however, the street protests meant the end, at least temporarily and until the time of writing. Minera Yanacocha suspended the construction work at the Conga site in November 2011 following a request by the national authorities (Newmont Mining Corporation 2016, 22). In April 2012, the government in Lima decided that the project would be suspended for two years and demanded that the company make improvements in the protection of water resources (Grieco and Salazar-Soler 2013, 154). In the following years, it was unclear whether the project would ever be realized, as the company remained active in the region with CSR projects and continued to build the infrastructure necessary for the mine. In 2016, parent company Newmont Mining announced that "[u]nder the current social and political environment, the Company does not anticipate being able to develop Conga for the foreseeable future" and that it would reallocate the project's capital to other world regions (Newmont Mining Corporation 2016, 22, see also: Sydow 2016, 219). Therefore, although the company did not officially announce Conga's end, there were many indications that the mine would not be built in the near future.

However, the social conflict between the mining company and parts of the local population did not cease after the project's suspension but repeatedly broke out into smaller confrontations. A typical example is the dispute between Minera Yanacocha and the Chaupe family, a *campesino* family who owns a piece of land within Conga's planned mining area. The Chaupe family inhabits and cultivates this plot of land and refuses to sell it to the mining company. Minera Yanacocha, for its part, claims to have acquired the land several years ago from the *comunidad campesina*, to which the family belongs, and has therefore repeatedly attempted to clear the land and to evict the family, sometimes by force.[23]

In view of such incidents, members of the local protest movement expressed doubts that they had been able to definitively stop the Conga project once and for all. Many of them told me that they believed to "have won a battle but not yet the war." They considered these doubts to be confirmed by Minera Yanacocha's CSR programs, which they interpreted as the mine's attempt to obtain the "social license to operate" by means of development projects and gifts to the population. In light of these programs, many activists feared Minera Yanacocha would one day relaunch the project – for example, if the price of gold rises again and the mine becomes even more profitable. For this reason, many of them tried to maintain their resistance and to remain active in the movement.

Since the end of the political mobilization on the streets, the resistance against Conga changed its shape and shifted to other areas, including the courtrooms. On the one hand, as in Piura, the social protests were criminalized; many of the activists were prosecuted by the authorities for their participation in the protests or were charged by the mining company for crimes, such as property damage. On the other hand, the social movements, along with local and national NGOs, have sought to demand justice for the human rights violations committed during the conflict. This has mainly concerned people who were injured or killed by state security forces during the conflict. In the further course of this book I will focus on various court cases that have arisen in this context and that exemplify both the legal mobilization *from above* (Chapter 4) and *from below* (Chapter 3).

Plataforma Interinstitucional Celendina (PIC)

Regarding the Conga conflict, my field research has mainly focused on the *Plataforma Interinstitucional Celendina*[24] (PIC). The PIC was founded in 2010 as a grassroots organization bringing together civil society groups from Celendín, its surrounding villages and *comunidades campesinas* (Tello 2013, 372). As its members told me, the PIC was born out of the efforts of various local groups, which, since 2009, had organized public meetings to inform about the Conga project and its environmental impacts (see also: Tello 2013, 371, Paredes Peñafiel 2016, 192). "At that time, we followed the idea that 'nobody defends what he or she does not know (*uno no defiende lo que no conoce*)'," as I was told by Milton Sánchez, who was the co-founder and secretary general of the PIC (Paredes Peñafiel and Li 2017, 13) at the time. Many PIC activists recounted that before the social conflict they – like the majority of Celendín's popula-

23 In Chapter 5, I go into more detail about the land conflict between Minera Yanacocha and the Chaupe family.

24 Interinstitutional Platform from Celendín.

tion – knew nothing about the mountain lakes in the higher areas of the countryside that supply the city with drinking water and that would be destroyed by the Conga project.

From the outset, the PIC was made up of various urban groups, such as members of the teachers' union SUTEP[25], women's organizations, or church associations. From rural areas, various *rondas campesinas*, *frentes de defensas*, and other loose associations and individuals joined the PIC, thus forming a broad alliance of *ronderos* and *ronderas*, teachers and students, housewives, urban professionals, active members of the Catholic and of Evangelical churches, *campesinas* and *campesinos* (Sullivan 2014, 131, Sánchez and Vargas 2019, 114). As has been discussed at length by others, women played an important role in the resistance against Conga (see, for example: Grieco 2016, 138–43, Silva Santisteban 2017, Li and Paredes Peñafiel 2019). Within the PIC, a separate women's group was founded. In addition, the PIC became one of the protests' most important coordinators in Celendín and also – through the exchange with other organizations in Bambamarca and Cajamarca – an important regional player.

At the regional level, *Grufides*, the environmental and human rights NGO from Cajamarca, became the most important ally for the PIC, especially in the initial phase of the conflict when gathering information on the Conga project and its impacts. With the outbreak of violence and when activists were increasingly criminalized for their participation in the protests, *Grufides* also provided legal assistance. In addition, lawyers from the *Coordinadora* in Lima intervened in the court cases. This resulted in a close cooperation between *Grufides*, the *Coordinadora*, and the PIC. Another important ally of the PIC was the *Programa Democracia y Transformación Global* (PDTG), an NGO bringing together activists and (former) researchers from the San Marcos University and other universities in Lima. In addition, the PIC also succeeded in establishing a strong international network. Particularly relevant for my research in this regard is the collaboration with EarthRights International, a U.S. NGO with an office in Lima. This cooperation resulted in various lawsuits against Minera Yanacocha and its U.S. parent company Newmont Mining, which I will discuss in the following chapters.

After the temporary suspension of the Conga project, the PIC's work shifted from coordinating protests to, first, upholding the exchange between the individual organizations. To this end, the PIC, along with activists from PDTG, organized the so-called *Escuela de Líderes y Lideresas "Hugo Blanco Galdos,"*[26] a capacity building

25 *Sindicato Unitario de Trabajadores en la Educación del Perú*, Unitary Union of Workers in Education in Peru.

26 "School of male and female leaders;" the *escuela* was named after Hugo Blanco Galdós, a revolutionary who led the *campesino* movement in southern Peru in the sixties and seventies, and who later became a politician for various left-wing parties. His book "Nosotros los indios"

workshop in which activists discussed ideas and strategies for social resistance against large-scale industrial projects. The *escuela* became an important framework for maintaining the social mobilization in Celendín. I participated in one of these *escuelas* in 2017 as part of my field research.

Second, dealing with court cases became an increasingly important focus of the PIC's work. On the one hand, as mentioned above, many legal NGOs with which the PIC cooperated attempted to use the law to seek justice for those who had suffered human rights violations during the Conga conflict. The PIC's activists helped to obtain information, established contact with the people directly concerned and mediated between them and lawyers from Cajamarca, Lima, and abroad. Although they were not the driving force behind the court cases and, in many cases, they were not directly involved as parties of the lawsuits, the members of the PIC thus became important actors within the judicialization of the Conga conflict and acted as a kind of "intermediary" or "translator" (Merry 2006b) in the court cases.

On the other hand, the activists and members of the PIC themselves came into the focus of the judicial authorities and thus involuntarily became actively involved in court cases since many of them had been charged with criminal offenses because of their participation in demonstrations. This increasing criminalization posed a great danger to the organization and its participants, as I demonstrate in Chapter 4.

Beyond the Conga conflict: protests against the hydroelectric dams in the Río Marañón

However, there were additional reasons why protests in Celendín continued after the suspension of Conga, as another social conflict broke out. This time, the protest emerged in resistance to the Brazilian infrastructure company Odebrecht, which planned to build several dams in the Río Marañón, a river running east of the province of Celendín. As one of the main tributaries of the Amazon, the Río Marañón is of great importance for the entire region. The national government promoted construction of several dams in this area by arguing that they would produce "clean" energy and would ensure Peru's economic development.[27] The protest movement that began mobilizing in 2013 against the construction of the dams in the Río Marañón complained, in turn, that the energy would not benefit the local economy or the local population, but only the planned mining projects in the area.

is considered one of the most important intellectual texts for the peasant movement in Peru (Blanco Galdós 2017). In recent years, Hugo Blanco has been involved in Peru's environmental and human rights movement.

27 In 2011, the Peruvian government in Lima declared the construction of twenty hydroelectric dams in the upper reaches of the Río Marañón to be in the "national interest." *Decreto Supremo*, N° 020–2011-EM, 26.04.2011.

At the same time, the costs to be borne by the local population would be extremely high, the opponents argued. They feared that many would lose their homes and livelihoods in agriculture because areas would be flooded, forest would be cut down, and the course of the river would be irrevocably altered (Amancio 2015, Lo Lau 2016).

Among the planned hydroelectric dams were the projects Chadín 2, Río Grande 1 and Río Grande 2, and Odebrecht was awarded the concession for all of them (Hill 2015a, 2015b). Within the sphere of influence of these three projects were several communities whose members had been already involved in the protest movement against Conga. Chadín 2 would particularly affect the *centro poblado* or village of Yagen, whereas Río Grande 1 would have a major impact on the district of Oxamarca. Activists from Yagen and Oxamarca had established close contacts with the social movements from Celendín during the Conga protests. In turn, they received support from this movement, in particular from the PIC, in their struggles against the dams. In the province of Celendín, the resistance against Conga thus merged into the struggle to protect the Río Marañón.

As I discuss in Chapter 4, many activists from Yagen and Oxamarca were criminalized for their resistance against the dam projects. In addition, there were violent clashes among the inhabitants of the village in Yagen, who were sharply divided into supporters and opponents of Chadín 2. Several people were killed as a consequence of these clashes, including Hitler[28] Rojas, who was one of the leaders of the movement against the dams. In 2015, Rojas was shot dead by another community member and supporter of Chadín 2 (Hill 2016). His death demonstrated how social conflicts over large investment projects penetrate the communities and how they lead to violent outbreaks at the local level. Thus, the social conflicts have not only involved the use of violence by state security forces against demonstrators. Moreover, the violence has also taken on much more personal or, following Kimberly Theidon's (2013) notion, "intimate" forms between people who share their daily lives in a community. However, in this research I focus on the former form of violence, i.e. on human rights violations committed by corporate and state actors. The decision to focus on these aspects also brought with it another type of data collection, which I describe in detail in the following section.

28 As in other Latin American countries, it is not unusual that parents in Peru choose exotic sounding names like Jhonny, Sindy or Pamela, or names of historical figures like Lenin, Stalin, or Hitler for their children. A lack of knowledge about world history may be one reason for the fact that even within the social movement in Cajamarca the name Hitler hardly caused any unease or discussions.

An ethnography of Peru's mining conflicts

This research is primarily based on eight months of fieldwork that I conducted in Peru between January and May 2017 and January and May 2018. I spent most of that time in the capital, Lima, and in Celendín. In addition, I went to the regional capitals of Cajamarca and Piura and to the province of San Ignacio for various shorter stays. Thus, my data collection was relatively strongly tied to two particular places. This is related to the fact that I worked with two specific organizations and accompanied their members for several weeks. In Lima, I focused on the work of *Fedepaz*, whereas in Celendín, I mainly collaborated with the PIC.

However, as Wendy Coxshall (2005, 209) wrote, ethnographic research is "open-ended," and my data collection continued long after I left Peru. I continued collecting data within Europe, traveling to Berlin, Aachen, and London to conduct interviews with employees of German and British NGOs as well as with a lawyer of a British law firm. All these people have worked closely with social movements and NGOs in Peru in the past or were involved in the court cases I am analyzing in my research. In these ways, I was able to complement the views and perceptions I had captured within Peru with the perspective of outsiders who were, however, in close contact with my field. Additionally, I also met activists from Cajamarca at a conference in Barcelona, conducted interviews via Skype with lawyers from the United States and Canada, and participated three times in the United Nations Forum on Business and Human Rights in Geneva. In this sense, my research also has the aspect of a "multi-sited" ethnography (Marcus 1995), but with strong ties to the places the social conflicts and the court cases took place. By tracing the court cases' different sites, I attempted to do justice to the fact that my research field is by itself multi-sited. The social conflicts have circulated beyond Peru through the cooperation with international NGOs, transnational court cases, and transnational advocacy networks. In this sense, I also attempted to be "there... and there... and there..." and to trace my multi-sited field as proposed by Ulf Hannerz (2003).

Furthermore, my data collection continued after the end of my actual fieldwork because I remained connected to the field to a certain extent via the Internet. Social media play an important role for protest movements in Peru. Especially via Facebook, NGOs and activists inform about their activities, share photos of meetings, broadcast live presentations, or record court hearings on video, which they then share online. When judgments are reached, copies of the documents are uploaded to Facebook shortly afterwards, supplemented by video recordings in which the people involved or their lawyers comment on the outcome of the court case. This allowed me to deal with the challenges I confronted, such as the fact that court cases I analyzed often lasted a long time and that the important steps in these lawsuits rarely occurred while I was on site.

Besides the protest movements, which are at the focus of this research, there are other groups of actors involved in Peru's mining conflicts. First, there are the companies, their employees, and local supporters, who in Peru are referred to as *pro-mineros* or simply *mineros*. Second, government institutions and their employees also play an important role in the conflicts. These groups also actively contribute to the judicialization of social conflicts by invoking the law to assert their interests. Thus, the judicialization of mining conflicts could also be analyzed from the perspective of these other two groups.

In the field, I initially attempted to gain access to these other groups of actors, too, and to establish contacts with the mining companies and judges, for example. However, I learned that studying a social conflict in a region like Cajamarca also means choosing sides, especially in the case of ethnographic research. I went to the court hearings with the activists, and as such, the judges did not perceive me as an independent observer but as part of the group of activists who accompanied the defendants. Consequently, they were not willing to talk to me about the court cases or about their work. In addition, the *mineros*, for example in Celendín, were difficult for me to grasp and remained an indeterminate group of opponents who, as the activists told me, follow what we do, where we go, and with whom we meet. Celendín is a small town where everyone knows what other people do; the activists, however, felt that they were under additional surveillance by the *mineros*. This also affected my own perception over time. Moving back and forth between the two sides, establishing contact and building trust with both groups soon proved to be unrealistic. Thus, even after eight months of fieldwork, my research remained focused on the social movements and their perception of the mining conflicts' judicialization.

Access to the field

In both cases, regarding the PIC and *Fedepaz*, the aim of my stay in the field, from a methodological viewpoint, was to accompany the employees and activists for a longer period of time and to participate in their daily (working) life. In the case of *Fedepaz*, this proved to be relatively easy, as I spent several weeks at the NGO's office. However, my expectation had been that the lawyers would constantly go to court hearings and that I could spend a lot of time with them in the courthouses. As it turned out, however, this idea was incorrect. As I explain in detail in Chapter 3, human rights litigation in Peru proceeds slowly and rarely reaches the stage of a trial. Most of the lawyers' work, therefore, is paperwork and occurs in their offices.

Furthermore, actual litigation was only a small portion of the lawyers' work; more often they were involved in legal capacity trainings with communities. Thus, my participant observation at *Fedepaz* mostly took place in the context of these activities. I studied the NGO's records on court cases, sorted files for the staff and helped them with minor research, documentation work, and the preparation of workshops. In addition, I accompanied the team to workshops and on a field trip to Supayaku, one of the indigenous communities in the province of San Ignacio. This allowed me to gain insight behind the scenes and a deeper understanding of the relationship between the NGO staff and a local community.

Establishing contact with *Fedepaz*' team and gaining its consent to participate in the daily life at the office was relatively simple. Regarding the PIC in Celendín, by contrast, I was initially confronted with various challenges, first in establishing contact with and getting access to the organization, and then in actually collecting data. At the beginning of my fieldwork, I approached the PIC and asked its members for permission to accompany them. Milton, the PIC's leader, was skeptical about academic research dealing with social movements on the ground. "Scientific work is of no use to us," he told me from the beginning, "if the results do not return to their place of origin and if the people involved cannot themselves learn from what academics write about them. We want researchers to give something back to us." As mentioned above, the mining conflicts in Cajamarca have been studied thoroughly in recent years, which led to an overflow of academic researchers visiting the region and the local organization. The PIC had also been affected by this wave of academic interest, which did not really help the movement, as the activists complained. Despite this clear position, however, Milton was willing to discuss my aim to do research with the *compañeras* and *compañeros* from the PIC. He invited me to a meeting where I was able to present and discuss my research proposal with the group.

So, I already had a foot in the door, but I was still far from having convinced the group that I had come to Celendín not to stay for a week or two and to do a few interviews like previous researchers, but that I had come to accompany them for a longer time. However, shortly thereafter the trial began in a criminalization case in which Milton and other members of the PIC were prosecuted. The activists asked me to accompany them and to approach the judges to make them aware that foreigners were following the case. The weeks that the trial lasted were a time of great tension, as I discuss in Chapter 4. At the same time, however, it was precisely this difficult situation that helped me build trust with the activists. By accompanying them to court and by supporting them merely by being present there, I was able to "give something back" to them, like they had asked. Thus, contrary to my initial expectations, it was not the lawyers in Lima who were constantly going to court but the activists from Celendín with whom I spent much time in the courtroom.

The second challenge in collecting ethnographic data with the PIC, in contrast to *Fedepaz*, was that there was no regular working day with office hours during which I could accompany the activists. The PIC had its own locations where meetings were held. A group of activists organized the group's regular activities. Part of this also involved running a blog and, at the time of my fieldwork, a weekly radio program, and a *revista*, a magazine. These activities, however, took place on an irregular basis. Many activists followed the PIC's activities after finishing their normal jobs, as teachers or mototaxi drivers, for example. Thus, while my participant observation with *Fedepaz* was tied to its office hours, with the PIC it was mostly limited to the activists' spare time.

In addition, my original research plan had involved the intention of spending several weeks in Ayabaca or Huancabamba to collect data within the social movement against the Río Blanco project. However, during my field trip in 2017, the environmental disaster *El Niño Costero* severely hit Peru and especially the region of Piura. Heavy rainfall, floods, and mudslides cut off road connections, which complicated traveling and made my trip to Piura impossible in the first year. Thus, I was stuck in Cajamarca for longer than I had initially planned.

When I returned to Peru in January 2018, the situation had normalized in terms of possibilities to travel, but social tensions had arisen within the communities in Piura. Despite the Río Blanco project's suspension, there were enormous social disputes occurring between the mine's supporters and its opponents. Consequently, there was a great deal of mistrust, especially toward unknown foreigners. Various people familiar with the region advised me not to travel to the communities alone my first time. Thus, I planned to accompany *Fedepaz'* team, which regularly travels to Ayabaca and Huancabamba to conduct capacity workshops with the communities.

Unfortunately, however, it was precisely at this time in 2018 that an internal conflict broke out within the local social movement, which also affected the relationship between parts of the grassroots organizations, their leaders, and *Fedepaz*. For reasons of caution, the *Fedepaz* team was unable to travel to the region for several months, which meant that my attempt to establish contact with their help also failed. I then traveled on my own to the capital of Piura and attempted from there to find an access to Ayabaca or Huancabamba through local contacts, which also turned out to be difficult. In consequence, I limited my analysis concerning the Río Blanco conflict to the work of *Fedepaz*.

"Voices of the victims"

Ethnographic research that deals with aspects of justice, human rights violations, or more generally with the processing of suffering often focuses on the perception of those directly affected, those who otherwise have no voice, "the governed" (Chatterjee 2004), the "subaltern" (Marcus 1995, 101–2), or "the weak" (Scott 1985). "Justice means many things to many people," as Sikkink (2011, 12) wrote. In addition, Sally Merry (2017, xii) noted that "[w]hat justice means, and for whom, must be answered in terms of contexts and situations," which for many anthropologists has led to the focus on the voice of the directly affected. I was confronted with this imperative to reflect the "voices of the victims" when I presented preliminary findings at conferences and discussed my research with colleagues. "And what about the victims? What do the victims say? What is their perception?" were questions I learned to prepare for early.

This research focuses on activists of social movements, human rights lawyers, and NGO staff. These actors are all in close contact with the "directly affected persons" or the "victims" – a term my interlocutors would, however, avoid whenever possible. Nevertheless, they represent a different group of actors. During fieldwork, I had conversations with some of the directly affected people, for example, the relatives of the men who were shot dead during the protests against Conga in Celendín. In some cases, however, I was reluctant to contact the people and to ask them to talk about their experiences. I am a social anthropologist and not a psychologist, and I had considerable fear of causing re-traumatization among my interlocutors. In other cases, I was also directly rejected, for example in the case of torture from Piura. I contacted some of the detainees, but was met with rejection, which was also related to my lack of access to the *comunidades* in that region. Therefore, the "directly affected people" only appear marginally in the following chapters. The aim of this book is to contribute to the discussion about the ambiguous forces of law for social movements in their struggles for social change. A study of the "voices of the victims," in turn, would have required a completely different research approach, and would therefore mean a completely different kind of investigation, which I can neither do nor have intended to do with this book.

Chapter 2. Expectations of Law

Introduction

In their book on U.S. citizens' legal consciousness, Patricia Ewick and Susan S. Silbey noted that "[l]egality is a social structure actively and constantly produced in what people say and in what they do" (1998, 223). Like other authors writing about legal consciousness, Ewick and Silbey's research examined the everyday understanding of law as it shapes the social relations of people interacting with, using, or coming into conflict with legality (see also: Merry and Canfield 2001, 538). While stating that "the law incorporates countless, varied, and often ambiguous rules" and that, therefore, "the law appears to us in varied and sometimes contradictory ways" (1998, 17), Ewick and Silbey also defined three different "stories" (*ibid.*, 31) of how interlocutors framed their legal experiences: First, they observed the story of people who stand "before the law;" these interlocutors described legality as a sphere detached from everyday life, which follows its own rules and formalities, and thus appears to be objective but at the same time intimidating and elusive (*ibid.*, 47, 57–108). In the second story of legal consciousness, which Ewick and Silbey categorize as "with the law," legality is perceived as a kind of "game" or, more specifically, "a bounded arena in which preexisting rules can be deployed and new rules invented to serve the widest range of interests and values" (*ibid.*, 48). In this perception, law provides tools or, rather, is instrumental by itself and thus enables those who (strategically) utilize it to assert their own interests (*ibid.*, 180–164). Finally, there is the dark side of legality, which Ewick and Silbey sum up as the story "against the law" (*ibid.*, 165–222). This includes stories of people resisting legality, its rules and its institutions, or simply avoiding it because, as a "product of arbitrary power, legality is seen as capricious and thus dangerous to invoke" (*ibid.*, 192).

In the process of judicialization that I describe in this book, I observed many of the stories of legality described by Ewick and Silbey. As I mentioned in the introduction, I noticed a significant difference in the field in terms of expectations regarding the law between the legal NGOs in Lima and the social movements in Cajamarca. Activists who were criminalized by the state for their political involvement have a different perception of legality than, for example, human rights lawyers, whose profession includes seeking social justice through legal processes. In this book's discussion on the different forms of legal mobilization *from below* (in Chapter 3) and *from above* (in Chapter 4), as well as in the analysis of the strategy of litigating cases *abroad* (in Chapter 6), these different forms of legal consciousness will be a recurring theme that accompany and shape my analysis. This chapter is intended to serve as preparation for this analysis. Since I consider the legal NGOs and human rights lawyers in Lima to be among the main drivers of the judicialization processes in Peru's mining regions, and since their work is at the center of my analysis, I focus this chapter on their expectations of the law. Thus, I provide insight into their belief in the law and their hope to use the law as a counterhegemonic means for social change.

In this sense, I deal with the form of legal consciousness that Ewick and Silbey have described as "with the law," i.e. with the instrumental, strategic use of law. In the first part of the chapter I describe what Peruvian human rights organizations understand by the concept of "strategic litigation," an approach that has often been used in recent years to describe the systematic use of legality by civil society organizations. In the chapter's second part I then discuss the various expectations that legal NGOs and human rights lawyers have of the law and categorize these different expectations. In doing so, I examine what the NGO lawyers seek to achieve for the people they defend in court, but also, in a broader sense, what they seek to achieve for larger population groups, specific social movements, and society in general.

Strategic litigation

In Ewick and Silbey's (1998) book, it was mainly individuals who recounted the history of acting "with the law" and who took advantage of legal mechanisms to pursue their personal interests or to resolve private disputes. The aspirations these individual followers of the law are similar, however, to a more institutionalized form of legal mobilization which has in recent years been discussed as the so-called "strategic litigation" approach. Strategic litigation is a concept that takes into account the instrumental use of rights by civil society organizations such as NGOs or legal aid centers, which use the law in emblematic court cases in order to have an impact not only for the plaintiffs, but also for other groups affected by the same violation of rights.[1] The approach became particularly popular in relation to public health care,

1 Various lawyers who are active in strategic litigation wrote about the approach and its implementation; see for example the work by lawyers working with the European Center for Constitutional and Human Rights (ECCHR) in Germany, Claudia Müller-Hoff (2011), and Miriam Saage-Maaß and Simon Rau (2016), or by lawyers working with the Argentine *Centro de Estudios Legales y Sociales* (CELS 2008) and the *Asociación por los Derechos Civiles* (ADC 2008). For a general overview from an academic perspective, see for example the work by Helen Duffy (2018), César Duque (2014), or Rachel Sieder (2017, 35–7).

for example during the HIV movement (Ezer and Patel 2018), but also more generally in struggles to defend fundamental human rights of vulnerable groups. The idea is that the legal system offers instruments that can be used strategically to force a political change in society through precedents via the legal system (Müller-Hoff 2011, 24). Comparable to the individuals who, in Ewick and Silbey's work, reproduce the story of legal consciousness of "with the law," legality for these civil society organizations thus becomes "a space 'within' which to operate and something 'with' which to work" (Ewick and Silbey 1998, 123).

In recent years, the strategic litigation approach also reached Peru, where it has been pursued by parts of the human rights movement, especially by legal NGOs in Lima, such as IDL and *Fedepaz*. IDL and *Fedepaz* were both founded during the internal armed conflict with the aim of defending human rights and, since then, have pursued the strategy of using legal mechanisms to get justice for people affected by state violence and human rights violations – for instance, in the context of the extractive industries. As civil society organizations, their legal mobilization is aimed at the persuasion of clear political goals and at the promotion of social change. For the lawyers of *Fedepaz* and IDL, to litigate is a political act, as various lawyers working with these NGOs told me during fieldwork. According to them, to litigate notorious human rights violations is a matter of shaping public discourse and of "pushing forward public policies (*empujar políticas públicas*)," as one IDL lawyer framed it.

According to David, one of *Fedepaz*' lawyers, strategic litigation comprises various methodological elements. A court case, usually based on a so-called "emblematic case" of (fundamental) human rights violations, serves as a starting point. By taking the case to court, the aim is to have the judicial authorities address the infringement and provide an official response to it. However, as David explained to me, it is not just a matter of filing a complaint or a lawsuit and "then waiting for the court to respond," but at the same time a political process must be initiated to accompany the court proceedings. This includes, on the one hand, making the case publicly known through press releases, press conferences, and other forms of cooperating with the media. According to David, lobbying among political allies, for example in Congress, or the cooperation with autonomous state institutions such as the *Defensoría del Pueblo*, Peru's ombudsperson, is also part of strategic litigation.

Furthermore, *Fedepaz* has regularly participated in the sessions of the IACHR, in which the NGO attempted to address the political demands raised by its court cases at the international level. This internationalization of its judicial struggles also includes the use of transnational advocacy networks to exert pressure on the national authorities from abroad (see Chapter 5) or to turn to foreign courts to support court cases at home, as *Fedepaz* did in the torture case in Piura by bringing a civil complaint against the parent company in the United Kingdom (see Chapter 6).[2] In all these endeavors, the initial lawsuit acts as the pivotal point, and all the further efforts are aimed at supporting this specific case. However, even if the human rights lawyers are ultimately unable to win a particular case in court, the lawsuit may lead to a favorable outcome through the political debates or processes it triggered. Ideally, this will result in political or social changes and thus bring the NGO closer to its political goals, for example by initiating a public debate, which then leads to a change in the legal framework (see also: Müller-Hoff 2011, 26).

Thus, strategic litigation comprises a range of measures to support a court case from outside the legal sphere. A second important characteristic of this approach is that it pursues goals that not only affect the plaintiffs directly involved, but also, as already mentioned, a larger population group. The aim is to litigate "structural" human rights violations and to change the conditions that allowed for the infringements, as David told me. In this context, it is telling how Pedro, who worked as a lawyer with IDL and as a Bertha Justice Fellow[3] at EarthRights International's Peruvian office, explained his work to the participants of the *Escuela de Líderes y Lideresas* in Celendín. In doing so, he addressed the approach of strategic litigation and said that it consists of different components:

> I want you to understand that it's not just about taking a bunch of paperwork to a judge and dropping it there, so that's not what it is, right? It's not just about bringing a lawsuit before a judge. [...] Usually when a lawyer gets out of college, he learned to litigate cases in the following way: "Just present a case and it's [a discussion from] lawyer to judge and [from] lawyer to lawyer. Nothing else." In strategic litigation it's not like that. It has components, one of which is the social component. For me, this is the most important component. Because you're the ones who are going to build the legal action. The second component is the legal component. The lawyer has to do the legal component. That's our job. But then again, strategic litigation also has a communicational component, doesn't it? Furthermore, it has a public policy component. Can you question a public policy [by initiating] a legal process? Yes, of course you can! – *Pedro, human rights lawyer,* Escuela de Líderes y Lideresas, *March 2017, Celendín (field notes, own translation)*

The aim of Pedro's legal capacity training was to give the *escuela*'s participants insight into the possibilities of filing constitutional complaints when large investment

2 For a detailed discussion of how David and Rosa reflected *Fedepaz*' strategic litigation approach in relation to the torture case from Piura itself, see: Velazco Rondón and Quedena Zambrano 2015, 32–42.

3 The Bertha Justice Fellowship is a program financed by the Bertha Foundation which aims to train young lawyers or the "next generation of social justice and movement lawyers" (Bertha Foundation n.d.) at international legal NGOs, such as EarthRights International, for example.

projects threaten the rights of local communities. At that time, IDL and the Peruvian office of EarthRights International were preparing a constitutional complaint, a so-called *proceso de amparo* or an injunction, against the Peruvian state to stop the hydroelectric dam projects in the Río Marañón. Pedro participated in the *escuela* to inform the members of the social movement in Celendín about the possibilities of this constitutional complaint. As I explain below, constitutional complaints are one of the human rights movement's key instruments to ensuring that the state assumes responsibility for protecting the rights of the population and for preventing human rights violations in the context of large-scale investment projects.

In a personal conversation during the *escuela*, Pedro described what he means by the social component he referred to when explaining his understanding of strategic litigation. He said that the social component is about involving the plaintiffs of a court case in the preparation of the case and about making them understand how the process is conducted and what can be achieved with it. This includes, as I explain below, the expectation that by conducting legal proceedings, the persons concerned will be "empowered" to exercise their rights and to strengthen their negotiating position, for example *vis-à-vis* the state or other powerful actors. Thus, according to Pedro, strategic litigation also includes *"un proceso de fortalecimineto,"* a process of empowerment, which gives an idea of the extent to which human rights lawyers in Peru perceive law and legality as an emancipatory means for the social movements and marginalized groups they represent in court.

Strategic litigation thus constitutes the methodological framework with which legal NGOs in Peru attempt to mobilize the law *from below* in order to defend the rights of specific population groups – including in the context of mining or other social conflicts. This makes the approach fundamental to understanding the case studies I discuss later in this book. As I demonstrate in the following chapter, however, human rights litigation in Peru is characterized by many hurdles and obstacles and the legal NGOs face considerable challenges when filing cases. In view of these circumstances, a question arises regarding the extent to which legal actions can actually be planned and strategically pursued and thus how *strategic* litigation can actually be in practice. As we see in the further course of this book, human rights lawyers do make strategic decisions, for example by leaving out the responsibility of the mining company, as in the torture case in Piura, so as not to jeopardize the entire process against the police officers directly involved (see Chapter 3). Beyond that, however, the actual *strategy* is using all possible means in the law and exhausting all instruments available to lawyers to get ahead with court cases. As we will see, the approach of strategic litigation therefore represents the theoretical ideal rather than the actual legal practice with which the lawyers are confronted. As I discuss in this chapter's second section, this is also related to the different expectations lawyers have of the law.

Categorizing expectations of law

The question of the expectations, aspirations and hopes placed on the law is, from a theoretical perspective, related to the question of the function of law in society. As I discussed in the introduction, legal anthropologists examine law as a social process. Merry and Canfield noted that "'law' refers broadly to the rules, processes, and norms that regulate social life" (2001, 535). Sally Falk Moore (2001, 97) defined the function of law, *inter alia*, as "problem-solver," thus pointing to the central role of law in resolving disputes and conflicts. Following these considerations, law is ascribed an ordering power on the basis of its established rules and formal procedures because "[l]aw provides a set of categories and frameworks through which the world is interpreted" (Merry 1990, 9). People adhere to the law because of its ability to determine the rules of the game for the disputes that are carried out within the "juridical field" (Bourdieu 1987). Individuals who enter the juridical field – or who are brought into or pushed into it – approach the law with specific expectations that are shaped by their legal consciousness, by previous experience with the law, or by other aspects related to their personal background. Expectations of law are thus strongly person-related; but we can, however, categorize these expectations in order to observe common patterns of how the law is "anticipated" (Eckert 2017) under specific conditions and circumstances.

Second, the question of the expectations of law is also related to the question of justice, an issue that has also played a major role in current legal anthropological studies and beyond (see, for example: Fraser 2009, Clarke and Goodale 2010, Faulk and Brunnegger 2016, Bens and Zenker 2017). Anthropology has made an important contribution to this field, especially in relation to truth and reconciliation commissions and in the context of transitional justice.[4] Despite the variety of these contributions, however, the concept of justice has theoretically remained difficult to grasp. "Justice means many things to many people" (Sikkink 2011, 12) and is difficult to define because it includes both "procedural and substantive aspects" (Merry 2017, xii). At the same time, however, justice works as a "utopian goal" (Goodale and Clarke 2010, 1), which is sought by individuals, but also by movements, and which serves as a political demand that is often universally understood. Justice is thus contextual and universal at the same time. This book aims to contribute to these discussions and to give the blurred picture some clearer lines.

This book deals with cases of human rights violations committed by corporate and state actors in the context of social conflicts. These abuses have mostly been dealt with in the field of criminal law, which already gives a first indication of the expectations of the law that are pursued in these court cases. In the following sections,

4 See, for example: Wilson (2001) on South Africa, Shaw (2007, 2010) on Sierra Leone, Theidon (2013) and Laplante and Theidon (2007, 2010) on Peru.

I categorize and discuss five forms of expectations that the actors in my research place on the law. These are, on the one hand, personal expectations such as, first, financial compensation and reparation, and second, justice and truth. Third, the expectations of law that I observed in the field also include expectations toward the state in the sense that legal processes lead to the redirection of violent conflicts into institutional channels. This indicates the extent to which the legal processes are also perceived as political processes by the human rights movement. Additionally, this links to the aim of, fourth, empowering and strengthening communities and movements by mobilizing legal means on their behalf. Finally, the fifth expectation that I observed in the field is directed at social change. As I argue below, it encompasses an overall societal dimension and thus aims at the change of previously existing, in this sense "hegemonic" norms and structures.

Financial compensation and reparation

> I always say, the worst enemy of dignity is poverty. If I have never had money and suddenly a foreign lawyer says, "It's easy, I will obtain compensation and you will be paid," people forget their rights, they don't even focus on [access to] water anymore, they focus on money and accept any strategy. In other words, it is not because they are greedy people, but because they have never had anything and they feel that it is fair. *—Jorge, human rights lawyer, February 2018, Lima (interview transcript)*

Within the human rights movement in Peru and elsewhere, financial compensation is a controversial issue, since demanding money and defending human rights do not seem to go together according to certain perspectives. The issue therefore causes a great deal of controversy, as I also observed during fieldwork.

Juliana, who worked in the office of EarthRights International in Lima, told me that lawyers as well as complainants or plaintiffs both face accusations when they demand financial compensation for suffered human rights violations. As she recounted, there is, first, the allegations that "lawyers are only interested in money" but that the complainants or plaintiffs they represent would seek "something else, something more related to justice than just demanding money." Second and in contrast to this first point, many human rights lawyers also believe, as Juliana told me, that financial compensation always involves the risk of negative effects on plaintiffs, their families, and their community and that these lawyers therefore argue for other means of reparation, although plaintiffs often need and demand financial compensation. Compensation payments would, according to these concerns, lead to an individualization of claims and could thus cause divisions within plaintiff groups or social movements. Maritza, a lawyer working with IDL in Lima, was particularly concerned about this aspect and told me,

> In the communities they often do not have the necessary conditions to have a decent life, right? So they see that opportunity where [the opposing party in the lawsuit] says, "We're going to offer you so much money in reparation." Then, of course, they see that opportunity and say, "Wow." I mean, "Yes, I was beaten, I suffered, so I want to be compensated." – Which is normal, right? [But] then the rest, I mean, it's forgotten. [...] Then [the plaintiffs say:] "I forget about my organization, I forget about the *asamblea*, I forget about everything, and that's it. I don't care what the community thinks, I care about my process because in that process, I'm going to get paid." So, it's that change in thinking that it is. It's also fine, it's normal, it's fair that everyone gets compensation, but not in the way that in the end you break the [social] structures and there's a whole problem within the community.
> *– Maritza, lawyer with IDL, February 2018, Lima (interview transcript)*

As I explain in Chapter 6 with reference to the torture case from Piura and the resulting transnational lawsuit against the parent company, these concerns mentioned by Maritza are not unfounded. The risk of negative effects is particularly high if the financial compensation is based on an out-of-court settlement and not on a court decision, i.e. if an agreement is reached outside the legal sphere. The expectations placed on the law to *award* financial compensation through a judgment must be considered and evaluated separately from this.

In addition, Juliana argued that "from an office in Lima it is easy to say" that moral values must be upheld and that "human rights claims cannot be about demanding money," while, at the same time, the people directly affected often live in precarious conditions and their lives are marked by poverty, so money is a real necessity for them. This illustrates how complex the considerations of human rights lawyers must be in assessing the risks of legal activism. I refer to this point when dealing with the relationships between plaintiffs and lawyers in Chapter 7.

The third accusation that Juliana raised in relation to the issue of human rights struggles and financial compensation concerned the fact that a person who receives indemnity is often judged on what he or she spends that money on. Juliana told me about a young *campesino* who had received financial compensation through a court case and who had invested this money in material things such as a moped and a television, for which he was later harshly criticized by people of the social movement he belonged to. According to Juliana, a person living in the city would never have been confronted with such accusations, which in her view indicates the clear ideas that prevail as to how a *campesino* should deal with such a compensation payment and for what he is allowed to use the money. In Juliana's experience, the notions of who, from a moral point of view, is entitled to claim financial compensation thus fundamentally shape the ideas of what a "victim of a human rights violation" should be. Furthermore, these moral considerations also define on what the obtained financial compensation should be spent.

Nevertheless, within the Peruvian human rights movement, financial compensation represents an important expectation of what court cases can achieve for the injured parties. This is particularly true in lawsuits on behalf of people belonging to marginalized parts of the population who are being killed, seriously injured, or tortured, thus in cases like those that this research is dealing with. The majority of the persons involved as aggrieved parties in the cases I am investigating came from modest backgrounds; many worked in small-scale farming or as simple employees in the urban area. As *Fedepaz* lawyer David put it, financial compensation could help improve the lives of these complainants, "a life that until now has been a hard life, [marked] by misery, by needs, by shortcomings." At least in material terms, financial compensation could be a relief, as David told me.

Furthermore, in various cases I am dealing with, the human rights violations have resulted not only in psychological, but often also in physical long-term consequences, for example the *campesino* Elmer, who was shot in the back by the police during a protest march against Conga (see Chapter 3 and 6). Before the incident, Elmer had lived in a *comunidad campesina* in the region of Cajamarca and had earned a living in agriculture for himself, his wife, and his children. Due to the gunshot wounds, Elmer became paraplegic and has been dependent on a wheelchair ever since. He had to give up his work in agriculture and move to the city. In addition, for a long time afterwards he was still dependent on complicated medical procedures, for which he had to travel to Lima because of the inadequate health care system in the highlands. For this reason, the criminal complaint, which the *Coordinadora* filed on Elmer's behalf (see Chapter 3), was, among other claims, clearly aimed at a compensation payment in order to improve Elmer's personal situation.

Similar to this is the situation of the women whose family members were shot dead by state security forces during the Conga protests. The women had lost their husbands or their sons and thus not only a beloved person, but often the main breadwinner of the family. As a result, many of the bereaved families found themselves in precarious living conditions and had difficulty making a living for themselves and their families. Mar Pérez, the *Coordinadora* lawyer who has represented the families in court, therefore hoped to achieve financial relief for the women through the court case. The criminal proceedings in this case were, however, dropped several times, as I explain later, and during my fieldwork, it looked like there was little hope that the men's deaths would ever be legally investigated. Adelaida, one of the widows, therefore searched for other ways to make the demands to which she had a right to, as she herself put it.

On the occasion of the fifth anniversary of her husband's death, Adelaida spoke on the radio show *Resistencia Celendina*, the program that the PIC broadcasted. Adelaida recounted that she had gone to the municipality of Celendín to ask for support for herself and the other surviving families. In doing so, she did not directly ask for money but for work to be able to sustain her family. Adelaida justified her claims by saying that if the father of her children was still alive, she would not make any demands, but since her children were now orphans, she would "embarrass herself" (*avergonzándome*) and ask for work. For Adelaida, asking for help is shameful, but financial compensation is an important part of justice, and she claimed to have a right to demand for this form of reparation. In addition, she justified her demand with the fact that her children had lost their father, and not directly with her own rights and that she had lost her spouse. She said that everyone knew that her husband had been a good father who took care of his children and that she wanted to offer her children the opportunity to get a good education, but she needed a job to do that. In this sense, Adelaida did not admit to herself the right to demand financial compensation for herself personally, but instead established her family's right to compensation with her children, who lost their father and who have thus been deprived of the security they would have had for the future.

This example again demonstrates the complex situation in which plaintiffs find themselves when demanding financial compensation for the harm they have suffered. My intention in the following chapters is to provide insight into how human rights lawyers have dealt with this issue in individual court cases and how they seek to meet the expectation of financial compensation through legal proceedings.

Establishing and knowing the truth

The second category of expectations of law, which plays an important role in my research, is, in a sense, the counterpart of financial compensation and includes what Juliana described by saying that plaintiffs are often expected to demand "something else [other than money], something more related to justice." Several human rights lawyers differentiated in our conversations between "compensation" and "other forms of justice." Mar, for example, spoke of the complainants demanding "compensation and justice," thus she referred to this differentiation, too. David, for his part, said, in relation to the torture case in Piura, that financial compensation could improve the lives of the complainants and that it was "a manifestation of justice," but that compensation is "not the justice that [the complainants] actually want." And he continued,

> Justice means concretely that the truth is known, that they [the complainants] know this truth and that it is made public, that the [system of] justice says that the policemen were criminally responsible and that they were victims of torture and kidnapping. This is what they want. – *David, lawyer with* Fedepaz, *May 2017, Lima (interview transcript)*

Thus, obtaining public acknowledgment about the suffering experienced is an important goal in the legal processes with which NGOs like *Fedepaz* seek to intervene on behalf of the complainants. In addition, David attributed this expectation of law to bring about justice by establishing the truth not only to the plaintiffs whom he and the other lawyers of *Fedepaz* represent in court, but also to the legal NGO itself. For *Fedepaz*, the search for truth is a central part of the legal process and is related to the fact that law, as a public process involving state actors and based on norms and processes on which a society has agreed, has the function of establishing justice. Establishing justice by establishing the truth thus implies a political recognition of the violations by the state and its institutions. This testifies to the anticipation that a judgment establishes a "definitive narrative" (Rubin 2008, 268) about an event. Furthermore, the NGO hopes that such a judgment will have a broader impact beyond the individual complainants, an aim which *Fedepaz* strives for with its strategic litigation approach, as described above.

There has recently been considerable research in legal anthropology into the relationship between truth and justice, for example by Rosalind Shaw on the TRC and the Special Court for Sierra Leone. Shaw argued that Sierra Leone became a "laboratory" for international legal experts who "viewed the Special Court's concurrent operation with Sierra Leone's TRC as an 'experiment' to answer the question of whether mechanism of truth and justice could work together" (2010, 211). Shaw questions, however, whether the mechanism of law enforcement – as executed by the Special Court – and the search for truth – as executed by the TRC – could work in harmony. In Shaw's opinion, the example of Sierra Leone illustrates that the binaries of the *politically* motivated search for "truth" and the *legal* processes focusing on "justice" are difficult to overcome.

What I have found in my research, however, is that truth is an essential component of justice for both human rights lawyers and the people they represent in court, precisely because of its political dimension. The fact that many legal NGOs in Peru emerged from the context of the internal armed conflict, that they later contributed to the Fujimori trials and that, in addition, many members of the human rights movement had worked with the Peruvian TRC may explain this strong link between the idea of justice and the search for truth. The movement's greatest success in recent years may have been the moment when the judgment against Alberto Fujimori was given and when the court secretary read, in a firm and loud voice, the Supreme Court's decision, confirming that "yes, it is proven" that Fujimori was guilty of crimes against humanity.[5] This marked the moment when some of the most serious human rights violations committed by state actors during the internal armed conflict were recognized by that very state and its legal authorities. This category of expectations of the law is thus nourished by the function of law to express official

5 The video recordings of the *relator judicial* Yanet Carazas Garay reading this judgment are widely known in Peru and symbolized the historical moment that confirmed the Fujimori regime's defeat.

recognition, based on the power of the state. In addition, this example also indicates why criminal law, as a legal body with which the state prosecutes and sanctions crimes against its norms, plays a central role in the struggles of human rights organizations such as *Fedepaz* or the *Coordinadora*.

In addition to this political dimension, however, learning the truth also has a remedial effect on the directly affected people. For many plaintiffs and complainants in the court cases I am dealing with, knowing the truth is also related to "being right" (*tener la razón*), a term widely used in this context. Behind this phrase, we can identify the hope that through a court case, the harm one had personally suffered would be acknowledged. The idea is that by a court decision, state authorities "recognize the right of those who have it" (*dar la razón al que la tiene*), as a teacher in Cajamarca expressed it. In this sense, Adelaida, the widow from Celendín, had hoped to obtain public recognition of her husband's death through the criminal lawsuit. In the PIC's radio program, she expressed her anger about the judicial system as follows,

> The poor person is ignored, the poor person is not given an answer as it should be. What we claim together with our relatives is that there must be justice. How many years have already passed by! Now it's going to be five years since they got lost, and we don't have any answers. – *Adelaida, radio broadcast* Resistencia Celendina, *July 2017*

What Adelaida demanded from the judicial system was a response, an official statement of the recognition of what happened to her husband. These aspects also influence the expectations of the law raised by Mar, the *Coordinadora* lawyer who represented Adelaida in court and who has previously represented many relatives of people killed in social conflicts. Mar expected a court case to establish, through public recognition of the truth, that the suffering that the individuals experienced was inadmissible and against the law. As I discuss repeatedly in the following chapters, large parts of the rural population in Peru not only feels marginalized by the nation state, but also abandoned and forgotten. They see themselves treated as second-class citizens who are denied fundamental rights. As I argued elsewhere (Lindt 2015, 90), people consequently perceive themselves as a kind of *homo sacer* in the sense of Giorgio Agamben (2010, 92), that is, as someone who loses all rights and can be killed with impunity (see also: Drinot 2006, 16–7, Nuijten and Lorenzo 2009, 113, Silva Santisteban 2013, 453). The fact that the death of demonstrators during social confrontations often goes unpunished confirms this perception of the population. By obtaining a court judgment that clearly condemns the death of demonstrators, this "state of exception" (Agamben 2010) of being without rights is overcome. Mar expressed this as follows,

> It strikes me very much that in several places [...] people say something like, "Our relative was not an animal." No? Everyone repeats that. I mean, it's like that the [judicial] process in itself is also a form of... reparation. That is, the sentence is a form of reparation, meaning that it is recognized that your relative was a human being who had rights, who was killed unjustly, right? – *Mar, lawyer with the* Coordinadora, *January 2018, Lima (interview transcript)*

This second expectation that human rights lawyers place in litigating human rights violations thus arises from the function of law to rule on admissibility and inadmissibility, on compliance and infringement, and on right and wrong.

In addition, establishing truth through litigation is also a matter of deciding *who* is responsible for the death of a relative or for the abuse suffered. Interestingly, in some cases the focus is not on the perpetrator directly involved, for example the individual police officer who fired at protesters, but rather on the "intellectual" perpetrators who gave orders or otherwise made the crime possible. For example, the mother of Joselito Sánchez Huamán, another man killed during the Conga conflict, told me that she hoped for the day when former President Ollanta Humala would receive a prison sentence for a corruption scandal he was suspected of at that time. Humala held the presidency during the Conga conflict's violent confrontations that led to the death of five people in Celendín and Bambamarca. From the social movement's perspective, Humala was regarded as the commander in chief of the military and police operations against the demonstrators.

Humala had nothing to fear from the court case in which the death of the demonstrators was investigated, but at the time of my field research, Humala was under investigation in the so-called *Lava Jato* case, a corruption scandal involving the Brazilian company Odebrecht, which bribed all the former presidents of Peru in the last twenty years. *Doña* Santos Huamán Solano, Joselito's mother, told me that she hoped Humala would finally go to prison, "even if it is not because of the death of my son but because of the money that he has stolen. The day Humala goes to jail, I'll be happy." At that time, the court case to investigate the death of her son had already been dismissed several times and the hurdles that arose in the proceedings seemed insurmountable at that time (see Chapter 3). *Doña* Santos therefore hoped that Ollanta Humala would face punishment through another trial. The expectation of knowing the truth through litigation thus also includes the hope for the punishment of those responsible.

Finally, the expectation of knowing the truth also involves striving for an admission of guilt. In the case of Elmer, the *campesino* who was shot in the back during protests, this element was particularly strong within the lawsuit. As Mar explained, a central aim of the court case was to get Minera Yanacocha and the police to apologize for the violence against the people of Cajamarca, thus, to get them to publicly acknowledge their mistakes. This recognition of guilt seems to be an important expectation toward legality particularly in cases dealing with corporate liability and thus with a powerful, but intangible perpetrator, which a corporation is. Jaime, an NGO employee from Cusco, who was involved in a social conflict involving the mining project Glencore Antapaccay, also emphasized this point. He told me that it is important that in a court case there is "some kind of sanction against the company, some kind of 'justice,' in quotation marks." He justified this by saying that there is a great powerlessness among the population in the face of the abuses committed by corporations and that the Peruvian government "does not say anything about it" and does not impose any sanction on these companies. In Jaime's opinion, a court case could help in this regard and help to regulate the corporation's behavior.

Thus, to sum up, the expectation of law to establish the truth comprises three different aspects: First, it aims at the public and official recognition of human rights violations by state authorities and thus involves a political dimension; second, it seeks recognition of the suffering of those affected or their survivors and recognition that they have been wronged; and finally, it aims at holding perpetrators accountable by getting them to admit responsibility and by imposing sanctions or regulations. These three aspects illustrate why establishing truth through a judicial process is so central to the human rights movement in Peru.

Redirecting violent conflicts into institutionalized structures

The third category of expectations of law that I observed in the field points specifically to the role and the responsibility of the state in social conflicts. According to the fundamental principles of international law, the nation state acts as the guarantor of the rights of its citizens and is the main addressee of human rights provisions. As such, the nation state holds a duty to respect, protect and fulfill human rights (Karp 2020). One expectation of the Peruvian human rights movement in conducting human rights litigation is to remind the nation state of this duty and to enforce the human rights framework set by international and domestic law.

Human rights discourses are particularly well suited to make demands to the state (Keck and Sikkink 1998, 12, Martinez-Alier 2002, 202–3, Nash 2012, 805). The state is not seen as the only bearer of responsibility for human rights violations in social conflicts, and, as previously indicated, attempts are being made to attribute responsibility to companies or third parties, as well. Nevertheless, a central responsibility is ascribed to the state because of its special role as guarantor of rights. Many legal NGOs see the use of law as particularly suitable for holding the state and its authorities to account. As I discuss in this section, the aim is thereby not to use the "law against the state" (Eckert *et al.* 2012b, see also: Eckert 2006, 51), but rather to demand the implementation of its administrative functions and to (re-)establish the rule of law, i.e. to strengthen the state and its institutions. When I speak about "the state", I thereby rely on an emic perspective of the people I worked with, who, by using this term refer, on the one hand, to the national government, the administration in Lima and the state institutions they are in contact with in their daily lives; and on the other hand also to the very *idea* of the state as the totality of different institutions that hold together and organize social life. These notions of statehood and of the perception of the state are closely linked to the hopes and expectations people place in the law as a social practice.

As mentioned above, the nation state is difficult to grasp for the population in the Peruvian highlands. Social movement activists in Cajamarca, for example, complained that the state's institutions are often absent in the *sierra*, or if they are present, they are weak or even act against the population, such as in the case of police and military operations controlling social protests. At the same time, the population's opportunities for democratic participation are for the most part limited to the participation in regional or national elections every four or five years, respectively. The national authorities and the administration of the central government decide on major economic projects such as industrial mines, with the local population generally having little say in these matters. Even with the implementation of its international obligations regarding the rights of the indigenous population to previous consultation, the Peruvian state has taken only hesitant steps these last years. As recent developments have revealed, however, parts of the local population oppose the promotion of large-scale projects. Since democratic channels to express the dissatisfaction with this form of economic development are lacking, there is a constant risk that social conflicts will escalate into violence.

However, the law provides an alternative. As Sieder *et al.* noted "the weakness of effective citizenship rights, the insecurities and hardships produced by economic crisis, and the failure of neoliberal policies to alleviate poverty have prompted ordinary people to resort to the courts or court-like structures to try to press their claims and secure their rights" (Sieder *et al.* 2005, 1). Eckert (2006) argued along the same lines by discussing the importance of citizenship rights in everyday struggles in India. In a similar manner, by using the judicial system, legal NGOs in Peru attempt to prevent these outbreaks of violence. Juan Carlos, one of the leading constitutional lawyers working with IDL explained to me in this regard,

> The idea is to redirect these conflicts to institutional mechanisms. By winning them, on the one hand, we affirm the rule of law; on the other hand, it is to give back to the state the confidence, to close the way to violent options, where in the end the dead are paid by the poor. And to force the justice system to assume its responsibility. So our first concern is not academic, but in a country with so many social conflicts… [our concern] is to provide a legal service to these vulnerable sectors in order to solve their conflicts within the justice system, thus, [we have] to appropriate legality. *–Juan Carlos, lawyer with IDL, February 2017, Lima (interview transcript)*

According to Juan Carlos, to bring a lawsuit is thus to remind the state of its duty and to hold its institutions responsible for resolving disputes within the society. By "appropriating legality," as Juan Carlos framed it, the legal NGOs make use of the state's inherent mechanisms. Thus, they "enact" its norms and rules in order to overcome the country's social conflicts and to strengthen the marginalized segments of the population.

Furthermore, Juan Carlos referred to a function of law, which Rodríguez-Garavito described in his research in Colombia and which I briefly mentioned in the introduction: Due to its "intrinsic procedural nature" (Rodríguez-Garavito 2011b, 273), the law lays down clear rules and prescribes fixed instructions as to how certain procedures – for example those involved in resolving conflicts – are to be carried out. In this context, the origin of the Peruvian human rights movement during the period of internal armed conflict is relevant again. The experience of both human rights activists and the general population of what can happen when conflicts are not steered along institutionalized lines but erupt into violence seems to me to be a major reason why people place their trust in the law. Through legal proceedings, conflicts can be steered into predetermined paths, and an escalation into violence can be prevented. As Rodríguez-Garavito argued using the example of consultation processes between indigenous groups and the Colombian state, the law provides not only the guidelines for procedural aspects, but also a *lingua franca* that facilitates negotiation between conflicting parties (*ibid.*).

To be able to use this ordering power of law, as I would frame it, or legality as "a structural component of society" as Ewick and Silbey (1998, 43) put it, a great deal of hope is placed within the Peruvian human rights movement in a specific legal body – that is, in constitutional law. With constitutional complaints, legal NGOs seek to persuade state institutions to protect the rights of the population, also in view of economically significant investment projects. As in other Latin American countries, social movements and civil society organizations in Peru make particularly frequent use of so-called *procesos de amparo* (injunctions) or, less often, *acciones de cumplimiento* (enforcement actions).[6] As mentioned above, the Peruvian office of EarthRights International, together with IDL, filed an *amparo* claim in favor of the population of the Río Marañón area by arguing that the hydroelectric dam projects will violate the population's right to a healthy and "balanced" environment (*el derecho a un medio ambiente sano y equilibrado*, Quispe Mamani and Barboza López 2019, Prado 2018, see Chapter 7). *Fedepaz* used the same mechanism in favor of the *comunidad nativa* Supayaku in Cajamarca to support the population in its fight against a mining project that threatened its livelihood and environment. In this *amparo* claim, *Fedepaz* argued

---

6 In recent years, there has been considerable research on the *amparo* or *tutela* processes in Latin America. See, for example, the work of Catalina Smulovitz (2005, 2006, 2010) on Argentina or of Sieder *et al.* (2005) on the Latin-American context in general.

that the Ministry of Energy and Mines, by granting a mining concession, had violated the community's right to a prior consultation on development projects that affect their territory.[7]

The aim of these constitutional complaints is thus to *prevent* an infringement of rights. In this research, however, I am dealing with human rights violations that have already been committed in the context of social conflicts. In the court cases that I am analyzing, the aim is to investigate and prosecute committed crimes, not to prevent them. For this reason, constitutional complaints play only a minor role in this work and are dealt with only marginally. Much more important for my considerations are the expectations that are placed on criminal law and that aim at the process of acknowledging the violations.

Empowerment

The human rights organizations and legal NGOs discussed in this book have set themselves the goal of defending the fundamental rights of those who they refer to as the "marginalized," "vulnerable" or "weak." From a socioeconomic perspective, there are great disparities between the lawyers and activists of legal NGOs and the people they represent in court. The vast majority of Lima's human rights lawyers have attended and graduated from one of the country's two leading universities, either from the *Universidad Nacional Mayor de San Marcos* or the *Pontificia Universidad Católica del Perú*. Most of them come from middle-class families, and most were born in Lima, although it is not uncommon to have a history of migration within the family and family ties to the highlands or other regions. The parents of several of the NGO employees I met in the field had moved from the rural provinces to the capital, which is typical for the development of Peruvian society in the twentieth century.

In turn, people affected by human rights violations in the mining regions often belong to the economically and socially marginalized population. Most of them work in agriculture or in the informal sector and have, compared to the lawyers, a lower level of education. The "marginalization" of these population groups by the Peruvian state and society is manifold and does not only include geographical aspects, with these people often living in remote areas, and economic aspects that allude to their marginal economic position. As Veena Das and Deborah Poole (2004, 10) described, marginalization of particular groups does not only involve a spatial or an economic

7 *Fedepaz* had filed the constitutional complaint on behalf of the *comunidad* in 2013; in 2016, a constitutional court in Lima ruled in favor of the plaintiffs by confirming that their right to prior consultation had been violated by the Ministry of Energy and Mines. In consequence, the mining project was suspended, at least temporarily. The lawsuit was a great success for the *comunidad* Supayaku and *Fedepaz*. It was the first judgment in which a Peruvian court granted a *comunidad nativa* the right to the *consulta previa* in the context of a metallurgical mining project (Fedepaz 2018a).

exclusion. Rather, hegemonic discourses, social narratives and political intentions also contribute to the fact that these population groups are pushed to the margins of society. Different aspects of manifest or latent racism play a major role in the Peruvian context. In this sense, I follow Poole, who wrote that

> "marginalization" is a powerful technique of power precisely because the margin is both a real place where roads do not penetrate, commodities seldom reach, and schools barely exist, and a discursive and ideological position from which people learn how to speak about things like justice to the state and among themselves. (Poole 2004, 38)

At the same time, however, this marginalization does not mean that the state has no importance for the population concerned. As I have discussed at length elsewhere by using the example of the Cajamarca region (Lindt 2015), the nation state and its institutions play a fundamental role for the population of Peru's highland area. This is particularly linked to the citizenship rights that the local population invoke and demand from the state, for example in social conflicts. Thus, the highland population does not avoid the state, but rather seeks to turn to it again and again and to receive its attention. The juridification of their social protests contributes significantly to these attempts. Through the use of law, human rights advocates seek to bridge this gap between the periphery of society and its center and to protect the rights of those who have been marginalized. It is therefore a matter of empowering people and demanding their rights as citizens of the Peruvian state, but also a matter of their fundamental human rights.

Legal NGOs seek to achieve this empowerment not only through actual court cases, but also through legal capacity training or workshops in the communities. Examples of such trainings are the *Escuela de Líderes y Lideresas* in Celendín or the workshops that *Fedepaz* conducted in the *comunidad* of Supayaku (see Chapter 7). The aim of these workshops is to raise awareness of the rights, legal frameworks, and norms available as a means of defending individual and collective interests. "Generating access to information" (*generar acceso a la información*), "training" (*capacitación*) of leaders or of communities and "providing empowerment" (*fortalecer* or *aportar el fortalecimiento*) are keywords that people used in the workshops I attended in Lima, San Ignacio and Cajamarca.

Pedro's contribution to the *escuela* in Celendín, which is briefly mentioned above, exemplified these intentions. He had the participants of the workshop read specific articles from the Peruvian Constitution regarding their right to file an *amparo* claim and then discussed those articles with the group. It was apparent how carefully the participants themselves dealt with legal terms and specific vocabulary and brought into the discussion the knowledge they had acquired in previous legal capacity trainings. Among the participants there were some who turned out to be actual experts, for example, on the law concerning the *rondas campesinas*. This acquisition of legal expertise also struck me when talking to Adelaida, the woman from Celendín who had lost her husband. Adelaida explained to me in great detail the various stages and specifications of the criminal proceedings, using the legal expertise she had acquired through the criminal proceedings.[8] The expectation that legal proceedings lead to an empowerment of the people involved includes, on the one hand, the aspect that people know their rights and know how to apply them.

On the other hand, empowerment is also about creating understanding and trust in the judicial mechanisms. For the Peruvian human rights movement, relying on legal mechanisms also means strengthening the faith of marginalized population groups in the judicial system and in the law itself. Mirtha Vásquez, a lawyer and the then director of *Grufides*, formulated this as follows after the pronouncement of the Court of Cassation in Lima in favor of the *campesino* family Chaupe against Minera Yanacocha (see Chapter 5),

> We believe that this [lawsuit] is worthwhile not only for Máxima, for her family, who have suffered so much mistreatment over the years. It is worth it for the justice of the weakest people in this country and especially for the people who are being abused by economic powers like these big corporations. I think there are many Máximas in this country; people who are abused by corporations, there are many in this country. And in those terms, I also believe that this court ruling serves to restore hope in justice and let communities know that, like Máxima, they can stand up and be right in confronting these big corporations and these big powers. What we are doing here is ratifying that the weak, the poor also have rights that have to be respected. –*Mirtha, lawyer with* Grufides, *declaration made in front of journalists and activists, May 2017, Lima (field notes, own translation)*

This court case in which criminal action was taken against the Chaupe family is one of several examples of how the law in Peru's mining regions is also applied against social movements. In Chapter 4 I discuss several of these criminalization cases. As I illustrate from the discussion of these examples, in the context of this kind of legal mobilization from *above*, as I call it, the aim of human rights lawyers is to restore the confidence of the criminalized persons in the legal system. The lawyers' aim in these criminalization cases is to strengthen the people in their right to defend their rights.

This in turn refers back to a point I mentioned in the previous section, that the legal NGOs do not seek to use the law "against the state," but rather to strengthen its

---

8 Eckert observed a similar development among young Muslim men in Mumbai, who, due to their experience with the police and judicial authorities, became experts in certain areas of law and proved to be "somewhat of a legal counselling body within their neighbourhood" (2006, 52).

institutions and to reinforce the rule of law. In contrast to the struggles of, for example, anarchist, libertarian, or even indigenous movements, the efforts of Peru's human rights movement are thus characterized by the fact that they seek to strengthen the state and its institutions themselves through the use of law, instead of fighting it or withdrawing from its influence. The expectation is that the law in itself can be an "ally" (Merry 1990, 4) for vulnerable groups and that the judicial system offers marginalized parts of the population the necessary tools and instruments with which they can defend their interests even against otherwise powerful actors. This aspect thus refers to the emancipatory possibilities of legal mobilization and to the expectation of using the law as a counterhegemonic tool, an aspect that is repeatedly taken up in this research.

Social change

Finally, the fifth category of expectations placed on law by Peru's human rights movement includes the hope to achieve social change by mobilizing the law. This category thus links to the aim of strategic litigation that I referred to above and to the forms of legal mobilization described by so-called counterhegemony theorists that I discussed in the introduction. Many counterhegemony theorists who addressed the emancipatory potential of law and legality have dealt with the aspirations of the users of law and their goals of changing existing political and social conditions through legal activism. However, most of these authors remained rather vague on the question of how this social change through law should then be enforced in concrete steps. In addition, their explanations often remained unspecific with regard to what they actually mean by the vague concept of "social change."

From the perspective of Peru's human rights advocates, the hope for social change includes, above all, the demand for institutional change and for the consistent implementation of the existing legal framework. The difficulty in Peru to get justice for human rights violations lies in the vast majority of cases not in the lack of laws or in an insufficient, deficient legal basis, but rather in the lack of implementation of these norms. Many of the cases that I analyze in this book are, at their core, about police violence used against demonstrators in the context of transnational mining conflicts. This involves killing, assault, or torture and thus classic offenses in criminal law. For the human rights lawyers involved, bringing about social change in these cases means regulating the actions of the state security forces and of the corporations and thus overcoming the impunity of corporate and state actors.

As David told me when explaining *Fedepaz'* aims of litigating such cases of human rights violations, he referred to the torture case from Piura and said that one of the legal actions' objectives was to induce the legal authorities to deal with the responsibility of the police officers and their superiors, as well as of the corporate actors.

On the one hand, as mentioned above, the aim was to establish the truth and thus provide certainty and public recognition of the suffering of the persons concerned. However, on the other hand, this also aimed to prevent a repetition of this crime in the future. Specifically, the aim was to influence the way the police act against protesters during operations in the context of social conflicts. Citizens' rights to participate in demonstrations should again be seen as a right of the population and not as a crime that can be misused as a pretext for committing human rights violations.

In Peru as elsewhere, the law offers mechanisms to promote such social change in an institutionalized form, for example with so-called guarantees of non-repetition. *Coordinadora* lawyer Mar told me that in recent years they relied on this mechanism in many criminal cases relating to police violence in social conflicts. The legal NGOs *Coordinadora* and *Fedepaz* attempt, in these lawsuits, to address not only the responsibility of the directly involved police officers, but also of the Ministry of the Interior as the state institution responsible for the police. In the ideal case of a court ruling acknowledging the Ministry's responsibility for the committed abuses, the human rights lawyers hope that institutional reforms will subsequently be initiated.

In the case of police violence during protests, for example, the lawyers demanded that police officers no longer be equipped with "weapons of war," such as assault rifles, when they are sent on operations against demonstrators, but with rubber shotguns or other non-lethal weapons, as Mar explained in one of our conversations. In her words, the idea is to induce institutional reforms to ensure that the police act in accordance with domestic legal frameworks and international human rights standards during demonstrations. In the human rights lawyers' opinion, these small steps of institutional change can then lead to social change.

Additionally, as a civil law country, legal change in Peru is normally not brought about through judicial precedents, but rather through the parliamentary process. The focus is therefore not on sensational rulings which establish completely new norms and upend the previously existing legal texts. It is less about legal activisms that help "create precedents that can become law," as Kirsch (1997, 136) put it; rather, it is a matter of gradually initiating institutional reforms through favorable court rulings which then changes the state officials' behavior.

Furthermore, it is mostly not a matter of demanding and implementing new law, but rather of securing existing rights for the benefit of marginalized population groups that have hitherto not been able to enjoy these rights. In this regard, I again follow Eckert (2006), who pointed out in her research on "citizens' practices of evoking state legal norms" (*ibid.*, 70) that different types of "legalism from below" give rise to changes on the normative level, in particular changes to what counts as "right or wrong" according to a society's norms. These forms of legal activism do not strive for an actual creation of new norms or new forms of law, but rather the reaffirmation of already existing norms. This in turn connects back to the expectation that legal proceedings will strengthen the rule of law and thus ultimately the state and its institutions, as I explained above. Moreover, this example illustrates how law can act as a counter-hegemonic means by granting power to socially marginalized groups of people through institutionalized channels.

In addition to Eckert's approach, I also rely on the work by Sikkink (2011) on individual criminal accountability. She followed a theoretical path similar to Eckert's, but in a completely different context. Sikkink dealt with transitional justice cases that followed military dictatorships in various European and Latin American countries. She argued that the power of law in these cases is that the norms of domestic criminal law, which had been applied for hundreds of years against "ordinary" criminals, are now used to hold former political and military elites accountable for their crimes (*ibid.*, 12). This "justice cascade," as Sikkink described it, has led to social change by applying the law to the powerful. Thus, what she observed was, again, not the appearance of new forms or norms of law, but rather a new way of enforcing the existing norms, as they were previously laid down in the legal code. This is the kind of process I trace in the analysis of the judicialization of Peru's mining conflicts.

Conclusion

The Peruvian human rights movement places great hopes in the law and expects to achieve a number of goals through legal mobilization – for the individuals it represents in court, their communities and social movements, but also for Peru's society as a whole. In doing so, the legal NGOs and their lawyers place so much hope in the law as a social process, because the law as a social practice, as a "problem solver" (Moore 2001, 97) or as an "ally" (Merry 1990, 4) for vulnerable groups provides for a multitude of possibilities. The different categories of expectations that I have discussed in this chapter encompass these different forms of hopes placed in the law. At the same time, however, they also highlight the many different possibilities that can be achieved through the mobilization of law. This explains why it makes sense for Peru's human rights movement to rely on law and legal mechanisms and why they attempt to achieve their goals "with the law," as Ewick and Silbey (1998) have categorized it.

Ideally, litigating a case of human rights violations in Peru considers different aspects. For example, in the case of *campesino* Elmer, who was shot by the police during the Conga protests, his lawyers made different claims to the court: First, they demanded financial compensation for Elmer as the injured party; second, they demanded a prison sentence for the responsible police officers who committed the crime; third, they demanded a public apology from the mining company and the police to the population of Cajamarca; and finally, they demanded the modification of the legal norms that regulate the actions of the police in interventions against demonstrators. By using the different possibilities the law provides for, it was thus possible to demand both justice for Elmer and social change for society and thereby to fulfill different legal expectations.

At the same time, as this chapter has also illustrated, legal processes not only raise expectations of the law, but also expectations of the persons involved, especially the "victims" and the lawyers. These expectations can lead to conflicts, especially if there are mediation difficulties in the negotiation processes between plaintiffs and lawyers or if there are major power differences. This highlights the fact that human rights ligation entails not only a legal but also a social process. Pedro, the lawyer who conducted the legal capacity training during the *Escuela de Líderes y Lideresas* in Celendín, focused on these aspects when he told me,

> The outcome of the lawsuit must not only be considered from a legal point of view, because sometimes the lawyer is very narrow-minded (*muy cuadrado*), sometimes very much limited to the law, and well, I can achieve a very good legal result, wow, spectacular, which, however, only serves the lawyers. So we have to think of a result that serves the people (*la gente*) and not the lawyer. I mean, I tell you, once we won a very good case, we got the best judgment [laughs], we could write a whole thesis about the judgment, but we didn't achieve anything for the people. [...] And well, I think you always have to think about the effects of what you are going to achieve [...] with a lawsuit, with a judgment. You always have to think not only about the legal effects, but about the social effects, the effects within and outside the community. Everything has to be thought about before developing the legal strategy. You also have to think about... if you win the process, what effect will it have? That's why you have to think very carefully about the strategy, not only with a lawyer's vision, but a vision of what could happen. If you win, if you lose, what would be the community's reaction? Because if you lose, it is more likely that the community no longer believes in justice. – *Pedro, NGO lawyer, Lima, February 2018 (interview transcript)*

Chapter 3. Human rights litigation from below

> La justicia es lenta, y la justicia no siempre es justa.[1] *–Juliana, human rights lawyer, Lima*

> Before the Law stands a doorkeeper on guard. To this doorkeeper there comes a man from the country who begs for admittance to the Law. But the doorkeeper says that he cannot admit the man at the moment. The man, on reflection, asks if he will be allowed, then, to enter later. "It is possible," answers the doorkeeper, "but not at this moment." *– Franz Kafka, The Trial (cited in: Ewick and Silbey 1998, 74)*

I sit with Marina in the meeting room of the human rights NGO for which she works. Marina is a young lawyer in her mid-twenties. On the table in front of us lies a thick court file containing various letters from the public prosecutor's office, a whole series of notifications, resolutions and orders, letters from Marina and her colleagues to the prosecutor, copies of documents and certificates they have submitted, and the criminal complaint they filed some months ago. Marina leafs through the file and explains step by step how she has proceeded in this case.

The complaint concerns an incident in which a mining company's security forces allegedly attacked a group of people, threatening them, insulting them, and damaging their property. Marina's aim is to make me understand how difficult it is to get the responsible public prosecutor to start a preliminary procedure, a so-called diligencia preliminar *– that is, to begin with the first phase of a court case under Peruvian criminal law. "This case is being handled by [local prosecutor]* doctor *Walter," Marina explains. "When* doctor *Walter receives the complaint, what does he have to do first? He has to investigate! It's called a preliminary procedure. Preliminary procedures are carried out by the prosecutor himself, with the help of the police, if necessary. So what is done? The most urgent statements are taken – that is, all the acts of investigation, the most urgent ones, for example, the inspection of the place, right? As it just happened, we go to the place to see so that the scene of the events, let's say, is fresh, that it hasn't changed much over time. That's an urgent procedure. The statements of all the people involved are taken."*

1 "Justice is slow, and justice is not always just."

Marina continues to leaf through the folder and comments on the documents. The incident occurred on March 16, and the NGO filed the complaint on behalf of the injured party shortly after. On April 6, the prosecutor's office confirmed to have received the complaint and ordered a judicial inspection for May 30. "However, this inspection did not take place," Marina adds, "because, if I remember correctly, the prosecutor's office car ran out of gas." She reads the file and adds, "No, that's not true. This time it was, as you can see here, because the other prosecutor working in the same office needed the car, as well. There is only one vehicle available at the office." Marina says that this is the way it always works: Sometimes there is no fuel, sometimes the car is not available, sometimes the assistant to the prosecutor is sick, and sometimes the weather is bad and they cannot go out to the countryside. In the case before us, the judicial inspection was postponed four times for such reasons and finally took place on August 9, almost five months after the incident. Marina explains that it is often difficult to detect damages and gather evidence on site after such a long period of time.

*In the present case, the preliminary procedure ended with the inspection of the site. Another five weeks passed between this inspection and my conversation with Marina. She must now wait and see how the prosecutor proceeds. According to the legal requirements, in the next step, the prosecutor should decide whether to open preliminary investigations: "He studies the case and sees if there are sufficient indications for the commission of a crime." In case he decides to open a preliminary investigation, more evidence will be gathered, the case will be further studied, and, based on this, the prosecutor submits a request to a judge of preliminary investigation (*juez o jueza de la investigación preparatoria*) for an indictment or for a so-called* sobreseimiento, *a dismissal.*[2] *Whether charges will ever be brought in this case remains unclear. In Marina's experience, such complaints are usually dropped by the prosecutor on the grounds that there is supposedly no evidence for the alleged crime, that the perpetrators supposedly could not be identified, or for other reasons. The prosecutor's office then closes the case and puts it on file.*

Human rights litigation in Peru requires much patience, tenacity, knowledge about legal proceedings, and, above all, *time*, a lot of time. In Peru, "[j]ustice is slow, and justice is not always just," as Juliana, a lawyer working at EarthRights International's office in Lima, noted in a presentation before law students at the *Universidad Católica*. The other human rights lawyers with whom I came into contact in the field would likely all agree with this statement. Peru's judicial system is full of hurdles and barriers, it is slow, and whether justice is finally obtained is not guaranteed. However, they all use the system of justice and bring cases of human rights violations to court. One could argue that of course these actors use the law because, after all, they are lawyers who are trained in law. There are, however, further reasons for these attorneys to use the legal system other than just their professional relation to law. We can

---

2 For a discussion of the various stages of the Peruvian criminal procedure, see: Oré Guardia and Loza Avalos 2005.

observe these different reasons in the way they use the legal system, in the norms they invoke, and in the strategies they apply.

In this chapter, I analyze different court cases brought before local courts by legal NGOs in connection with the mining conflicts in Piura and Cajamarca. The chapter is structured in three parts. In the first part, I discuss the obstacles that have arisen in these lawsuits and examine the approaches the lawyers have used to overcome them. Thus, I provide insight into the hurdles and the strategies of legal mobilization *from below*. In the second part of the chapter, I focus on the public prosecutor's office, which plays a crucial role in most of these lawsuits. In doing so, I shed light on the prosecution by examining its role as a kind of doorkeeper guarding the access to law's doors. Finally, in the chapter's third part, I discuss how the presence of transnational mining companies influenced these court cases. There are reasons, both in law and beyond, that complicate litigation when powerful actors such as TNCs are involved as defendants. At the same time, there are different strategies human rights NGOs use to attribute legal responsibility to these corporate actors.

"Slow and not always just"

Filing a complaint, initiating an investigation

The torture case from Piura is one of the court cases that exemplified human rights litigation as practiced by legal NGOs in Peru's mining conflicts. As I mentioned in Chapter 1, this case concerns a group of twenty-eight protesters who were detained and tortured within the Río Blanco mine camp in 2005. *Fedepaz* brought this case to court with the support of the *Coordinadora*, the umbrella organization of Peru's human rights movement. As described earlier, a prosecutor visited the mine site to interrogate the detained demonstrators. Thus, the local prosecutor's office had knowledge of the abuses. When the group of protesters was released after three days, however, the same prosecutor did not open an investigation into the allegations of torture, but, on the contrary, took action against the detainees and against nearly eighty demonstrators for participating in the protest march.

Under these circumstances, it took the NGO lawyers nearly three years to file a complaint about the abuses the twenty-eight detainees had suffered. One reason why this took so much time was the lack of evidence for proving the abuses. In January 2009, *La República*, one of Peru's most important daily newspapers, published pictures that revealed the protesters' detention (Prado 2009). The photos showed the detainees sitting on the floor with their hands tied, blindfolded, and surrounded by armed police officers. With these pictures in mind, it is difficult to understand how it could take the judiciary so long to deal with this incident. However, the photos only became public after the complaint had already been filed. An anonymous source leaked them to the newspaper a few months after *Fedepaz* and the *Coordinadora* had lodged the complaint. When they began building the case, the lawyers did not have any such evidence and only relied on the declarations of the detainees.

Due to its long-standing cooperation with the social movements in the region, *Fedepaz*' team knew some of the persons involved, especially the social leaders who had been detained. But among the detainees were also ordinary members of the protest movement whom the lawyers did not know. As the two *Fedepaz* lawyers David and Rosa told me, it was difficult to reconstruct the events and to establish contact with the affected people who came from remote communities. Some of them lived a several hours' walk from the nearest towns and did not have a telephone connection. Due to this spatial marginalization, keeping contact with the complainants was a challenge, which was also related to the fact that the NGOs' offices are located in Lima, more than one thousand kilometers away from where the complainants live. Rosa told me that, later on, when the proceedings had started and when they had to inform the complainants about appointments with the prosecutor, for example, they used personal messages sent via local radio stations because there was no other way to contact them. In Peru's rural areas, radio stations were – and still are – an important means of communication. Early in the morning, before people went to the *chacra*, to their agriculture field, they would listen to the radio. *Fedepaz* used this as a platform to keep the complainants informed about their lawsuit. This example illustrates the practical hurdles the lawyers faced when preparing the complaint.

The situation was further complicated because, as a consequence of the severe offenses, many of the complainants had suffered a psychological shock, which made it difficult to organize them as a group. *Fedepaz*' team had the difficult task of convincing them to turn to the judicial system, a system that worked closely with the police officers who had abused them. To make matters worse, the heavy repression of the social movement and the criminalization of its members continued for a long time after the incident. In general, the rural population's distrust of state institutions, including the judiciary, is widespread in Peru's highlands, as Deborah Poole discussed in detail (2004). According to Monique Nuijten and David Lorenzo's (2009) research on Peru's central highlands, this mistrust is rooted in, among other things, the weak presence of the state in these regions and the local perception that the authorities in Lima had not only marginalized them, but also had abandoned and forgotten them. This description also applies to the Andean region in Piura. The state is present in these areas through institutions such as schools and basic health care facilities. However, these institutions often function inadequately, are poorly equipped, and underfunded. The local population therefore perceives the state primarily through the presence of repressive police forces, and the absence of the state as an institution that would support the population is a recurrent complaint.

The group of complainants in the torture case included a teacher, a journalist and a woman who had studied at a university; thus people who had frequent contact with the state in their daily lives. The remaining complainants, however, were almost all *campesinos* and *campesinas* who lived off subsistence agriculture, had low incomes and education levels, and from whose daily lives the Peruvian state was largely absent. Instead of the nation-state, by contrast, institutions of local social organization played a significant role in the lives of these *campesinos* and *campesinas*. Many of them had taken a prominent role and led the local protest organizations within the social movements against Río Blanco. Due to their political commitment, some of them had come into contact with the legal system earlier, in particular because they were criminalized for participating in the protest movement. However, in view of the powerful opponents they faced, I would classify the group as rather inexperienced in the field of judicial processes. In terms of power, financial resources, and legal expertise they were so-called "one-shotters" in the sense of Galanter's (1974, 97) terminology. In the judicial proceedings, they depended on the human rights lawyers who had the experience and the knowledge of the law and who acted on their behalf before court as "repeat players" (Galanter 1974, 114).

The fact that they lacked evidence and that they received no support from the public prosecutor's side hampered the work of the human rights lawyers. In their efforts to support the case, *Fedepaz* and the *Coordinadora* turned to foreign partner organizations, among them the international NGO Physicians for Human Rights, which helped systematize the complainants' statements. Physicians for Human Rights sent two medical specialists to Peru to examine some of the complainants and to evaluate the physical and mental consequences they had suffered. In doing so, doctors working for an international NGO fulfilled a task that would typically fall under the responsibility of the prosecution in a criminal investigation. According to Mar, a lawyer working with the *Coordinadora*, this NGO report finally made it feasible to file the complaint to the Provincial Criminal Prosecutor's Office in Piura in June 2008. Thanks to their integration in a transnational advocacy network, it was thus possible for the lawyers to take the decisive step toward opening a criminal proceeding.

The complaint[3] focused on the offenses of torture and aggravated kidnapping; other crimes were included, as well. The main allegations were brought against three different groups of actors: first, three high-ranking and personally named superior police officers who were responsible for the region where the alleged crime took place; second, the police officials directly involved in the protesters' detention and mistreatment; and third, the security staff of the mining company. The mining company's officials were also named as accused parties. Moreover, the complaint mentioned, first, the killing of the *campesino* who was shot during the police's repression of the protest march; second, the "acts against the modesty" (*actos contra el pudor*) of

3 Criminal complaint to the *Quinta Fiscalía Provincial Penal de Piura*; document on file with author.

the two detained women; third, the "omission of criminal proceedings" on the side of the prosecutor who visited the mine site but who did not intervene; and, finally, the issuance of false medical certificate by members of the criminal investigation division in Piura, who had examined the demonstrators after their release and allegedly issued false documents about the state of their health, thus concealing the traces of torture. Accordingly, the complaint was extremely detailed and included many pieces of information that the lawyers of *Fedepaz* and the *Coordinadora* had researched.

Leading a case through criminal proceedings

The torture case garnered national interest some months after the complaint was filed when *La República* published a series of pictures revealing the abuses in January 2009. Despite the publication of these images and despite the detailed complaint *Fedepaz* and the *Coordinadora* had filed, however, the prosecutor's office decided in March 2009 to take action against only the low-ranking police officers and dismissed the other allegations brought forward. *Fedepaz* appealed this decision and requested the reopening of the case (Fedepaz 2009).

In the following seven years, this process of closing the case, on the side of the authorities, and the process of appealing and demanding the investigation's reopening, on the side of *Fedepaz*, was repeated several times, not only on the level of the prosecution, but also later when the charges were brought and when the courts dealt with the case. The filing of appeals became *Fedepaz*' most effective tool. At each new stage, the prosecutorial and judicial authorities found new reasons to obstruct the continuation of the proceedings, attempting to close the case and to stop the legal investigation of the incident. The human rights lawyers' efforts were mainly to keep the court case going and to prevent a definitive dismissal, as David told me in retrospect.

Finally, the judicial authorities split the initial complaint into different lawsuits. The proceedings concerning the killing of the one *campesino* were soon dropped because it could not be established who was responsible for his death. After exhausting all legal possibilities to appeal against this decision, *Fedepaz* had to accept this dismissal. In other aspects of the complaint, however, the NGO was more successful. The allegations of torture and kidnapping were investigated in two separate cases: one against fourteen police agents directly involved, and another against the high-ranking police officers (Velazco Rondón and Quedena Zambrano 2015, 51). Behind this separation was allegedly the attempt to split the responsibility of the "ordinary" police officers from that of their superiors, thus from the direct perpetrators, on the one hand, and the "intellectual actors" (*autores intelectuales*) of the abuses, on the other hand, as *Fedepaz* called them. In the following years, the NGO's legal team sought to prevent this fragmentation of responsibility and, in March 2016, managed to combine the two cases again (Fedepaz 2016). The allegations of torture and kidnapping were then again investigated as a single case. The legal proceedings, however, still did not lead to a trial. There were delays because detailed aspects of the accusation needed to be clarified.[4]

During my stays in Peru in 2017 and 2018, I was repeatedly told that the proceedings in the torture case would "soon" enter into the phase of the *control de acusación*, in which the charge is "controlled" by a judge, who decides whether all the procedural requirements are fulfilled. After this step, a case proceeds to the final phase, the *juicio oral*, the oral hearing (Hurtado Poma 2009). Thus, nearly ten years after filing the complaint and more than thirteen years after the human rights violations occurred, the lawyers working with *Fedepaz* finally expected a trial to start sometime "soon," as they told me.

Due to the location of the incidents, all the proceedings were conducted in Piura, which meant that *Fedepaz*' lawyers had to take a flight for each hearing or appointment with the prosecutor. For *Fedepaz*, which finances itself on a project-by-project basis through partner NGOs, the long process was a financial challenge. In addition, with this temporal aspect in mind, Rosa stressed the importance of keeping complainants updated about their case. Since the justice system is so slow, the human rights lawyers' task is to convince complainants that there is still hope of getting justice one day, even though proceedings seem to get stuck. Their efforts involve assuring that the processes are "slow" but still "just." Rosa told me, however, that the long wait and the associated feeling of being forgotten by the judicial system is often difficult for complainants.

In her research on the justice system in Peru's central and southern highlands, Poole analyzed historical court cases and described how people who file a complaint with a prosecutor had to wait years for a response. She used a specific case to illustrate how a complaint was passed from one judicial authority to another, moving back and forth between different locations. Poole called this "the *expediente*'s [the court file's] routings, or 'driftings,'" (2004, 48). She noted that "the vast majority of legal cases that are 'directed' to the next level of the judicial apparatus do indeed seem to drift more or less aimlessly from one office to the next, before finally being returned, unresolved and often years later, to their points of origin" (*ibid.*, 42). In the cases I examined, the files are sometimes moved back and forth between the authorities, but from the complainants' point of view, they do not drift around but rather get stuck and do not move on. A man from a *comunidad campesina* in Cajamarca, for

4 For example, *Fedepaz* demanded that the involvement of the Ministry of the Interior, as the institution responsible for the police, to be discussed in the court case, too (see third part of this chapter). Moreover, the NGO requested the aggrieved party to be included as "civil actor," which allows for the active participation in the oral hearing (Fedepaz 2018b). These issues had to be clarified before the hearing could start.

example, once noted that "it seems that the papers are sleeping in the courts," in reference to a complaint his community had filed. So, from the point of view of these plaintiffs and complainants, it is not the drifting, but the actual immobility that captures the cases, and this immobility is linked to the inactivity of the authorities.

In the perception of the human rights lawyers, there are several reasons for this inaction of the authorities. I explore these aspects in the second section when discussing the role of prosecutors as gatekeepers. For now, I would like to emphasize that it is these long and exhausting procedures which represent the greatest difficulty in the cases of human rights litigation that I analyzed. The cases that I summarize in this book as "human rights violations" actually involved assault, killing, torture, and kidnapping. Some of them also involved less serious crimes such as property damage, harassment, or threats. All these criminal offenses are clearly regulated in Peru's criminal code and are categorized as inadmissible. Thus, the problem does not lie in the law – that is, in law's code itself – but rather in law's proceedings and in the way the institutions administer them. Once a complaint is filed, cases often get stuck in the system, which in turn results in litigation being "slow and not always just." However, there is one specific area in which the legal basis does present a difficulty, and that is when it comes to regulating state security forces; I address this issue in the following.

Opening investigations against state security forces

Social conflicts between corporate actors and social movements in Peru have repeatedly resulted in outbreaks of violence in recent years. However, the violence often did not originate directly from company employees but from state security forces. The *Coordinadora* records the number and the names of the people killed under such circumstances (see, for example: CNDDHH 2012, 163–4, 2015, 62–93, 2017, 72–81).[5] According to these statistics, from Peru's return to democracy in 2000 to 2017, over 150 civilians were killed by state security forces during social conflicts.[6] Human rights NGOs and activists complained that in many conflicts, in particular those arising from large investment projects, state security forces did not take on the role of mediators but instead sided with corporations by using force against protesters.

As *Grufides* lawyer Mirtha Vásquez wrote, the military and police personnel would "confront protesters as 'criminals' or 'enemies'" (2013, 425, own translation). Former executive secretary with the *Coordinadora* Rocío Silva Santisteban noted that the state would use narratives to portray the demonstrators in mining conflicts

---

5 These numbers include not only mining but also other social conflicts.

6 See, for example, the contribution of Ana María Vidal, representative of the *Coordinadora*, during the hearing on "Human Rights and Extractive Industries in Peru" held on May 25, 2017 in Buenos Aires, Argentina, during the 162nd Period of Sessions of the IACHR.

as "terrorists" or as "inferior others" who "oppose the economic development of the country," thereby discursively legitimizing the use of violence against these population groups (2013, 2016). Many activists in Cajamarca told me about their experiences of being labeled "resistant" or "violent enemies of the state" during the Conga conflict. They said that, in this way, the state had attempted to "discredit the protest movements' legitimate protests" and to "justify the use of violence." The use of force by the state was thus discursively negotiated within the social conflict. In addition, this form of state violence is structural in nature and there is a legal framework allowing for such abuses. In this sense, the state institutions secure themselves in the use of force not only through discursive argumentation but also based on legal norms.

One condition laid out in the law that facilitates the use of force by state actors in social conflicts is the possibility of contracts for "extraordinary services" between Peru's National Police (PNP) and private parties.[7] These contracts allow members of the PNP to carry out missions for the benefit of private actors, such as corporations. Companies operating in the extractive industries have made frequent use of this possibility in recent years and have "rented" officers to protect their properties. When providing these extraordinary services, the officers wear their usual uniform, equipment, and weapons (Velazco Rondón and Quedena Zambrano 2015, 23). Therefore, it is not always possible to determine whether they are providing such private security services or acting as public servants. Various authors have argued that this practice has led to a partial privatization of the Peruvian police (Kamphuis 2011, 72, 2012a, 540, Jaskoski 2012, 96, Silva Santisteban 2013, 446).

For this research, I analyzed several such contracts between transnational mining companies and the PNP.[8] These contracts stipulate that the individual police officers perform the extraordinary services "on a voluntary basis" during their holidays

7 Supreme Decree No 004–2009-IN; *Decreto Supremo que aprueba el Reglamento de Prestación de Servicios Extraordinarios Complementarios a la Función Policial* ("Supreme Decree approving the Regulation on the provision of extraordinary supplementary services by the police forces").

8 The analysis included a total of five contracts concluded between the PNP and the mining companies Minera Yanacocha, Empresa Minera Xstrata Tintaya, and Empresa Minera Las Bambas. The conventions were issued between May 2011 and October 2017. All documents are on file with the author. Three contracts were publicly available on the website of the Ministry of the Interior (2020), whereas two contracts were published by the information platform Servindi (2016). With regard to the Río Blanco project in Piura, it is not known whether the company had a contract with the PNP when the torture case occurred in 2005. However, the company coordinated with the police on the deployment of the special unit to protect its facilities when the incident occurred. Moreover, as Kamphuis (2011, 77) reported, a general of the National Police publicly explained that the company did not pay the police officers directly for their deployment but for their food and transport. This statement was also confirmed by David of *Fedepaz*. It therefore seemed that this case was more of an informal collaboration, rather than a contract-based cooperation between the PNP and the mining company.

or at a time when they are released from their normal duties (see also: Kamphuis 2011, 70). The conventions regulate the number of officers, the location of the operation, and the officers' tasks. In addition to the salaries that the officers receive based on these contracts, the companies also pay for their transport and food. However, all documents I examined explicitly stated that the contracts did not imply a direct employment relationship between the police officers and the mining company and that, consequently, no pension entitlements would arise for the officers. Most of the contracts stated, in addition, that "nothing in this convention shall be construed to mean that the PNP, or any of its members, are agents, partners, employees or representatives" of the concerned mining company.[9] Thus, according to the contracts, there is no subordination of the police, the company has no power of command, and the police must not be restricted by the extraordinary services in performing their functions of "maintaining internal order."

The legislation that allows for such private contracts dates back to the internal armed conflict. At that time, mines recurrently became targets of attacks by insurgent groups because they stocked large amounts of dynamite (Jaskoski 2012, 91). Peru, as a "weak" state that lacked financial resources, thus "invited" private companies to "subsidize state security forces," as Maiah Jaskoski (2012, 81) put it (see also: Avant 2005, 181). However, this practice was not limited to the time of the internal armed conflict but was also maintained after the return to democracy in 2000. Civil society organizations have argued that the legal basis allowing for such contracts is against the constitution since they violate the state's monopoly on the use of force in the sense of Max Weber (2014 [1919], 9). Legal NGOs have argued that by breaking its own monopoly on the use of force, the state would no longer fulfill its fundamental task, i.e. the protection of the rights of its citizens, and would instead place itself at the service of private economic interests. Therefore, it comes as no surprise, the NGOs argued, that the PNP has repeatedly used violence in conflicts between protesters and mining companies, since these same companies hold contracts with the police.

State authorities have repeatedly responded to this criticism from civil society by invoking the law. For example, in a hearing before the IACHR, a state representative argued that "there is a constitutional framework, a legal framework, a normative framework that allows the Peruvian state [to sign] these extraordinary agree-

---

9 See, for example: *Convenio específico de cooperación entre Minera Yanacocha S.R.L. y la Policía Nacional del Perú* (Specific cooperation agreement between Minera Yanacocha S.R.L. and the Peruvian National Police), issued in October 2017; document on file with author; own translation.

ments."[10] To underline this argument, he referred to the "Law on the Peruvian National Police,"[11] which regulates services of state security forces. Based on this example, I argue, first, that the exercise of state violence in social conflicts in Peru is structurally determined and made possible by law.

A second institutional aspect that allows the exercise of violence by state agents within social conflicts lies in the legal basis that, under certain conditions, grants impunity to members of the police and the army if they kill or seriously injure someone "in the performance of their duties" (*en el cumplimiento de su deber*). The legal basis that established this form of impunity has been revised several times in recent years. During the government of President Alan García, the regulation in the Peruvian Criminal Code on the "in-imputability" (*inimputabilidad*) was extended to include "reasons which exempt or diminish the criminal responsibility" of someone who violates the law. The corresponding article declares that, for example, minors cannot be held criminally liable. With a legislative decree adopted in 2007, the article was supplemented by a clause concerning the personnel of the armed forces and the police, which then read as follows:

> Article 20.- To be exempted from criminal liability is [...]
>
> 11. The personnel of the Armed Forces and the National Police, who in the fulfillment of their duty and in the use of their weapons in a regulated manner, cause injury or death. *–Article 20.11, Peruvian Criminal Code, as applied from 2007 to 2014, own translation*

As Kamphuis wrote, it was the first time in Peru's history that "this type of immunity [had] been legally codified" (2012b, 236). In 2013, the Congress went even further by passing Law 30151, which again modified Article 20, paragraph 11 of the Criminal Code. With this modification, the term "in a regulated manner" was removed; instead, the phrase was supplemented and stated that to be exempted from criminal liability are police and military forces who "in the course of their duty and in the use of their weapons *or other means of defense*, cause injury or death."[12] Within the human rights movement, this change in the law caused great criticism and objection. Several legal NGOs protested against Law 30151 by declaring it a "violation of fundamental rights," a "carte blanche" for the state security forces, or even a "license to kill" (IDL 2013, 3, Vásquez 2013, 427). They feared that the change in the law would result

10 Hearing on "Citizen Security and Reports of the Irregular Use of Police Forces in Natural Resource Exploration and Mining Activities in Peru" held on 1 October 2018 in Boulder, United States, during the 169th Period of Sessions of the IACHR.

11 Article 51.1, *Ley orgánica de la Policía Nacional del Perú*.

12 Article 20.11, Peruvian Criminal Code, own translation, emphasis added. This version of the article applied until March 2020, when it was again modified.

in human rights violations committed by state security forces remaining in "absolute impunity" (Velazco Rondón and Quedena Zambrano 2015, 14). This is a second example that demonstrates the structural nature of police violence in Peru's social conflicts and the codification of impunity in the country's legal code.

IDL, a national human rights NGO based in Lima, argued that the law would award the state security forces a license to kill, even "when they act under the sponsorship of privates" (IDL 2013, 3, own translation), thus referring to the extraordinary services the PNP provides to companies. This also demonstrates how the various legal texts intertwine and form a pattern that allows for the use of state violence, which in most cases remains unpunished. There is thus a clear legal basis favoring the use of violence by state security forces.

Public prosecutors as doorkeepers

Peter Brett (2018, 45) noted that "[j]udicialisation requires courts willing to hear cases, and lawyers willing to support them." I agree with this statement, but I would add that in criminal law there is above all a need for prosecutors who are willing and prepared to accept and support a case and thus to enable legal mobilization. In this sense, I follow Johanna Mugler who wrote that:

> Prosecutors occupy an important function in the court process where the accountability of people who are accused of having committed a crime is discussed, interpreted and established. They can be pivotal in assisting victims of crime to seek "protection" from further harm and to obtain "justice". It is up to them to ensure that "everyone is equal before the law" by holding also the "rich, powerful and well-connected" to account for wrongdoings. And it is amongst their responsibilities that every accused receives a fair trial. (Mugler 2019, 24)

In Mugler's view, it is thus the public prosecutors who should uphold and defend the principles of legal liberalism of equal treatment before the law. They should ensure access to the courts.

Standing before the law's doors

Marina, the human rights lawyer mentioned at the beginning of this chapter, underlined the prosecutor's pivotal role by telling me that in an initial phase of a criminal proceeding, a case's success "doesn't depend on me, nor on the injured person, nor on anyone else, only on the prosecutor, right? That the prosecutor feels like saying: 'Well, that's what happened; let's go and see how it was' – so, that he's *concerned* with investigating." Thus, it is the prosecutor's decision whether to follow a specific case or not. Since the opening of an investigation is the cornerstone of any criminal proceeding, a prosecutor thereby decides who has access to the system of justice and who does not (see also: Michel 2017, 196).

Therefore, I argue that prosecutors act as gatekeepers of the law, comparable to the doorkeeper in Franz Kafka's "The Trial." Kafka used a parable to describe how a guard stands "before the law" and prevents a man from the country, who wants to appeal to the law, from entering. He wrote that:

> The man from the country did not expect such difficulties; the Law is supposed to be available to everyone and at all times, he thinks, but when he takes a closer look at the doorkeeper in his fur coat, with his large pointed nose, his long, thin, black Tartar moustache, he decides he had better wait until he is given permission to enter. The doorkeeper gives him a stool and lets him sit down at the side of the door. He sits there for days and years. (Kafka 2009 [1925], 154)

Over the years, the man from the country repeatedly attempts to convince the doorkeeper to grant him access, but he fails. Shortly before his death, though, he asks the guard why he was the only one to ask for admission, in all those years, despite the fact that everyone is striving for the law. The guard replies, "No one else could ever be admitted here, since this gate was made only for you. I am now going to shut it" (Kafka 2009 [1925], 155).

I propose that in Peru's criminal proceedings the position of persons affected by human rights violations in relation to mining conflicts is comparable to Kafka's man from the country. They "stand before the law" and ask to be admitted but are hindered from doing so by a guard, which, in Peru, is the public prosecutor.[13] To the persons standing before the law it is not comprehensible which criteria the gatekeeper uses to decide whether to grant them admission. With the support of lawyers who represent and advise them, they submit evidence and invoke the existing procedural norms in order to convince the prosecutor of the necessity to open a criminal investigation, thus to let them access the law, but they often fail.

Mugler stressed that prosecutors "decide *who* to charge with a criminal offence, *what* charges to file and *when* to dismiss or withdraw a case" (2019, 21, emphasis added). In a similar manner, Verónica Michel noted, with regard to several domestic human rights trials worldwide, that "a prosecutorial organ dictates *what*, *when*, and *whom* to prosecute" (2017, 193, emphasis added). In this regard, "prosecutorial discretion" plays a major role, as both Michel and Mugler stressed. Mugler explained that prosecutors are equipped with "extensive powers of discretion to initiate or discontinue criminal proceedings on behalf of the state, backed by the power of the state"

13 In a similar manner, Michel described prosecutors as "key gatekeeper[s] of the courts" (2017, 193).

(2019, 21). In the mining conflicts in Peru, it is precisely this power of discretion prosecutors have to decide *when* and *who* to investigate for *what* alleged crimes.

According to the country's new procedural code, "[t]he Public Prosecutor's Office is in charge of exercising criminal action. It acts *ex officio*, at the request of the victim, upon popular action, or police report."[14] In addition, the prosecution is obligated to be independent, "adapting its acts to an objective criterion and being governed solely by the Constitution and the law."[15] In doing so, however, it enjoys discretionary powers. Discretion is part of the very nature of law. In any interpretation of the law – i.e. in the application of a legal principle to a specific case – there is a certain degree of discretionary power that allows for different outcomes. To rely on discretionary power is thus not against but, in contrast, inherent to law. In Peru's mining conflicts, human rights lawyers have argued, however, that there is a misuse of this discretional power on the part of the involved prosecutorial authorities.

To underline these accusations, the NGO lawyers referred, for example, to the collection of evidence, which is a central task of the public prosecutor's office. The reasons put forth by prosecutors to postpone judicial inspections and thus to gather evidence on site, such as in the case described by Marina, are perceived by the lawyers as inadmissible pretexts. Mar, the *Coordinadora* lawyer, told me that due to the prosecutors' unwillingness to gather evidence, this task often falls to the complainant side. She told me that:

> It's just that [the prosecutors] – *ex officio* – would have to see what evidence could help to know what happened. But no, it's never like that. If the [complainant's] lawyers do not constantly expedite things themselves, proposing evidence, and sometimes even bringing them the evidence, they would not do it. – *Mar, lawyer with the* Coordinadora, *January 2018, Lima (interview transcript)*

By gathering and submitting evidence, the complainants undertake tasks which, according to the law, are the responsibility of the prosecutor. Furthermore, if prosecutors close a case, it is up to the aggrieved party to appeal against this action in order to reopen the law's doors and to keep a case going. This was particularly evident in the torture case, in which *Fedepaz* repeatedly appealed against the orders to dismiss the claims. The lawyers had to exert constant pressure to ensure that the authorities would fulfill their duties as encoded in the law.

A specific characteristic of criminal proceedings is that, in contrast to civil law, the state is also among the aggrieved parties. A prosecutor is therefore a public lawyer who investigates, in many cases, *ex officio* when norms of the state were violated (Michel 2017, 196). Thus, the prosecutor's role is to defend both the rights

---

14 Article 60.1, New Peruvian Criminal Procedure Code, own translation.

15 Article 61, New Peruvian Criminal Procedure Code, own translation.

of the complainants and the interests of the state. Mirtha, an NGO lawyer from Cajamarca, told me in this regard, "The public prosecutor's office itself must be the defender of legality and normally plays the role of siding with the complainant because it is he who is reporting a crime, not only against him but against society, as well." A prosecutor who does not take action, even though he or she has knowledge of a violation of rights, acts not only against the interests of the injured party but also against the state.

The human rights lawyers argued that, furthermore, the prosecutors also act against the law, not because of relying on their discretional power not to investigate but because of their alleged misuse of this power not to do so. The NGO lawyers thus acknowledged that prosecutors hold a certain discretion to decide whether to investigate; they complained, however, that in cases of human rights violations involving corporate and state actors, the margin of discretion is improperly or even unlawfully interpreted against the complainants. According to the NGO lawyers, the reason for this is the alleged "lack of a political will" to investigate against powerful actors.

"A lack of political will"

The reasons for this alleged lack of political will to initiate investigations in the context of mining conflicts are probably as diverse as the public prosecutors and their personal backgrounds. One reason, which social movements' activists and human rights lawyers have repeatedly mentioned, is corruption. As Palujo, an activist from Celendín told me, "corruption changes people," thus the best trained and most dedicated prosecutor "is worth nothing" if he or she begins taking bribes. Another activist told me that corruption in the authorities leads to the fact that "they do not care about the truth."

Corruption[16] is a particular problem in regions like Cajamarca, where mining companies act as powerful regional players. At the same time, the phenomenon is also a central issue at the national level. During my stays in the field, discussions in Peru's national media and in public space were strongly influenced by the then recently revealed corruption scandal surrounding the Brazilian corporation Odebrecht. As in other Latin American countries, this scandal uncovered the bribery of a number of Peruvian politicians, including *all* five presidents who governed the country after the transition in 2000 until 2020, as well as many high-ranking politicians

16 As in other humanities and social sciences, a growing interest in corruption as a field of research can be observed within social anthropology in recent years (for an overview see, for example: Haller and Shore 2005, Torsello and Venard 2016, Anders and Nuijten 2017). Although I recognize the phenomenon as an important object of research, too, it would go beyond the scope of this book to include the theoretical approaches of the anthropology of corruption in my analysis. Rather, I consider and include corruption in this book as an emic concept that has emerged from the field.

and members of Congress. Because all the former presidents were investigated for corruption, social movements activists saw their suspicion confirmed that a network of high-level corruption links the government, members of Congress, and the judiciary to corporations. For many grassroots activists, corruption is one of the most striking features of the local judiciary. I have been told many times that "all prosecutors and judges are corrupt." This perception has led many activists to adopt a hostile attitude toward judicial and prosecutorial authorities, and it explains why many people are critical of legal proceedings. Interestingly, however, people direct their distrust mainly at the people who embody the law, i.e. judges and prosecutors, and the judicial system they represent, but not at the law itself as an idea and a social institution. Thus, people make a clear distinction between, on the one hand, judges, prosecutors, and the institutional system with which they come into contact due to the juridification of social conflicts, and, on the other hand, the law, of whose functioning they have a fixed idea and towards which they have a social expectation. In this context, corruption is seen as something that attacks and challenges the purity of law and its social function. This explains the supposed contradiction that people criticize the judicial system as corrupt and as therefore untrustworthy, while at the same time invoking the law and its ordering function in society.

In addition, the experience with corruption has also shaped the attitude of the lawyers who generally ascribe an emancipatory or counterhegemonic effect to the law. Mirtha told me that it is "obvious to everyone in Cajamarca" that mining companies use bribery to influence the judicial authorities and that this constitutes a large disadvantage for social movements. Despite the fact that the corruptibility of the judiciary is publicly known, however, it is difficult for human rights organizations to take legal action against corruption. Mirtha noted that:

> It's very easy for companies to collude with and corrupt authorities. It's very common here. So, you have to litigate in a context where you have a judicial power or a prosecution that is "presumably" corrupt [laughs], ... and we say "presumably" corrupt because, for us, corruption does not leave any real traces. It is very difficult to prove, but it is evident that the actions of ... for example, the public prosecutor's office, the mining company would almost not need lawyers because they have the public prosecutor's office defending them and trying to pull their chestnuts out of the fire, as we say here, right? – *Mirtha, lawyer with* Grufides, *February 2017, Cajamarca (interview transcript)*

With her statement that "the mining company would almost not need lawyers because they have the public prosecutor's office defending them," Mirtha also pointed to the social networks that link members of prosecutorial and judicial authorities with corporate actors. At the national level, it is the "revolving doors" through which individuals move back and forth between the private sector and the state administration, thereby creating personal linkages and, consequently, an interdependence between institutions and corporations (Urteaga-Crovetto 2012, Durand 2016). At the local level, activists and lawyers complained about the revolving doors between the prosecutor's office and Minera Yanacocha, for instance. In addition, they also alleged direct personal networks and family ties between state and corporate actors that called into question the independence of the institutions.[17]

Corruption and other forms of personal linkages are thus a major obstacle to legal mobilization from below. At the same time, attributing the problem of influential public prosecutors and judges only to corruption would mean oversimplifying the situation. Rather, there are also subtle ways in which powerful actors control the judicial system. Various lawyers from Lima as well as their colleagues in the provinces told me about "trustworthy" and "just" prosecutors and judges who were known to be independent and incorruptible. The lawyers repeatedly observed how exactly these officials were transferred to other places, presumably as a measure of promotion. In Cajamarca, for example, a judge who was "*más o menos probo*" – "more or less righteous", as the activists described him – was "promoted" and transferred to the province of Chota. There he held a higher position in the institutional hierarchy, but he was, at the same time, far away from the court cases related to the mining conflicts in the southern provinces of the region. In the perspective of the lawyer who told me about this transfer, the judge's colleagues, who had proposed his promotion, had acted strategically to "get him out of the way."

Having the prosecutors and judges' individual situation in mind, I argue that judicial officers are personally exposed when they are involved in lawsuits dealing with corporate or state actors. They directly face pressure to close cases or to delay or even disrupt proceedings. Various other authors have written about disciplinary measures within judicial authorities in Peru and in other countries. Coletta Youngers (2000, 15–6), for example, described a tendency toward self-censorship in her research on Peru's judicial system during the Fujimori regime. Similarly, Matthew Hull (2003, 289, 300–1, 2012, 128), in his ethnographic research on Pakistan's bureaucracy, described how officials attempt to avoid personal sanctions by producing as little written material as possible that would allow conclusions to be drawn about their person. In this way, the officials attempt to "collectivize" the responsibility for individual decisions and actions. It goes beyond the scope of my research to discuss how individual officials of Peru's judiciary perceive such challenges, but these examples provide insight into the assertion that corruption is far from being the only reason for prosecutors' and judges' reluctance to investigate politically sensitive cases such as those involving human rights violations.

17 I discuss this point in Chapter 4 when analyzing a specific criminalization case from Cajamarca.

Furthermore, there are also structural reasons that lead to the prosecutorial organs lacking willingness. In court cases dealing with police violence, a state authority – the prosecutor's office – is required to investigate and punish the involvement in human rights violations of another state authority: the police. In Peru, prosecutorial and police authorities are institutionally close to each other and collaborate in everyday work. The NGO lawyers see this as a reason why judicial authorities are reluctant to take action against the police. Despite this institutional closeness, however, the human rights lawyers also claim that the prosecution often lacks the specific expertise to take action against police forces, as Mar noted:

> They also don't know about the procedures of the police, nor do they know how the police work administratively, how decisions are made within the police; and so, they don't know what evidence, what documents to request, who to call to testify. And of course, the police and the army don't help them at all, right? – *Mar, lawyer with the* Coordinadora, *January 2018, Lima (interview transcript)*

The case of the five men killed during the Conga conflict confirmed this allegation. All the attempts made by the *Coordinadora* to investigate these deaths were ultimately unsuccessful since the authorities argued that it was not possible to identify the direct perpetrators – that is, the police officers or the members of the armed forces who had shot the demonstrators. Although forensic investigations, the so-called *peritajes judiciales,* proved the involvement of the police and the military in the killings, the case was repeatedly dismissed. The state security forces allegedly withheld information by claiming that the *cuaderno de afectaciones,* the list in which the distribution of weapons to the units was recorded, no longer existed. Without this information from within the institution, it was impossible for the prosecution and the complainant's lawyers to trace who the shooters were.

Furthermore, and as explained above, Peruvian police officers and members of the army are exempt from punishment if they seriously injure or kill people "in the fulfillment of their duties." In a few cases, the judicial authorities invoked this law to justify the termination of prosecution against members of the police.[18] Mar confirmed to me, however, that in the actual proceedings it is not this legal norm which causes impunity, but rather the fact that the prosecution does not investigate other state authorities, such as the police or the army. This means that the cases never reach the procedural level where the law on police impunity would be applied. The

18 The first case that came to light in this regard concerned a group of police officers who had violently attacked student protests in the Huancavelica region in 2011. The four police officers were under investigation for the deaths of four students. In the first instance, however, they were acquitted on the basis of Law 30151, the law on police impunity (court ruling on file with author, see also: Fowks 2012).

law on impunity was therefore, in Mar's opinion, a political decision to provide reassurance to the state security forces and also served as a political message to the public. In practice, however, the security forces do not need the law on impunity at all because the public prosecutor's office protects them from criminal prosecution anyway, as Mar claimed.

Finally, there are also institutional issues that complicate criminal proceedings. *Fedepaz'* lawyer David complained that the actual "administration of justice" was, in large part, not functioning properly. As in many other parts of the world, the high case load is a major issue in Peru. To overcome this difficulty, a judicial reform has been underway for several years. This reform involved the introduction of a new procedural code in criminal law. The aim of the reform is to make the system of justice more "efficient," for example, by simplifying processes and by including innovations such as electronic court files and the digital notification of the parties (Ministerio de Justicia y Derechos Humanos 2016, 9–10). According to David, under the old procedural norms, the process of notifying parties – i.e. informing the parties about a further step taken by the authorities – can take two months. In Cajamarca, I observed the false notifications repeatedly leading to problems because complainants or defendants were not correctly informed at their *domicilio procesal* (officially registered address) and thus had no knowledge of upcoming court hearings, which led to delays in the proceedings. The human rights lawyers' hope is that the situation will improve somewhat with the new procedural code. However, it will still take time for this reform to be fully implemented.

All these points illustrate that complaints about human rights violations get stuck in the system not just because of the "lack of political will" of the public prosecution authorities or because of corruption. Rather, there are many other causes and preconditions that also impede legal mobilization from below.

Altering the opportunity structure for legal mobilization

Given these circumstances, to what extent does it make sense for lawyers in Peru to invoke the law and use judicial means to support people affected by human rights violations? To return to Kafka's parable, I argue that in the light of prosecutors' wide discretion in criminal proceedings, it is the role of these lawyers to guide the "people from the countryside," who stand "before the law," through the criminal process and to ensure their access to the justice system, thus to ensure that they may pass through law's door. From a theoretical point of view, this is what Gloppen (2018) labeled altering the involved actors' *legal opportunity structure*.

This includes, first, the attempt to change the opportunity structure of judicial authorities by improving the "courts' responsiveness" (Gloppen 2018, 18) to cases of human rights violations. As already mentioned, many legal NGOs in Peru form part of transnational advocacy networks. Within these networks, the NGOs ask international partner organizations to write and submit so-called *amicus curiae* letters to the courts in Peru.[19] These *amicus curiae* letters serve, first, to demonstrate a judicial case's international support. In this sense, they allow one to "put the spotlights on a judge," as a lawyer working with IDL noted, and to make a judge feel that an international audience is closely following the case he or she is dealing with.[20] Second, the aim of *amicus curiae* letters is also to provide judges with information concerning, for example, developments in international law. In complex lawsuits, judges must often decide on specific details on which they lack expertise or in relation to which there is not much jurisprudence. Maritza, an IDL lawyer, told me that *amicus curiae* letters may be of great support. She said, "As the name suggests, it is an advice from a 'friend of the court,' and a judge may or may not consider it." In her experience, however, many judges in Peru accept the statements provided by foreign legal experts, which is, in a global comparison, not always the case.[21]

This supply of legal expertise and technical support can also come from the directly involved human rights lawyers or from the complainants themselves, as another example revealed. According to the *Coordinadora*'s reports, it has only been possible in one case to hold police forces accountable for the killing of protesters during social conflicts. A lawyer from Lima told me that, in this one exceptional case, three police officers and one superior were sentenced for the shooting of student activists in the Huancavelica region. The favorable ruling was made possible because of constant pressure of the students' families and because "the prosecution was given technical support and that the prosecutor accepted that help."[22] To alter prosecutors' and judges' opportunity structure thus means to strike a balance between placing external pressure on the authorities and at the same time providing them with support.

19 Some lawyers also rely, in these attempts, on contacts with law clinics, for example of universities in the United States. An activist from Celendín told me that they prefer the intervention of foreign law clinics to that of foreign NGOs because the foreign law clinics are often considered by Peruvian judges to be "more independent" and therefore more trustworthy than NGOs.

20 In Chapter 5, I discuss this strategy of using external pressure, which is widely used by transnational advocacy networks, not only in Peru, but in many other countries (Keck and Sikkink 1998).

21 A lawyer working with ECCHR in Germany told me that in India, unlike in Peru, for example, there was, in her experience, no point in filing an *amicus curiae* letter because Indian judges would interpret such an intervention as "legal imperialism" and would reject it on the grounds that they did not allow foreign lawyers to explain to them how to dispense justice. Judges in Peru, in turn, are said to be more receptive to such interventions, although this does not mean that they follow the foreign advice in their ruling.

22 This is the same case from Huancavelica that has already been mentioned regarding the application of the law on impunity for police officers. In the first instance, the police officers were acquitted on the basis of law 30151. However, the higher court then issued a conviction against the police forces. Court ruling on file with author.

This strategy also considers that prosecutors and judges are under great pressure from other state institutions or corporate defendants, as I mentioned above.

A second way of influencing prosecutorial or judicial authorities' behavior is by relying on the state institutions' ratification process, thus on the official accountability mechanism. At the time of my fieldwork and until June 2018, judges and prosecutors in Peru were elected and appointed by the plenary of the National Council of the Judiciary (*Consejo Nacional de la Magistratura, CNM*).[23] Every seven years all judges and prosecutors had to undergo ratification by the CNM, which should ensure the authorities' accountability. Several human rights lawyers in Lima and Cajamarca told me that they had made active use of this ratification process to put pressure on the authorities, for example by filing complaints about specific judges.

Third, there are also legal means of intervening against the inactivity of authorities who do not follow their duties. In the torture case from Piura, for example, the inadmissible actions of the responsible public prosecutor were especially obvious. The complaint filed by *Fedepaz* and the *Coordinadora* included allegations against the local prosecutor for his failure to report the committed crimes despite being present during the events. This led to a criminal investigation. In 2012, the public prosecutor was sentenced to a three-year imprisonment, a disqualification for public functions for one year, and the payment of 6,000 Nuevo Soles (approximately US$3,000) for civil reparation (Velazco Rondón and Quedena Zambrano 2015, 51). This demonstrates that prosecutors cannot be sure that they will be protected from prosecution for their inaction.

Thus, the human rights movement in Peru reacted to the set of obstacles and hurdles in the judicial system with various strategies from the legal field, as well as beyond. As Mar told me, "In reality, these cases are not only defined by what the rules say. They are super political cases, so you have to use all the tools." In the following chapters, I discuss various examples of how the Peruvian human rights movement has applied these strategies and tools to make a difference in human rights litigation and to guarantee access to the legal system.

23 Article 150, Peruvian Political Constitution of 1993. The only exceptions were those judges appointed by popular vote, for example judges of the peace. The CNM was a constitutionally autonomous body, its members were appointed by various state institutions. Due to the involvement of members of the Council in a major corruption scandal, the body was suspended by President Martin Vizcarra in July 2018 and, following a reform, replaced by the *Junta Nacional de Justicia*, which took over the CNM's tasks in February 2019 (La Ley (online) 2018, 2019).

Attributing corporate liability

According to Peru's human rights movement, there are various reasons to take action in the judicialization processes over mining against the companies and not only against the direct perpetrators of the abuses, who often belong to the state. These includes moral, legal, and political considerations. In the third part of the chapter, I discuss this strategy of attributing corporate responsibility. First, I examine the specific hurdles that arise from the involvement of corporate defendants. With the so-called civilly liable third party, I then discuss a strategy used by Peru's human rights movement to overcome these difficulties. This provides further insight into the possibilities of legal mobilization *from below*.

Powerful opponents, insufficient resources

> There is an asymmetry – that is to say, you have to fight against someone who is much more powerful, who has various weapons at their disposal to act against you, against the aggrieved people, right? It's very difficult, it's very complicated. [...] We're always going to be at a disadvantage. – *Mirtha, lawyer with* Grufides, *February 2017, Cajamarca (interview transcript)*

There are several reasons why human rights lawyers are "always at a disadvantage" when facing corporate defendants, as Mirtha put it. One important reason is again the issue of corruption and, consequently, the lack of independence of judicial and prosecutorial authorities. A lawyer working with IDL in Lima told me about a case from Espinar, a mining region in the southern part of the country, where a mining company constructed the building in which the public prosecutor's office later operated. Such examples demonstrated, in this lawyer's view, how the independence of authorities is compromised because "you don't bite the hand that feeds you," as she said. Social movement activists and human rights lawyers in the provinces and in Lima all shared this complaint about the "corporate capture" of judicial institutions. Leo, an activist with the PIC, told me that judicial officials always "go against the ordinary citizen but never against the economic power," and Milton complained that "the state is captured by economic power, and [its institutions] act according to the needs of the companies, not the needs of the people." They all agreed that the complexity of judicial proceedings in Peru's mining regions is further aggravated by the entry of powerful players such as TNCs.

The fact that legal NGOs are at a disadvantage compared to companies in court proceedings is also related to financial and human resources. Elena, a former NGO lawyer who now works for a state institution, told me that "the mining companies' strategy is to tire us out (*cansarnos*)." She told me that companies would take advantage of the fact that NGOs have limited financial resources, and it would therefore benefit the companies if court cases were delayed. "Whatever step we've taken, they've always attacked us," she said. By using all possible formal and legal arguments, corporate defendants attempt to prevent, delay, or dismiss claims, which requires extensive resources and expertise from the side of the NGOs to oppose these efforts.

As mentioned in the second chapter, the leading human rights lawyers in Peru are well educated and experienced. Most of the lawyers in Lima graduated from prestigious universities. Many of them have been litigating human rights violations for years or even decades and have extensive legal experience. Nevertheless, many of them consider their counterparts to be dauntingly powerful. They complain that companies have infinite financial resources, which would allow them to hire an "army of lawyers." Marina told me about her experience of the judicial inspections, wherein the complainant and defense counsel, along with the prosecution, visit the scene of the alleged incident to establish evidence. She said that normally "about eight or nine engineers, about four, five lawyers, and all the staff of the mining company go to the site. In contrast, we went... Well, only one of our lawyers went there." Similarly, IDL lawyer Juan Carlos told me about a case in which he represented an indigenous community in the Amazon region that was affected by an oil exploration project. He recounted:

> In the hearing there was an indigenous leader, a young lawyer who had just obtained his title, and me. On the opposite side: Eighteen lawyers from the four main law firms in the country, including an ex-vice minister, who went to the judge and said: "I was vice minister, I was in the Ministry of Justice, just to make this clear." – *Juan Carlos, lawyer with IDL, February 2017, Lima (interview transcript)*

The difference in power between corporate and NGO lawyers also has, in the experience of the latter, a clear gender aspect. A large proportion of Peru's human rights attorneys are women; lawyers I worked with in the field – such as Mar, Rosa, Mirtha, Juliana, Maritza, Vanessa, and Marina – confirmed this picture. Although Juliana complained that the leading positions in many human rights NGOs are still held by men, the crucial and determining role that women play within the organizations is undisputed. On the opposite side, however, the situation is quite different. Elena told me that from her experience with litigating corporate abuses, on the companies' side "there were all male lawyers and all from Lima; there were no lawyers from here," from the provincial town in the highland where Elena lived and worked.

In addition, there are several legal obstacles in attributing corporate responsibility. From a legal perspective, the difficulty in suing corporate actors often lies in proving causality. In cases of contamination or environmental damages, for instance, the aggrieved party must prove the link between a company's activities and the harm that has occurred, for example the pollution of water sources. Various lawyers working for NGOs in Lima told me that they often lack the necessary technical reports to prove this link. An example of this are the attempts to bring legal actions in the Espinar region in Peru's southern parts against mining company Antapaccay, a subsidiary of Swiss mining company Glencore. As various lawyers working on this case told me, the judiciary would not recognize independent studies by universities. When the NGOs requested a technical study from the relevant state institutions, they learned that the authorities either did not have the capacity, the knowledge, or the will to carry out these studies. As no evidence could be provided, the company evaded judicial proceedings.

In cases of human rights violations, the difficulties lie in proving the causal link between a corporation's behavior and the misconduct of police officers, for instance, who shot or injured protesters. For complainants, it is difficult to understand how the collaboration between the police and the mining companies work in practice, how and by what means instructions are given, and how the chains of command function. The contracts between the mining companies and the PNP that I described above had, for a long time, been "confidential," meaning that they were not available to the public. Due to pressure from the human rights movement, this has changed, and all inter-institutional contracts currently in force are now publicly accessible on the Ministry of the Interior's website (Ministerio del Interior 2020).

However, these contracts only provide general information, such as the agreements between the police and the corporation concerning the area of operation, the supply of food, or the equipment provided to the police units. It remains unclear how the collaboration works in practice. Human rights lawyers who attempt to base their claims against the corporation on this collaboration with the police can only rely on this public information and lack access to documents from within the corporations or state institutions. Pedro, a lawyer who worked with IDL, told me that companies in Peru are not obligated to disclose their cooperation with the police and that they are also "not so honest" to do so on their own initiative. And state institutions, for their part, are likewise not transparent enough to inform about this, he added.

Furthermore, there is an ongoing debate among human rights lawyers in Peru regarding whether the legal basis is actually suitable to attribute corporate liability, especially with regard to criminal cases. Some lawyers in Lima and Cajamarca told me that the problem is that "in criminal law there's supposed to be personalized authorship" and that, therefore, "a legal person cannot be the object of criminal liability." If legal actions are taken against the natural persons – that is, against representatives of the company – it is often not possible to prove that this person was directly involved in the offenses. In addition, a lawyer told me that when managers are sued, the problem is that the company will simply replace them, but the company's behavior may not change. This in turn provides support for suing the corporation as a legal entity. However, as another lawyer told me, "it is still under debate whether this is possible." Pedro told me that he is observing efforts in academia in Lima to address corporate criminal liability but that political discussions have not yet reached this point and that "Congress is thinking more about other things." Therefore, the "norms are not designed to hold companies legally responsible for the crimes they commit," as Mirtha put it.

Mirtha added that some state institutions have now realized that the existing legal regulation is inadequate with regard to the field of business and human rights. She told me that Peru's authorities followed the international developments on this issue and made efforts to support and implement the many *soft law* approaches and multi-stakeholder initiatives which have emerged in recent years. The Voluntary Principles on Security and Human Rights played a pivotal role in this. Many of the transnational mining companies operating in Peru have committed themselves to these voluntary standards, which make legally non-binding recommendations on how companies should conduct their cooperation with public and private security forces.[24] According to Mirtha, however, the Voluntary Principles are only "*un saludo a la bandera,*" a symbolic gesture, which is based on the companies' self-regulation and not on state regulation. Mirtha said that this initiative would not work to sanction companies for abuses they committed. She referred to the so-called *governance gap* on corporate responsibility, which arises between the inadequacy of state regulation, on the one hand, and the lack of effectiveness of so-called *soft law* regulations, on the other (Zerk 2006, Simons and Macklin 2014). Thus, I learned that the legal framework is insufficient to attribute liability to mining companies in Peru.

However, I then talked to *Fedepaz* lawyer David about this issue and asked him whether the lack of corporate criminal liability in Peru was the reason the investigations against the company involved in the torture case had been dropped. David raised his eyebrows and asked, in a stern tone, "Who claims that there is no corporate criminal liability in Peru?" He then reached for the penal code lying on his desk, opened it, and read the following:

> Article 105: Measures applicable to legal persons
>
> If the punishable act was committed in the exercise of the activity of any legal person or by using its organization to favor or cover it up, the judge must apply all or some of the following measures:

24 For instance, Newmont Mining Corporation, Minera Yanacocha's main shareholder, joined the Voluntary Principles in 2002 and became an active member of a multi-stakeholder group that aims at implementing the principles in Peru (RESOLVE 2016, 14). For a detailed discussion of the Voluntary Principles on Security and Human Rights, see: Pitts 2011, Hönke and Börzel 2012, 22–35, Simons and Macklin 2014, 122–9.

> 1. Closure of its premises or establishments [...].
> 2. Dissolution and liquidation of the company, association, foundation, cooperative or committee.
> 3. Suspension of the activities of the company [...]. – *Article 105, Peruvian Criminal Code, own translation*

According to David, the legal basis for corporate liability is thus clearly stated, and it is, in his opinion, quite strict. To make this clear, he said, "In Peruvian law there is only one form of the death penalty," which is enshrined in Article 105, with the possibility of a judge ordering the dissolution of a company. The problems in attributing corporate liability are thus, in his view, not judicial but political problems.

Vanessa, a lawyer who worked with the NGO *CooperAcción* in Lima, agreed with David's opinion, and told me that this example revealed, once again, that the problem does not lie in the legal basis but in its implementation. She explained that by Latin American standards, Peru, "together with Colombia and maybe Brazil, has a progressive legislation with regard to the regulation of companies, even if there are still some gaps in the legislation." In her opinion, the problem arises not from the law itself but, first, from access to the legal system in order to use the legislation and, second, from the implementation and enforcement of this legislation.

By taking a closer look at the individual cases, we can observe what this actually means. In the torture case from Piura, for instance, *Fedepaz* also attempted to make the legal responsibility of the mining company Río Blanco and of the private security company Forza an issue in the criminal proceedings. In the complaint, the NGO lawyers demanded that an investigation be opened against the mining company's security personnel for the crimes of torture and aggravated kidnapping. In addition, in its further description of the incident, the complaint mentioned that several detainees alleged the involvement of corporate employees in the abuses (see also: Kamphuis 2012a, 546). In its concluding section, the complaint demanded to "clarify the level of participation of the company's employees in the commission of the crimes" and listed several indications "of the corporate managers and security personnel's responsibility in the reported events, by showing a high degree of knowledge of what was happening, as well as by the provision of assistance for the development of police activities."[25]

25 Criminal complaint to the *Quinta Fiscalía Provincial Penal de Piura*, p. 22; document on file with author; own translation. As David explained, for tactical reasons the degree of involvement of the company was not mentioned more specifically. For example, the company was not directly accused of "aiding and abetting" the police because it would have been possible that the company representatives were involved as "direct perpetrators," as David told me, and "it is not the complainants' job to clarify and define the degree of involvement of an accused," as he further noted.

In the proceedings, the task was then to effectively prove the corporations' involvement in the abuses. There was no available evidence that the company Río Blanco had a contract for extraordinary services with the police because, at the time, these contracts were still subject to a confidentiality clause. It was clear to the lawyers involved that corporate actors had decisively contributed to the torture and the kidnapping of the group of protesters, for example by providing logistical support to the police forces. But they lacked the evidence to prove this support. The fact that the incidents took place within the company's property supported their position. In addition, it became apparent during the criminal proceedings that key company representatives in Lima were informed of the events within the mining camp in which the abuses occurred (Kamphuis 2012a, 547). However, the investigation against the mining corporation and its employees as well as against the private security staff was dropped during the legal procedure. The public prosecutor's office decided that due to the lack of evidence, it could not find a responsibility for the alleged acts on behalf of the corporate actors.

Fedepaz' lawyers then decided not to insist on this issue because, as David told me, "this would have endangered the entire court case," and they would have risked the entire proceeding being dismissed. As I mentioned above, the case against the police officers had been dropped four times, and *Fedepaz* had managed to win the appeal against this decision four times, which, however, took much time. The NGO lawyers then decided, for strategic reasons, to leave the issue of corporate responsibility out of the proceedings for the moment and to move forward with the accusation against the police. *Fedepaz*' strategy was to bring forth the case against the police officers directly involved and against their superiors and to ensure that a trial would finally take place to discuss these actors' responsibility. Within or after the trial, it would then be possible to bring up the "indications of the company's responsibility" again and to request further investigation into this issue, as David told me. Thus, his strategy was "to leave something behind in order to achieve more in the end." In the torture case, the issue of corporate responsibility was abandoned in order to allow for a trial against the police. In this sense, the case was one of many cases of human rights violations in Peru in which the corporate actors – and, until the time of writing, also the state actors – have remained unpunished.

Addressing the civilly liable third party

If we take a step back and consider Peru's human rights litigation dealing with corporate and state actors' abuses as a whole and over a longer period of time, it is clear that the strategies of legal NGOs follow a kind of trial-and-error principle. Approaches that worked well in one case have been applied in other proceedings. The exchange in networks, such as within the *Coordinadora* – where NGO lawyers from different areas meet and discuss their cases – serves as an important platform for sharing and passing on experiences. This exchange in turn gives rise to new strategic approaches. Based on the cases that I have analyzed for this research, I see the approach of relying on the figure of the *tercero civilmente responsable*, the so-called "civilly liable third party," as the judicial approach that currently seems most promising to hold corporate and state actors liable.

According to the new Peruvian Code of Criminal Procedure, a *tercero civilmente responsable*, or a civilly liable third party, is a person who "together with the accused, bears responsibility for the consequences of the crime" and who can therefore be incorporated into the criminal proceeding.[26] Thus, it describes "not those who committed the crime, but rather those who, by virtue of a legal mandate, will be civilly responsible together with the accused" (de las Casas 2015, 222, own translation). This can be, for example, a contractor, a state institution, or an employer, such as a company. The idea behind this doctrine is that the legal subject with whom the perpetrator was in a dependent relationship – i.e. who exercised control over the perpetrator or on whose behalf the perpetrator was acting – bears a civil responsibility, as well. Within the criminal proceedings, the inclusion of a party under this legal figure occurs at the request of the prosecutor or the civil party and is decided on by a judge.[27]

The figure of the civilly liable third party represents an innovation in Peruvian criminal law, which was introduced with the new Code of Criminal Procedure. As Mar, a lawyer with the *Coordinadora*, noted, the use of this figure allows one to complement criminal law with civil proceedings and to take action against the authorities or a private party who gave instructions that led to rights abuses. Roberto Pérez-Prieto de las Casas (2015, 222) noted, from the perspective of legal theory, that, although the figure of the civilly liable third party is laid out in criminal law, the character of this figure is much more influenced by the idea of civil law. In principle, it is a figure used to secure a compensation payment, which is part of civil law. Consequently, with this figure, the complainants have the possibility of claiming civil compensation from a third party, but within the same criminal proceedings in which the criminal liability of the direct perpetrator is being discussed. As I will now illustrate with two examples, this approach serves as a valuable instrument to litigate against both state and corporate actors.

The torture case from Piura is one of these cases where the figure of the civilly liable third party was used. The case had begun under the old procedural order but was then transferred to the new regulations due to the long duration of the proceedings. This transfer allowed *Fedepaz* to file a request in 2011 to include the Ministry of the Interior as a civilly liable third party in the case (Fedepaz 2018b). The request was justified on the grounds that the ministry is responsible for the police and thus for

26 Article 111, new Peruvian Criminal Procedure Code, own translation (see also: de las Casas 2015, 218).

27 Article 111 and 112, New Peruvian Criminal Procedure Code.

the officers and their superiors who were prosecuted in the torture case. The intention of this judicial action was to urge the judiciary to deal, in the proceedings, not only with the responsibility of the individual police officers but also with that of the institution to which the police force is accountable.

It took the judicial authorities several years to respond to the request to include the Ministry of the Interior. In May 2017, during my stay in *Fedepaz*' office, the corresponding court ruled on the basis of a procedural, formalistic argument that the application was inadmissible and dismissed it. *Fedepaz* appealed and succeeded a year later when the Court of Appeal decided to admit the request and to include the ministry as a civilly liable third party in the proceedings (Fedepaz 2018b). This was a great success, as David told me, from a legal point of view, on the one hand, as it was the first time under the new Code of Criminal Procedure that the Ministry of the Interior was involved as a civilly liable third party in a case concerning human rights violations. On the other hand, and more importantly, it was also a success from a political point of view. According to David, it makes a large difference whether only the responsibility of the police officers and their superiors is addressed, or whether a lawsuit also negotiates the responsibility of the corresponding state institution for the abuses. Thus, if the trial in the torture case eventually begins, the authorities will also have to face responsibility, which is fully in line with the aims of the human rights lawyers to hold state institutions to account in order to impose a social change (see Chapter 2).

The second case in which the figure of the civilly liable third person was used in a promising way was the criminal proceeding in favor of Elmer Campos, a *campesino* from the Cajamarca region. During the Conga protests in November 2011, Elmer was shot and seriously injured by the police. Along with other *campesinos* who were wounded in the same protest march, he became a complainant in a criminal proceeding against the police forces. Mar, the *Coordinadora* lawyer, assumed the representation of the aggrieved party. Within the proceedings, the complainants' side requested that the judicial authorities include, as civilly liable third parties, the Ministry of the Interior and the company Minera Yanacocha, which had had a contract for extraordinary services with the police at the time the incident occurred (Ordoñez 2017).[28]

As in other similar cases, the complainants' lawyers faced the difficulty of proving that there was a causal link between the contract for extraordinary services and the committed abuses, thus the difficulty of proving that the mining company had control over the police forces who shot the *campesinos*. In this case, however, the human rights movement found a way to overcome the existing obstacles. As I discuss

28 *Convenio de prestación de servicios extraordinarios complementarios a la función policial entre la Policía Nacional del Perú XIV-Dirección Territorial de la Policía-Cajamarca y Minera Yanacocha SRL*, issued in March 2011. Document on file with author.

in Chapter 6, the international NGO EarthRights International used a legal mechanism in the United States that made it possible to obtain internal corporate documents from the U.S. parent company Newmont Mining. These documents contained detailed information about the coordination between the mining company and the police forces involved in suppressing the protest march.

The documents obtained abroad allowed the Peruvian human rights lawyers to introduce evidence into the proceedings about the police's subordination to the mining company. Within the proceedings, Minera Yanacocha argued that there was no such relationship of subordination because, first, the contract with the police stated that there was no employment relationship between the police officers and the company. Second, the company argued that the Peruvian Constitution does not allow the police to be subject to the orders of third parties. The company claimed that it did not give any orders but merely had a general contract that mandated the police to ensure security around the mining camp. In December 2017, however, a court in Cajamarca decided to involve Minera Yanacocha in the proceedings as a civilly liable third party. At the time of writing, the case was still in the phase of the *control de acusación*, i.e. in the last phase before the start of the actual trial, which would then lead to the judgment. Therefore, it remains to be seen whether Minera Yanacocha will actually be convicted and will have to pay compensation. However, the fact that the company was included in the process already represents a major political success for the involved NGOs.

The advantage of the strategy of using the figure of the civilly liable third party is, according to Mar, that more "emphasis is placed on the institutions rather than only on the individuals." This means that the responsibility of the mining company or the Ministry of the Interior is at stake instead of just the responsibility of an individual police officer.[29] David added that police violence in Peru is often structural in nature, so it is important to question the structures and processes within state institutions rather than just punishing individual perpetrators. The use of this judicial figure thus allows legal NGOs to raise the issue of the institutional responsibility of the state in these criminal proceedings.

In addition, Elmer's case illustrated the attempts to enforce moral responsibility, which the local communities ascribe to Minera Yanacocha, in the legal field. The use of the civilly liable third party makes it possible to negotiate the shared responsibility of Minera Yanacocha and the Ministry of the Interior. If only the company's criminal responsibility were being addressed, the case would be more likely to be dropped because there is no evidence that the company was directly involved in the crime. It was members of the police who fired at the demonstrators. The figure of the civilly liable third party reduced the complainants' burden to prove the causal link between

29 Eckert (2016, 252) also noted this focus in the attribution of responsibility to the "*Befehlsverantwortlichen*," i.e. the commanders, in her research on India.

the corporations' behavior and the police. Thus, by relying on this judicial figure, the human rights lawyers use a different narrative of causal responsibility and thereby attempt to overcome the obstacles that exist in criminal proceedings in Peru. To hold Minera Yanacocha responsible as a civilly liable third party, it must only be proven that there was a relationship of subordination between the police and the company, which is easier to demonstrate than the *direct* involvement of corporate actors in the abuses.

Conclusion

The examples of legal mobilization from below discussed in this chapter illustrate the obstacles faced by the legal NGOs. Litigating cases of human rights violations that involve transnational mining companies and in which the perpetrators have acted on behalf of the state is additionally challenging. Corruption, the alleged lack of political will on the part of the authorities to take action against powerful actors, difficulties in gathering evidence, and structural reasons, such as the poor functioning of the judicial administration, lead to court cases being dismissed, delayed, or protracted.

In the majority of cases, the door to justice remains closed for those people who live on the margins of Peruvian society. In order to be able to take it up with the doorkeepers of the law – the public prosecutors – and the enforcers of the law – the judges – these people need very specific knowledge of the legal process so that they can take advantage of the law and use it as an emancipatory tool. However, because those affected by human rights violations do not have this knowledge, as they are not experts, but rather "one-shotters" in law (Galanter 1974, 97), they depend on the legal NGOs' support.

The Comaroffs wrote that "it is neither the weak nor the meek nor the marginal who predominate in [legal processes]" (2006, 31). In legal proceedings, those who are able to utilize the means offered by the law prevail. I agree with the Comaroffs that it is often those who have the greatest financial resources and technical expertise who exercise the greatest power over the decision-makers in the law. However, this is at the same time a pattern rather than a fixed rule. Attempts to change the opportunity structures of legal mobilization and to use the existing legal basis strategically *from below* can, in certain circumstances, enable those who have fewer resources to succeed. This illustrates that the law is, in most cases, not a "weapon of the weak" (Scott 1985), but it may serve as an emancipatory means for those who try to empower the weak. In this sense, I follow Ewick and Silbey, who wrote that using the law in a strategic way means to "[incorporate] not only a pragmatic account of social practice, but also a normative aspiration" (1998, 227). The approach of strategic human rights litigation is based not only on the idea that it is possible to use the law to strive for social change, but also on the wish or the normative aim that this may be possible.

In her presentation to law students at the *Universidad Católica* in Lima, in which she said that "justice is slow, and justice is not always just," Juliana upheld the use of the legal system *despite* all the prevailing difficulties. She argued that the various mechanisms of the law must be used, for example, by adopting the approach of strategic litigation or by using political mechanisms that lie outside the legal system and thus beyond the law. I discuss these different mechanisms in the following chapters.

Chapter 4. Criminalizing social protest

We meet at the PIC's clubhouse for a last coffee before traveling to Cajamarca where the trial will start the following day. Before leaving the place, Milton briefly gives his shoes a shine. He puts a book in his pocket and grabs his backpack, then we leave. A mototaxi brings us to the corner where the colectivos *(shared taxis) leave for Cajamarca. While Milton looks for a car to take us to the city, Mallu, the Brazilian sociologist who accompanies us, and I stand around and talk. From the corner of my eye I see Milton speaking vividly to another man, but I do not pay attention to it because I assume that it is, as so often, a* compañero de lucha *or an acquaintance of Milton. When Milton comes back, however, he tells us that the guy he spoke to is the former governor of Celendín – thus, the man who filed charges against him and who will appear as complainant in court the next day. Milton relates that just now the former governor accused him again of being responsible for the deaths in Celendín during the Conga conflict because he had mobilized people for protest. Milton is confounded and shakes his head in bewilderment.*

We reach Cajamarca after a three-hour drive. Milton meets with his attorney, who works for the local NGO Grufides, *and with the representatives from the national NGOs, who have come from Lima for the trial. Mallu and I meet them later in a small café. Milton grins broadly when he spots us coming and shouts from afar: "Angelita! We have a task for you! For you and Mallu. You have to carry the Molotov Cocktails to the courtroom tomorrow!" He bursts out laughing and then explains what it is actually about. His lawyers feel that there is a need to put some pressure on the judges. "We want you to approach the judges to show them that someone from outside is watching the case. Tell them about your research. And take your camera along!"*

Early the next morning, we meet at the plaza de armas *and walk together to* Grufides' *office some blocks away. The mood has become tense. Milton says he was able to find some sleep last night, but he is unusually taciturn this morning. We are all a little nervous. At the NGO's office we do not see anyone yet, and we wait outside until the secretary shows up and opens the door, which is secured with several locks. While we wait in front of the office, a man in blue jeans and a baseball cap seems to be watching us. He stands half a block away at the corner and looks down the street in our direction. As we enter the office, I just see him turning around the corner and walking away in direction of the courthouse.*

We wait in the entrance room of Grufides' *office. Little by little, the other defendants arrive. Most of them are from the district of Sorochuco, a village located in the vicinity of the planned Conga mine. The defendants from Sorochuco had to leave at four in the morning to get to the city in time. Others arrived by* colectivo *from Celendín. The group of persons facing prosecution consists of sixteen individuals, among them five women. Some of them are dressed as if they were attending Sunday mass, others wear football shirts or other simple clothes. Everybody looks worried. Other people arrive in the office, among them Mallu; Palujo, who is responsible for communication tasks within the PIC; Juliana, who works at EarthRights International's office in Lima; and Victor, a representative of the* Coordinadora *from Lima. Mirtha, the principal lawyer working for* Grufides, *arrives with a woman who I have always thought was her friend or assistant, since I had seen the women together a few times before. Later, people will tell me that the "friend" is a plain-clothes policewoman who accompanies Mirtha for security reasons.*

Mirtha welcomes everyone and gives a short introduction about what the defendants have to expect today. She explains that the three judges responsible for the case have changed and that the situation has therefore become even more complicated. The new judges are "clearly against us", Mirtha explains, as they are said to have personal links with Minera Yanacocha. One judge is the son of a former consultant of the mining company. Mirtha told me in a conversation some weeks ago that she fears the bench will attempt to teach Grufides *and her personally a lesson with this case. Now she chooses her words more carefully so as not to frighten the defendants even more. But she makes clear how tense the situation is. Mirtha explains that she requested help from the* Coordinadora *from Lima and that, therefore, Victor traveled to Cajamarca to support her in the trial.*

Mirtha further describes how the hearing will proceed: "The judges will ask you how you see your guilt. You must explain individually whether you consider yourself guilty or innocent. The judge will tell you that there may be a reduction in punishment if you admit the deed. But because you have not committed this offense, you must all declare that you are innocent." Mirtha also explains that the judges will ask whether the defendants wanted to speak or to remain silent. In an earlier phase of the criminal proceedings, the group discussed who would give a declaration to the court. Those people are again reminded of their task. Milton recalls that the situation is serious and that it is therefore important to always arrive on time and to follow the lawyers' instructions. It becomes clear that the defendants will join the process initiated by the opposite side. They will follow the rules of the game – that is, the rules of the law – and participate in the trial as they are expected to, although they cannot be sure that they will receive due process and that the opposing party and the judicial authorities will respect the rule of law.

We then walk to the courthouse, which is only a few blocks away. The courthouse is an inconspicuous two-story building in a residential area. Our identity cards and bags are checked at the entrance, and then we are admitted. We cross a simple entrance area and reach a patio where we enter the courtroom. The room is small and offers little space. The three judges sit at a large desk at the front of the room. Next to them is a court employee who takes care of the audio recording and other technical matters. The judges are elegantly dressed in suits and ties. In front of them, the public prosecutor and a procurador[1] *representing the interests of the Ministry of Defense sit at a small table on the left side. Mirtha and Victor take a seat at the same level on the right. Microphones are placed in front of them. Mirtha wears the insignia of her bar association, a green medallion with a golden star.*

The furniture in the courtroom is shabby and worn out. The defendants, the complainants, the public defender, and we the visitors sit on four benches at the back of the room. There are far too few seats. Several people are leaning against the wall. I recognize the man from the taxi station the day before. He is standing next to one of the defendants. No attempt is made to keep complainants and defendants spatially separated. A Peruvian flag stands behind the judges in the corner. There is a wooden crucifix and a smaller version of the ensign on the magistrates' table. A thick court file and the penal code lie before them. The bench's speaker opens the hearing with the ringing of a small golden bell at nine o'clock sharp.

The hearing begins with the accreditation of the prosecutor, the procurador, *and the defense lawyers. All the defendants are then called up individually. They have to declare their presence and recite the number of their National Identity Document (*Documento Nacional de Identidad, *DNI). They are asked to provide their address, their profession, and their monthly income. Additionally, they are asked for their criminal record. Among the prosecuted are farmers (*agricultores*), housewives, a carpenter, an accountant, a single mother, and several teachers. Their ages range from mid-thirties to well over fifty. Most of them live either in the city of Celendín or in the district of Sorochuco. Some of them find it difficult to quantify their monthly income. For some, it is embarrassing because they have no steady income. Some people recite their DNI number quickly like a shot; others find it hard to recall the number that establishes their identity and makes them tangible for the state.*[2] *Three defendants are absent. Mirtha asks for patience and explains that the people had to travel from distant hamlets and probably did not make it in time. The bench decides to declare those absent in contempt of court (*declarados contumaces*), but to continue the hearing despite their absence.*

The prosecutor begins reading the indictment. The sixteen women and men are accused "of the alleged commission of the crime of aggravated abduction [...] and, as an alternative or subsidiary accusation, of the crime against freedom in the form of coercion [...]." In addition, one man is accused of "the alleged commission of the crime against the symbols and values of the homeland in the form of outrage to symbols of the fatherland." The prosecutor recounts the events that led to the alleged crimes. In April 2013, a capacity building workshop for lieutenant governors took place in the community hall of Sorochuco. The defendants are said to have burst into the auditorium and to have violently evicted the attendees of the event and forced them out of the building to the plaza de armas. *There, the two aggrieved persons – who were, at that time, governors of the district of Sorochuco and of the province of Celendín, respectively – were*

1 The *procurador* involved in this lawsuit is a legal expert representing the interests of the Ministry of Defense.

2 For a detailed discussion of the role of identity documents in Peru see: Skrabut 2019.

"deprived of their liberty during approximately one hour." The defendants are said to have "publicly insulted" the governors, "throwing eggs at them and pointing at them with sticks and then forced them through violence and threats to sign a document in which [the governors] agreed to [...] their own dismissal and they promised that [...] democratic election of the district governor of Sorochuco would take place." The prosecutor continues by stating that "[l]ater, the mob moved to the governor's office from where one defendant removed the national coat, which he showed and passed around publicly as if it were a trophy, offending and outraging the symbols of the fatherland. After committing these criminal acts, the defendants continued shouting their slogans and calling the governors mining agents."

Based on the criminal code, the prosecutor's office requests "the payment of a civil reparation of 10,000 Nuevo Soles [approximately US$3,000] to be paid to each of the complainants in solidarity by the defendants." As a penalty, it demands a prison sentence of between thirty-one years and eight months and thirty-three years and six months. With regard to the alternative or subsidiary classification of the alleged offense as coercion, the prosecutor requests a penalty of between eight and sixteen months of deprivation of liberty and a civil reparation to the complainants of 4,000 Nuevo Soles [approximately US$1,200]. In addition, for the crime of outrage to the symbols of the fatherland, the public prosecutor requests one year and four months of deprivation of liberty and the payment of a one hundred days' fine in favor of the state.

"That's all, señor juez,*" the prosecutor concludes.*

The dark side of judicialization[3]

In Peru's mining conflicts, it is not only activists and NGOs who strategically mobilize the law to enforce their claims. State and corporate actors likewise rely on legal means in these conflicts. They use the law with the objective of impeding political mobilization, silencing protest, and restoring the public order, which they see endangered by social movements. In this chapter, I examine this specific form of legal mobilization by tracing a court case in which sixteen leaders of the protest movement from Sorochuco and Celendín were charged with abduction. Two former local representatives of the central government, who were well-known for their support of the Conga project, filed the criminal complaint against the activists. In 2017, the case was dealt with before the Supra-Provincial Criminal Court of Cajamarca.

In the previous chapters, I discussed the (im)possibilities of mobilizing law *from below* to overcome corporate and state actor's impunity in Peru. I now look at the legal mobilization *from above*. To do this, I turn to a specific way in which corporate

3 Parts of the material on which this chapter is based were previously published in an article entitled "The Dark Side of Judicialization: Criminalizing Mining Protests in Peru", *Latin American Research Review* 58, 2 (2023).

and state actors mobilize law: the criminalization of protest. Reduced to a minimal definition, criminalization means to declare a certain behavior to be illegal or criminal. When I speak of the criminalization of social protest, I thereby mean the judicial prosecution of different activities typically linked with social protest, such as the participation in marches or rallies, for example. State and corporate actors rely on the accusation of specific criminal offenses in order to challenge the movements' mobilization against large-scale mining projects. Since these accusations then result in criminal prosecution by judicial authorities, I categorize it as a form of legal mobilization *from above*.

With regard to different Latin American countries, Alexandra Huneeus *et al.* observed an increasing use of criminal law in governance in recent years and described this as "a darker side of judicialization" (2010, 11). As an equivalent to social movements' legal activism, criminalization thus forms part of and contributes to the judicialization of social conflicts. In addition, criminalization is to be understood as a form of domination. In Peru's criminalization cases we can observe the state's increased use of law "to regulate [its] populations" (Merry 2017, xi) and to obstruct dissent and counterhegemonic aspirations. In this sense, criminalization reveals different forms of law's domination. The aim of this chapter is to identify these different forms and to discuss how law and legality become effective in these cases. The analysis of the different ways in which law is enacted by corporate and state actors will contribute to our overarching debate on the judicialization of Peru's mining conflicts. From a theoretical point of view, the criminalization strategy illustrates how the judicialization of social conflicts may lead to a "lawfare," to use the Comaroffs' (2006, 30) term. Therefore, this chapter explores how activists experience these lawfares and how they confront the criminalization processes. I am interested in the hegemonic use of law which political and economic elites apply to retain existing power relations and to impede social mobilization.

In addition, this chapter starts with the observation that the criminalization strategy not only has an effect on the social movements, but also on a personal level on the individual activists. Some of the sixteen people prosecuted in the Sorochuco case were leaders of local groups, such as the PIC or women and church organizations. Many, however, were ordinary members of the protest movement. They were teachers, grandmothers, *campesinos*, active church members, *ronderas*, or accountants. The danger of imprisonment caused them great concern not only for themselves, but also for the children, spouses, and parents they care for. Some of them had been criminalized before for their involvement in the Conga protests, but for most of them it was the first time that they had to participate in a trial. I provide insight into their personal experience and their strategies in dealing with the uncertainty caused by the court case. Thus, I describe what it means for activists to stand "before the law" (Ewick and Silbey 1998). How did they deal with the threat of being convicted? And to what extent did the criminalization processes influence the activists' legal consciousness? These considerations are central to my overarching research questions because they demonstrate the extent to which law is becoming effective as a hegemonic means of dominating social movements, but also individuals.

As described above, the defense lawyers in the Sorochuco case considered it an advantage to have foreigners in the courtroom. As observers from abroad, Mallu and I approached the magistrates during the trial. We asked for permission to take photos, for a copy of the trial's audio files and for further background information about the case. I still have my doubts as to whether the judges were in any way impressed by our presence. They only smiled mildly and told us that "unfortunately, they were not allowed to speak about an ongoing case." Accompanying the defendants for several weeks, however, allowed me to gain insight into how they experienced the proceedings. Moreover, the Sorochuco case was not the only criminalization case that was ongoing during my stays in Cajamarca. I also attended a trial against a group of *ronderos* from Yagen. They were accused of having kidnapped employees of Odebrecht's Chadín 2 dam project. More generally, the threat of criminalization was an issue people constantly talked about in the field, and there was a wide range of ongoing and already closed cases that I discussed with people in Cajamarca and in Lima. This ethnographic material forms the basis for this chapter.

Criminalization of mining critics in Peru

The criminalization of social protest is one of the main concerns of the grassroots organizations and the human rights movement I worked with in Peru. Activists involved in the movements against both the Río Blanco and the Conga project faced judicial prosecution for taking part in protests. In most of Peru's recent conflicts over mining, leaders, as well as the movements' ordinary members have been criminalized. The use of criminal law is thus a recurring technique of the Peruvian state for responding to social conflicts. Criminalization is enacted through prosecution and criminal investigations. It consists of pressing charges against individuals or groups of people, which result in years of investigation and litigation. At the end of these criminal proceedings, the complaints are often dismissed because they lack grounds and there is no evidence to prove the accusations. Nevertheless, even the pre-trial stages often place a great deal of emotional strain on those affected.

In the course of the Conga conflict, a series of charges was brought against the leaders and members of the protest movement from Cajamarca. Some leaders in the region had up to fifty charges against them. They were accused of riots (*disturbio*); encroachment (*usurpación*); damage to private property; crimes against public order or against public safety; abuse of authority; disruption of public transport (*perturbación de los medios de transporte*); simple and grievous harm; disobedience and resistance to authority, rebellion, and coercion; or kidnapping (*secuestro*). In some cases, the proceedings were initiated by the public prosecutor's office, but in others it was the mining company or local representatives of the national government who filed the complaints that led the prosecutor to open an investigation. Thus, the public prosecutor's office again holds an important role as a kind of gatekeeper who decides which suspected offenses are investigated. Most of the allegations that emerged from the Conga conflict concerned events that occurred between 2011 and 2013, when mobilization on the streets reached a peak. In some cases, proceedings were closed in the following years during the procedural stage of preliminary investigations. However, when I was in the region in 2017 and 2018, several cases entered the *juicio oral*, which is the final stage of criminal proceedings before a judgment is passed. In these cases, the risk of conviction was particularly high.

The incident and the alleged offenses that led to the Sorochuco case date back to April 2013. The defendants had participated in a spontaneously organized protest meeting in Sorochuco, which led to a public dispute with two governors, who represented the national government on the local level. In the aftermath of the events, the governors denounced a group of participants of the protest. According to the defendants, the governors had specifically denounced those protesters who had taken a leading role in the protest movement against Conga. A total of about two-hundred people had attended the protest meeting, but only sixteen had been denounced. Furthermore, defendants told me that the criminal investigation had been marked by irregularities. The activists recounted that the proceedings had initially been dropped by the public prosecutor's office, but had later been reopened, allegedly under pressure from the former governors and in violation of existing procedural rules.

In 2015, the *juicio oral*, the court hearing, had started but had repeatedly been postponed due to the absence of judges and other formalities. In accordance with a rotation principle, the judges responsible for the case were then changed and the trial was suspended for more than a year. Thus, when I accompanied the activists to the court in March 2017, they had already experienced some days in court. With this court hearing, the new panel of judges reopened the trial and continued the criminal proceedings. In May of the same year, the trial ended with the *lectura de sentencia*, the reading of the judgment. In between were four further court hearings, which we attended. For the activists, but also for us who accompanied them, it was a time of great uncertainty since it was not foreseeable how the trial would end and whether the defendants were effectively going to be sent to prison for a long time.

During the first day at court in March 2017, Mirtha was given the floor after the public prosecutor and the *procurador* had presented the accusation. From the very beginning, Mirtha challenged the prosecutor's accusation and the allegations made by the complainants. She started her first intervention to the court as follows:

> Distinguished magistrates. The defense pronounces itself rejecting the thesis of the prosecutor's office and the civil party. We recognize that freedom is a fundamental good that must be protected, and this is neither unknown to nor denied by my *patrocinados* [protégés], several of whom have held public positions. In this trial we will prove that our *patrocinados* are not responsible for any crime that has violated the freedom of any of the aggrieved here present, nor coercion, even less the crime of kidnapping. On the contrary, we shall prove that what took place [...] was an exercise of constitutional rights, the participation in the political life of a community and in public affairs. [We will prove] that a peaceful assembly took place, and that the right to freedom of expression has been exercised collectively. [...] The public prosecutor's office accuses the defendants of having used physical violence to commit these crimes, and we are going to demonstrate in the present trial that there is no evidence whatsoever to prove such an accusation. – *Mirtha, lawyer with* Grufides, *intervention to the court, Cajamarca, March 2017 (transcription of the hearing's audio file, own translation)*

Thus from the outset, Mirtha emphasized that the defense recognized the importance of freedom as a "fundamental good," and at the same time she stressed that there had been no violation of the governor's rights and that there was no evidence to prove the alleged crimes of abduction.

After Mirtha's first intervention, all defendants were called up individually and were asked whether they consider themselves guilty. As Mirtha had predicted, the judges told them that if they admit their guilt the sentence might be reduced. Everyone declared to be "innocent," "without guilt" or "totally innocent." The judges then proceeded with the questioning of the individual defendants. While most of them invoked their right to remain silent, Milton provided a declaration. He recounted how the events had occurred from his point of view:

> We were going from Celendín to a community called El Lirio, in the upper part of Huasmin. [...] When we were on our way [...] we were told that the authorities were in a meeting in the district municipality of Sorochuco. [...] When we entered the site, the ex-governor of the province of Celendín [...] was speaking. He was just referring to me, with defamations, saying that we are deceiving the people, that we are inciting the population to protest against the Conga project. I asked for permission to speak. [...] Then the population requested the assembly members to go out and to hold the meeting in the *plaza de armas* [...] because there were a lot of people, right? I deny that there was a kidnapping. We have even seen the presence of the police at that moment. This, in my opinion, shows that there has not been any kidnapping. – *Milton, intervention to the court, Cajamarca, March 2017 (transcription of the hearing's audio file, own translation)*

Thus, both Mirtha and Milton denied that an infringement of rights had taken place and that the governors had been deprived of their liberty. Instead, Milton described the events as a form of political intervention, which coincides with Mirtha's argumentation that her *patrocinados* participated in a political assembly and exercised their right to freedom of expression and to freedom of assembly.

In the eyes of Mirtha, Milton, and the other defendants, the prosecutor and the complainants used the offense of abduction as a pretext to initiate criminal proceedings against their opponents. Within the Conga conflict, the governors had publicly supported Minera Yanacocha's project and had entered into a fierce conflict with the protest movement. This conflict was waged in public, but at the same time, it was also a dispute that took place on a very personal level. The encounter between Milton and the complainant that I witnessed the day before the trial exemplified the conflict's everyday dimension. Through the process of litigation, however, this conflict was transferred to the courtroom, where it was waged under the supervision of the judges. The defense lawyers did not question this judicialization of the conflict in itself. They considered it a legitimate act to file a complaint, and they also agreed to participate in the trial, even though they repeatedly told me that the pretrial investigation had not followed procedural rules and that the complainants had exerted pressure on the prosecutor's office. More importantly, however, the defendants criticized the complainants and the prosecutor, stating that they had *misused* the criminal law in order to start an illegitimate lawsuit based on unfounded accusations. As I describe in the following section, this misuse of law is one among various forms of how law is invoked in the criminalization cases.

Law's domination

There are various ways in which law is used to govern people and to secure existing power relations. Like in other forms of legal mobilization from above, we can observe different ways in which domination is exercised in the criminalization cases. Based on the analysis of my ethnographic material, I propose three categories, which I discuss in the following section. First, there is a domination *by* law, thus by specific articles of the legislation. In this sense, criminalization is *encoded* in law. Second, we can observe a domination *of* law itself, i.e. through its institutions and its mechanisms. Then, there is, third, the *misuse* of law, which Mirtha and Milton criticized in the Sorochuco case. These different forms of law's domination all reveal the criminalization's potential to impede counterhegemonic struggles.

Domination *by* law

The domination *by* law is the most evident way in which legal mechanisms are used by judicial authorities and by political and economic elites to criminalize opponents. Legal norms in general and criminal law in particular determine which conduct and activities are permitted in a society and which should be punished. Within the nation state, it is the task of the judicial authorities to enforce these norms and to prosecute unlawful conduct. Marginalized groups who oppose the state and its projects are especially likely to breach the norms of a society. This is, on the one hand, due to their marginality; there are laws that are specifically tailored to groups who live at the state's margins (Das and Poole 2004, 9). On the other hand, states modify rules in order to make unwanted resistance an offense. This later strategy is especially effective if the people affected by legal modifications form part of marginalized groups.

The first aspect, law's tendency to be fundamentally hostile to marginalized groups, has long been a point of criticism of law. As early as 1894, Anatole France formulated his critique of law based on this aspect and ironically described the "majestic equality of the laws, which prohibit the rich and the poor alike from sleeping under bridges, begging in the streets and stealing bread" (cited in: Brinks and Gauri 2014, 375). Everyone is equal before the law, but some have a higher risk of getting into conflict with it. France claimed that the poor are especially vulnerable to this form of legal domination. In her book on the judicial system in South Africa, Johanna Mugler noted that "racially discriminatory laws created an illegal population" (2019, 26) during the time of Apartheid, which led to "criminalization of Black everyday life" (2019, 28). Likewise, Eckert described in her research in India how "illegalization and poverty are intricately connected" (2014, 295). The poor constantly come into conflict with existing norms, purely through their presence, for example, through the lack of a legal way to obtain land rights or to find work in the formal sector. In Peru's mining conflicts, to be involved in protest is, in a similar way, *intrinsically* connected with a breach of norms. If a protest march takes place in the urban area, the offense of obstructing public transport, for example, is very likely to happen. Thus, the activists run the risk of violating the law purely by participating in protests.

What has been much more striking in Peru's mining conflicts, however, is the second aspect of domination by law, which is how existing legislation has been tightened to criminalize participation in demonstrations. This development had already begun in the era of Alberto Fujimori in the context of the internal armed conflict (see Chapter 1, see also: Vásquez 2013, 416). In that time, the penal code was tightened with the aim of combating terrorism, i.e. fighting a specific group that revolted against the state. However, the stricter laws also affected persons who were merely suspected of supporting terrorism, although they did not belong to any subversive group. The Andean population was particularly affected by this policy and by the suspicion of supporting the insurgency.

After the transition, the democratically elected presidents who followed Fujimori tightened the criminal code with regard to social protest. With the increase of socio-environmental conflicts, a new population group became the target of the state's legislative adjustments. Social movements in Peru make their voices heard primarily through gatherings on the streets, for example through regional strikes, road blocks, and manifestations in the urban centers or in the vicinity of the contested mine sites. New laws have been created, and existing laws have been adapted to make these acts a prosecutable offense. Although the danger of terrorism was officially overcome with the state's victory over the guerillas, new threats to society were found to legitimize the tightening of laws. In many cases, the tightening of specific articles of the criminal code was legitimized by combating "organized crime" or "drug trafficking."[4]

Articles concerning "crimes against public tranquility" and "against public peace" were especially targeted in the efforts to tighten the criminal code (Vásquez 2013, 425). According to various human rights lawyers, this resulted in an "overpenalization" (*sobrepenalización*) of offenses related to social protest (see, for example: Velazco Rondón and Quedena Zambrano 2015, 12, Vásquez 2016, 14). Peru's constitution guarantees freedom of assembly and the participation in protests can thus not be directly punishable. However, criminal offenses were extended to make prosecution against protesters possible.

In 2007, for example, the offense of "extortion" (*extorsión*) was modified to punish protest-related activities. In its earlier version, the article defined the crime of extortion as when someone "by means of violence, threatening or holding a person hostage, compels that person or another person to give the agent or a third party an undue economic advantage." As a result of the modification in 2007, the article additionally defined extortion to include "anyone who, by means of violence or threats, takes over buildings, obstructs communication channels or impedes the free movement of citizens or disrupts the normal functioning of public services [...]."[5] Here, the explanatory statement (*exposición de motivos*) issued in conjunction with the legislative decree which gave rise to the modification is revealing. The statement directly referred to criminal conduct, which was said to occur "under the guise of strikes, protests or claims" (*bajo el disfraz de huelgas, protestas o reclamos*, Consejo de Ministros 2008). The document further noted that "claims for supposed rights" made in this context were "superimposed on the rights of the majority, attacking public and private property, freedom of work, public security and internal order, including socioeconomic development" (*ibid.*, own translation). This example clearly demonstrates how specific articles of the criminal code have been extended to provide the legal basis for criminalizing protest against large-scale development projects such as mining.

Thus, the first way law's domination works in the criminalization cases is through its written norms and through its code, which defines criminal behavior.

---

4 These are frequently used justifications, as Eckert (2008, 8) pointed out with regard to the anti-terrorism legislation created after 9/11.

5 Article 200, Peruvian Criminal Code, own translation (see also: Kamphuis 2012b, 236).

As David, *Fedepaz*' director stated, it is the "normative system which allows for the criminalization of social protest." In this form of law's domination, the danger of criminalization therefore emerges from the law's code and from the written norms.

Domination *of* law

The second way in which criminalization becomes effective is the threat to the accused that comes from law itself and its institutions. By domination *of* law I mean that legal institutions and legal mechanisms are dominant in their way of functioning. Because judicial authorities are built to defend the rule of law and to enforce the legal norms of a society, law's institutions are powerful; they are made to govern and to dominate people.

One reason for the domination of law lies in the persons who embody the institutions, in particular the judges. Pierre Bourdieu (1987) noted that judges universally belong to the dominant class of a society. He wrote about the "closeness of interests, and above all, the parallelism of habitus" between judges and political and economic elites (Bourdieu 1987, 842). This is also the case in Peru. Especially in rural areas, judges are authorities who hold considerable symbolic power and who represent the power of the state – a state that is, beyond that, not very present in these areas. In addition, Bourdieu wrote that the social proximity between judges and political and economic elites leads to the decisions of magistrates being "unlikely to disadvantage the dominant forces" (Bourdieu 1987, 842). Beyond this social proximity between the judiciary and the elite, we can observe the law's domination in the legal institutions and the legal mechanisms themselves.

To be confronted with the domination *of* law is what Ewick and Silbey (1998) have described as to be standing "before the law," which is one form of legal consciousness that they observed in their study on the justice system in the United States. Ewick and Silbey wrote that, in this form of legal consciousness,

> legality is envisioned and enacted as if it were a separate sphere from ordinary social life: discontinuous, distinctive, yet authoritative and predictable. In this form of consciousness, the law is described as a formally ordered, rational, and hierarchical system of known rules and procedures. (Ewick and Silbey 1998, 47)

They describe how the domination of law appears through the materiality of the institution of law itself, through its architecture, the staging of its prescribed processes, its language[6], and through the theatricality with which judicial processes are performed:

---

6 For a discussion on the limits that legal language "may place on law's democratic aspirations" see the work by Elizabeth Mertz (2007, 3).

> Aspiring toward grandeur and permanence, law houses itself in monumental buildings of marble and granite and arranges its agents behind desks, counters, and benches. It expresses itself in a language that is arcane and indecipherable to most citizens. The theatrical scripting and costuming of trials creates an unbridgeable distance from the interactions of everyday life. (Ewick and Silbey 1998, 106)

Law is, in this sense, perceived as a powerful apparatus following procedural rules, which dictate the course of legal processes, but which are often difficult for ordinary people to comprehend. In the Cajamarca criminalization cases I found it striking how little the defendants knew about how the trial would proceed and what they had to expect in which phase of the process. Due to their lack of legal knowledge, they depended heavily on their lawyers, who guided them through the process and who gave detailed instructions on when to speak and how to behave. Although many of the activists told me that they do not believe in the legal processes and in the law, all of them were obedient to the rules of the legal proceedings and actively participated as they were expected. This is how the domination *of* law became apparent.

As I mentioned at the beginning, the courthouse in Cajamarca was not particularly impressive. The Peruvian state's lack of financial resources was evident, for example in the shabby furniture. Nevertheless, a sense of awe gripped me every time I entered the courthouse with the activists. During the trial, the theatricality of the law was repeatedly demonstrated with small details, for example with the ringing of the bell at the beginning of each hearing, with the accreditation of the parties, and with the way the lawyers filed motions to the court. Social differences between judges and defendants became obvious during the proceedings. There were the judges – educated, well-dressed, and elegant in their appearance – who pulled the latest smartphone models out of their suit pockets during the trial. Before them stood the *comuneros* and *comuneras*, the ordinary, simply dressed people from the country side – the *gente humilde* (humble people), as they are often referred to – who have a simple way of expressing themselves, which is quite different from the law's official language. The defendants were unfamiliar with legal culture and had little to no experience with legal proceedings. They stood "before the law" and were at the mercy of its hierarchical structures and procedures.

The judges treated the accused with the necessary respect, but at the same time did not miss any opportunity to let the other side feel their superiority. In a trial against a group of *ronderos* from Yagen that I attended, for example, several defendants had trouble naming their date of birth. A judge made ironic remarks, for example when one man said that he was born in 1883, instead of 1983. During the trial, the judges hinted at jokes that were not understood by the defendants concerned. The situation was shameful for the defendants. In another instance, a witness made contradictory statements. A judge interrupted him and asked him about his level of education, a question that was in no way related to the issues on which the witness was supposed to provide information. The man was only asked about his education in order to subtly expose and embarrass him. The judges clearly demonstrated the domination of law, the power of the institution and their own social position. Thus, this is the second way in which law's domination works in the criminalization cases.

Domination through the *misuse* or the *manipulation* of law

Finally, a third way in which law's domination manifests itself in criminalization cases is the *manipulation* of legal means. The Inter-American Commission on Human Rights defines criminalization as the "misuse [*uso indebido*] of criminal law" (CIDH 2015, own translation). According to the commission, it is "the manipulation of the punitive power of the state" through non-state and state actors to "control, punish or prevent the exercise of the right to defend human rights" (CIDH 2015, 18). A central element is the notion that criminal law is misused to prevent the legitimate exercise of rights, such as freedom of expression or the right to protest. In Latin America, criminalization is often directed against (environmental) human rights defenders – thus against actors who collectively or individually and "in a peaceful manner, strive to protect and promote human rights" (Special Rapporteur on the Situation of Human Rights Defenders 2016, 4) and who "promote or procure in any way the realization of human rights and fundamental freedoms recognized at the national or international level" (CIDH 2015). The legal system is "manipulated" to silence legitimate but unwanted critics (Vásquez 2013: 423).

There is a slight, but important difference between the cases in which the law's code is modified so as to define a certain act as criminal and those cases in which the law is misused to criminalize an act, thus the difference between domination *by* law and the *misuse of* law. In the Sorochuco case, the prosecutor categorized the alleged deed as "aggravated abduction." The defense confirmed that the protest meeting had occurred and that the defendants had participated. Yet they denied that the complainants had been deprived of their freedom but insisted that a legitimate form of protest and political participation had occurred. They claimed that the crime of kidnapping was misused as a pretext for threatening heavy prison sentences. In their view, criminal prosecution became judicial persecution.

The offense of abduction (*secuestro*) has often been used in criminalization cases in Cajamarca in recent years. In many cases members of local *rondas campesinas* have been prosecuted under this offense, but, as the Sorochuco case revealed, the strategy has also been applied to other groups of mining opponents. Among the sixteen defendants and among approximately two-hundred other participants of the protest meeting in Sorochuco were members of local *rondas campesinas*. As during other protest events, some of them had brought their *binzas*, their whips, which is one of the *ronda*'s identifying marks, but during the protest meeting they had not intervened in their role as *ronderos* or *ronderas*.

In contrast to this, in the Yagen trial the defendants had acted in their role as members of the *ronda*. An important task of the *rondas* is to carry out patrols in the *comunidades*. In the case of Yagen, the *ronda* had stopped a group of Odebrecht workers during such a patrol and took them to the community house. In a similar manner, two *ronderos* from the comunidad of Quillamachay in the district of Oxamarca were prosecuted for having stopped four people who wanted to purchase land in their community for Odebrecht's Chadín 2 dam project. The two *ronderos* had been acquitted of the kidnapping charge about six months before the start of the trial in the Sorochuco case but had been sentenced to one year in prison for coercion. In both the Oxamarca and the Yagen case, the defendants were prosecuted for carrying out their tasks as *ronderos*, although Peru's legislation entitles the *rondas* to control and detain suspects in their communities.[7] In the context of the criminalization of social protest in Cajamarca, however, the local public prosecutor's office did exactly this and used the crime of kidnapping to prosecute the *ronderos*.

As mentioned in the first chapter, the *rondas campesinas* are local authorities responsible for "administrating justice at the margins of the state" (Gitlitz 2013).[8] They arose in the late seventies in Peru's northern highlands in response to the state's absence (Gitlitz 2013). The function of the *rondas* is encoded in the constitution, and their members have a clearly regulated autonomy to exercise justice for specific crimes. Furthermore, the *justicia ronderil* is an important pillar of the *campesino* population's identity in Cajamarca. *Rondas campesinas* have played a significant role in the struggles against Conga and against the hydroelectric dam projects in the Río Marañón. They were decisively involved in the protest movements' success since, in many *comunidades*, the *rondas* play an important role in the organization of social life. Therefore, the *rondas* were particularly effective in organizing local resistance and political mobilization. Challenging the *rondas campesinas* and their members meant targeting the core of the social movements in Cajamarca's rural areas. The state's strategy to prosecute and sanction the *rondas* for exercising their functions thus affected their political mobilization.

Beyond that, the attack on the *rondas* must be seen in a broader context of ordinary judiciaries' unease with legal pluralism. In many Latin American countries, indigenous and *campesino* communities have the constitutional right to autonomously

---

7 A plenary agreement of the Peruvian Supreme Court clearly stated that *ronderos* and *ronderas* cannot be charged with abduction if they arrest a person in their official capacity and if they respect the involved persons' fundamental rights (Corte Suprema de Justicia, V Pleno Jurisdiccional de las Salas Penales Permanente y Transitorias 2009).

8 The main legal frameworks that define and regulate the *rondas campesinas*' competences in administering justice within their territories are Article 149 of the 1993 Constitution, Law No. 27908 (*Ley de Rondas Campesinas*) and its regulations (approved by *Decreto Supreme* N° 025–2003-JUS). For further details on the role of the *rondas campesinas* in Cajamarca and Piura in general and within mining conflicts, see Chapter 1.

exercise justice. However, as Rachel Sieder and Anna Barrera (2017, 642) have described, representatives of the ordinary judiciary and the police are often "resistant" to recognizing legal pluralism and to accepting the existence of alternative judicial authorities on the local level. With regard the *rondas campesinas* in Peru, Julio Faundez wrote that "the legal profession and the judiciary [...] have difficulties accepting that community justice organizations have any role to play within the legal system" (2005, 201). To judges and prosecutors, legal pluralism constitutes a challenge to their own profession and they often meet community justice institutions with great mistrust.[9] The persecution of *ronderos* and *ronderas* on the pretext of kidnapping should be understood in this context. During the judicialization of social conflicts, the latent tensions between the *justicia ordinaria* and the *jusitica ronderil* have re-emerged and have been fought out in the courtrooms.

In addition, relying on the offense of abduction not only makes it possible to attack the *justicia ronderil* as an important social institution in Cajamarca, but also allows for demanding long prison sentences. According to Peru's criminal code, abduction is a serious crime which is to be punished with no less than twenty years of imprisonment. The penalty shall be not less than thirty years in particular cases, for example if the aggrieved party is a state official or a public servant (*funcionario o servidor público*).[10] The long prison sentences demanded could thus be attributed to the fact that the governors were in official service at the time of the incident. The criminal code also provides for this severe penalty when the aggrieved is kidnapped for his activities in the private sector, which was relevant in the Yagen and Oxamarca cases.

In the activists' perception, this threat of long prison sentences did not correspond in any way to the description of the events. The complainants in the Sorochuco case, for example, had great difficulty explaining in court why the protest meeting had been an abduction. It was foreseeable that a conviction under this classification would have been difficult to enforce legally. On the other hand, because this type of criminalization is a misuse or manipulation of the law, it was not clear whether the judges would follow the written norms and the criminal code's categorization of offenses. The case of the *ronderos* from Oxamarca, who had been convicted for coercion, had demonstrated this. The risk in such cases does not emanate from the law or its code itself, but from a misuse thereof. This makes these cases particularly dangerous because the rules of the game are not clear, and it is not possible to foresee the basis on which the judicial authorities will make their decisions.

In the case of domination *of* law or domination *by* law, the rules of the game are clear at the outset. Criminal law may be strict toward certain population groups or

9 Yet this distrust is mutual. I discuss the mistrust the rural population in Peru feels toward official judicial authorities in Chapter 1 (see also: Faundez 2005, 190).

10 Peruvian Criminal Code, art. 152.

with regard to specific behavior, or the law, as an institution, may be disadvantageous to those who have no litigation experience and do not speak the language of law. However, these two types of law's domination can be responded to with specific counterstrategies, as I discuss in the final part of this chapter. In law's domination through the misuse of the criminal code, however, the rule of law is eliminated and a situation of arbitrariness prevails. This contributed to the threat and the great uncertainty in the Sorochuco case.

The threat of criminalization

The first day of the Sorochuco trial continues with the questioning of witnesses. Both the prosecutor and the procurador, *as well as the defense may interrogate them. The prosecutor is a man in his late thirties who hectically leafs through his files. He seems poorly prepared for the case. The judges repeatedly rebuke and correct him during the witnesses' interrogation. The hearing ends with the questioning of a policeman who was on duty in Sorochuco when the protest took place. The officer's statements are of little help to the complainants. Although he confirms that a demonstration took place, he does not confirm the allegations of abduction, and his statement does little to clarify the issues at stake. After questioning that witness, the judges declare the hearing closed. They announce that the trial will resume ten days later. We leave the courtroom. The defendants seem relieved to have made it through the first day in court.*

After the hearing we meet again in Grufides' *office. Mirtha and Victor, the* Coordinadora *lawyer, are satisfied with how the trial has gone so far. The attorneys' observation is that the complainants were not able to attribute any concrete offense to the individual defendants. The prosecutor's performance was unconvincing, they say, since he made many formal mistakes and was repeatedly reprimanded by the judges. "Technically, there should be an acquittal," Mirtha concludes. But then she also expresses concerns and recalls the case of the* ronderos *from Oxamarca, who were sentenced by the same judges to a year's unconditional prison sentence, not for kidnapping as initially demanded, but for coercion, the subsidiary accusation. In the defense's view, there had been no evidence of a crime in this case either, yet a sentence was issued. The two* ronderos *were able to escape from the courthouse and to evade arrest but have been hiding ever since. Mirtha makes clear that this case demonstrated how unpredictable the judges are. Her experience with the Oxamarca case thus becomes a benchmark from which the Sorochuco case's threat is deduced.*

Then there is time for questions from the defendants. For some of the accused, the focus is on clarifying practical, everyday issues. Manuel, a teacher from Celendín, asks whether he should ask for permission to stay away from work next week when the trial continues. He is worried about getting into trouble with his superiors. Other defendants react by laughing at him, saying that if he was convicted next week, he could forget his work as a teacher anyway. Emperatriz, one of the women from Sorochuco, expresses concern as to how she would be informed about the further course of the proceedings. She explains that she no longer has a mobile phone because she was constantly receiving threatening phone calls. Therefore, she is difficult to contact at the moment. She says that she is being harassed in Sorochuco by the mine's supporters. Sorochuco is a small community. Those who, like Emperatriz and the other defendants, publicly speak out against the mine are exposed to harassment and threats. Because of her commitment, Emperatriz was ostracized by her family. She and her children now live in the market where she also works. The social defamation is a heavy burden on her. She says that unknown people have killed her dogs in order to intimidate her. But despite all her worries, Emperatriz smiles confidently and says, "They will not defeat me."

The strategy of criminalizing social protest is not limited to the legal sphere, but affects people's everyday lives, their social relations, and their political aspirations. Activists and human rights lawyers claim that there is a policy of criminalization in Peru. Part of this policy is, on the one hand, that the national government and its local allies construct a hegemonic discourse against those who question extractive projects. The adaptation of legislation with regard to crimes committed in social protest is part of this policy, but it also includes other strategies which go beyond the law. Criminalization is about defining and sanctioning criminal behavior, whereby it remains socially contested who retains the power of definition to determine what is considered criminal or legitimate behavior. Public defamation and the stigmatization of opponents through this hegemonic discourse plays an important role in criminalizing social protest. In the following sections, I argue that the law's threat emerges from different fields and affects the activists in their everyday lives, through the loss of time and money, but also in their political mobilization, through defamation and stigmatization. Furthermore, social conflicts in the Cajamarca region have revealed that the latter aspect permeates communities and families and leads to social tensions and even violence in the affected *comunidades*.

Losing time and money

The Sorochuco trial continues about ten days after the first hearing. As a precaution, only those defendants are present who did not attend the first hearing and who have therefore been declared in contempt of court, which theoretically means that a warrant can be issued for their arrest. The other defendants are not obliged to join the hearing because they have already been questioned. Since it is not clear whether the court will pass a judgment, they have stayed away to avoid being arrested in case of a conviction.

During accreditation, Mirtha states that she represents fifteen defendants. "Only fifteen?" asks the judges' spokesperson. A short discussion follows, in which it becomes clear that the one man who is not represented by Mirtha has no lawyer of his own and that he will therefore be represented by the public defender. In contrast to the first hearing, however, no representative of the public defender's office is present. The concerned defendant is not here either. The judges decide that the hearing cannot continue under these circumstances. The spokesman suspends the hearing and postpones the further course of the trial until the day after tomorrow. Mirtha is frustrated. She hoped that the trial would come to an end soon. The two defendants who are present today will have to travel again to Cajamarca two days later, which will mean a further loss of time and money for them because of the travel costs, but also because they will again be absent from work on that day.

Criminal proceedings against activists in Peru are lengthy and often drag on for years. Delays occur when new judges are appointed and when these judges must familiarize themselves with the cases. Every year in February or March, the judiciary is on holiday for thirty days; nearly the entire institution stands still for a month. In addition, strikes are not uncommon and often paralyze the judiciary. But even when it operates properly, delays and interruptions in criminal proceedings often occur. Hearings are suspended because public prosecutors, public defenders, translators, or judges are absent (Vásquez 2018). Another common reason is when the responsible authorities have not had the time to study the files and to prepare for the hearing. The lawyers of criminalized activists see this as a delay tactic to keep the court cases open for as long as possible (see also: Chérrez *et al.* 2011, 115). In other Latin American countries, this strategy is widespread too. The IACHR observed that criminal proceedings against human rights defenders often take a disproportionately long time. According to the commission, the underlying aim is to intimidate the prosecuted individuals and to restrict them in their political and social work. The constant postponement of hearings is described as a strategy to prolong court proceedings (CIDH 2015, 96–7).

The loss of time, and consequently of money, is one of the major impacts on the daily lives of prosecuted activists. The authorities considered the Sorochuco case to be a complex legal process. It was therefore not dealt with in Celendín, as it would normally be the case since the events took place within the province of Celendín. Instead, it was transferred to a court in the city of Cajamarca. For the people of Sorochuco and Celendín, each court hearing meant the loss of an entire working day. This high expenditure of time is related to the law's locality. As Ewick and Silbey (1998, 96) described, judicial institutions are placed in specific locations. For people living in geographically marginalized places, for example in rural areas, it is often a great burden to travel to the places where the law is administered. People who want or need to interact with the law often cover longer distances and "have to enter literally the space of the law" (Ewick and Silbey 1998, 96). This loss of time has a social aspect, too. Ewick and Silbey borrow E. P. Thompson's expression of "the law's time" to describe the temporal dimension of legal processes. "The law's time" is the "time spent away from work, or family, or neighbors, or leisure" (1998, 98). It is a disruption of people's routines and everyday life.

In many cases, it is the "physical distance of courts from local communities" (Faundez 2005, 202) that becomes an obstacle for defendants. For the *ronderos* from

Yagen, for example, a single court date in the city of Cajamarca meant a three-day trip. Their village is not connected to the national road network. Therefore, the *ronderos* first walked for six hours to Bella Aurora, where they took a shared taxi to Celendín. In Celendín they spent the night before going to Cajamarca the next day. When their hearing was suspended after fifteen minutes because the public defender and two of the defendants were not present, as sometimes happens, this led to great frustration among the *ronderos*. They left their families and their work behind for nothing and unnecessarily spent money on travel, money that was already scarce.

Thus, law is not only socially distant from rural people through the domination *of* law and through the peculiarity of its mechanisms and its language but is also distant through its geographical location. To stay away from work means the loss of a full day's income for the accused, especially for those who are self-employed or who work in agriculture. Thus, a court hearing has negative effects on the financial situation of the prosecuted. As the example of Manuel from Celendín revealed, for those who are formally employed, a court case is a burden, too, since it is difficult to conceal from superiors. Defendants must ask for permission to be absent from work for a hearing, which can result in sanctions.

In addition, the loss of time is characterized by a gender dimension with women facing particular difficulties. Due to court hearings they cannot fulfill their duties and care work at home. Among the defendants from Sorochuco was Cecilia, a woman who takes care of her grandchild because her daughter lives and works in Lima. Cecilia suffered accusations from her family because she had to abandon this task during the trial. For her, being confronted with the trial meant not being able to fulfill the role that her family expected her to take on. In addition, court hearings are a particularly heavy burden for young mothers. Tatiana, a single mother from Celendín, experienced this when she appeared during one of the court hearings in 2015 with her son, whom she had to breastfeed. She was not admitted to the courtroom with her child but was also unable to find someone to take care of her son during the hearing. She was threatened with being declared in contempt of court because she did not comply with the call to attend the trial. Thus, she was restricted in her right to defense and had to reckon with reprisals by the judicial authorities (see also: Silva Santisteban 2017, 85, 102). These examples illustrate how the legal sphere stands in stark contrast to the sphere of everyday life, how the criminalization affects the activists in their daily activities, and also how tasks of daily life limit defendants in their possibilities in criminal proceedings. This materializes in the loss of time and money, the first form of how criminalization threatens the individual activists.

Disputes and defamations

Beyond disrupting everyday life or working life, the criminalization strategy also has an emotional effect on the prosecuted activists. Eckert (2014) wrote about how the threat of criminal prosecution in the context of terrorism prevention affects the social relations of those prosecuted and how it limits their scope for action. In the Sorochuco case, we observed a similar phenomenon, which stems from two different types of threats. First, the legal proceedings were in-and-of-themselves threatening to ordinary people who had no experience with the judiciary and who had never before set foot in a courthouse. To stand before the law and to face the judges who interrogated them was an intimidating experience for many of the accused. It was a moment when the domination *of* law was clearly invoked by the judicial authorities.

Second, the prosecuted had to face the threat of a concrete sanction because of the domination *by* law and because of the *misuse* thereof, thus the threat emerging from law's consequences. During the trial, the threatened prison sentence of more than thirty years led to a quite dramatic situation for the activists, especially shortly before the judgment was passed. Precautions were taken within the movement, and discussions were held regarding which persons would take over the organizations' leadership in case of a conviction. In addition, the threat was effective at the individual level, too. Tatiana, the woman from Celendín, told me afterwards that on the day of the judgment she had set off toward the Ecuadorian border to escape a possible arrest. "I am a single mother," she told me. "I cannot go to prison. Who will then take care of my child?" This threat also stemmed from the activists' lack of knowledge of legal processes. They depended on the decisions of the court and the work of their lawyers and lost control over their future prospects. This uncertainty was difficult for many to bear.

Regarding their political mobilization, the criminal proceedings had, on the one hand, brought the group of activists closer together, some of whom had hardly known each other personally before the trial. On the other hand, however, some of the activists involved will in the future think twice about whether to participate in political protest and risk receiving another criminal complaint. Moreover, the threat of prosecution acts as a deterrent to those affected by such criminalization cases, and it also discourages other people from becoming involved in social movements. An activist from Sorochuco pointed out, for example, that there are hardly any young people involved in the social movement in his community. He said: "Young people ask themselves, 'Why do you put yourself in that situation?'" In his view, social protest is de-legitimized in order to gradually neutralize it and to deprive it of the population's support. Criminalization restricts the activists' political space and prevents other people from joining the protest. In addition, criminalization not only acts as a deterrent to future protesters, but it also reduces the probability that activists will be able to hold official political office, because criminal proceedings make it much more difficult for them to run for office. This was an important issue when it came to deciding whether members of the social movements in Celendín would stand as candidates in the regional elections. Many activists saw the court proceedings against them as attempts to keep them from running for office. This, too, reveals the dimension and impact of criminalization on political mobilization.

In addition, there is the social dimension of the consequences of criminalization. Criminalization also restricts people in their personal relations. The lines of social conflict often run across communities and even across families. Emperatriz, for example, was disowned by her family because of her involvement in the protest. Others recounted that they had conflicts with their partners, siblings, or other family members who accused them of being involved in criminal activities. Many of the activists said that as a consequence of the defamation they participated less often in public events and communal festivities. Participation in the carnival, for example, was repeatedly discussed by the activists. Many of them were afraid that opponents could attack them during these festivals. In order not to unnecessarily expose themselves, they stayed away from the events. Moreover, there was not only fear of assault, but also of social exclusion. Cecilia from Sorochuco is active in her church. She told me that, as a consequence of the social conflict, she no longer travels to other villages to attend masses because people there had discredited her for her commitment to the social movement.

The activists from Celendín complained that the defamation they experienced in their communities and their families was fueled from outside. In their opinion, untruths about the social movement were spread via local newspapers, radio stations, and social media portraying them as criminal, violent, or even associating them with terrorism. During the *Escuela de Líderes y Lideresas* in Celendín, these defamation campaigns were discussed. Mirtha led the discussion and asked the participants to share their experience:

> *Mirtha*: How do people look at us? How do they look at the one who says, for example, "I don't want this mining project to enter my territory because it's damaging my life?" How do they qualify us?
> *Activist*: They treat us like troublemakers.
> *Mirtha*: What else?
> *Activists*: [They call us] revolutionaries. – Radicals. – Terrorists. – Crazy. – Violent. – Anti-development.
> *Mirtha*: That's it. Those qualifications are part of the criminalization. Criminalization is a web of not only political, legal, but also communication strategies. The communicational part has contributed in a great way to construct the criminal subject as someone who, like us, thinks differently. – Escuela de Líderes y Lideresas, *March 2017, Celendín (field notes, own translation)*

According to Mirtha and the other activists, the media, but also state and private actors, play an important role in bringing up such defamation campaigns. Through defamation, the other side would try to delegitimize the role of human rights activists and to "construct the criminal subject." By being constructed as "criminal subjects," activists lose their fundamental rights, such as the right to protest or the right to political participation. Moreover, they become outlawed criminals who can be attacked with impunity. Thereby, activists become vulnerable, not only to attacks by mine advocates, but they "could be attacked by any ordinary person who believes that discourse," as Mirtha said.

In extreme cases, the social tensions caused by the defamation campaigns result in physical violence in the communities. During the workshop, Mirtha went on by saying the following:

> Because we are already criminalized, we are already qualified as a criminal subject. If one day someone kills us, people will say, "For being a criminal, for being violent, for being unruly, that happened to him." That's what they said about our *compañeros* who died [during the protests in July 2012 in Celendín], right? "For being unruly," or "for joining the *revoltosos* [rioters]." Or "What were they doing in the middle of the mob of *revoltosos*?" They have already created a criminal subject in us to legitimize even the aggressions we may suffer. That is the policy of criminalization which is being deployed. –*Mirtha, lawyer with* Grufides, Escuela de Líderes y Lideresas, *March 2017, Celendín (field notes, own translation)*

One case that strikingly highlights these violent conflicts in the communities is the case of the leader and *rondero* Hitler Rojas from Yagen. Hitler Rojas was a leading critic of the Chadín 2 dam project and was elected mayor in his district. Only a few days after his election, he was shot dead in December 2015 by a member of his community. The murderer was prosecuted and convicted, but various shortcomings marked the criminal proceedings. In the first instance, the murderer was sentenced to a six-year imprisonment, which in the eyes of the social movements meant a mild sentence. Only after Rojas' family appealed the ruling, did the judicial authorities tighten the sentence from simple murder (*homicidio simple*) to aggravated homicide (*homicidio calificado*) and increase the prison sentence to twenty-one years. According to Mirtha, who led the appeal, the message that the judges sent with the first judgment was clear: "This man's life is worth nothing." She repeatedly compared Rojas' case to the criminalization cases. The prosecutor demanded a prison sentence of more than thirty years for the participants of what she considered to be a legitimate protest, but an activists' murder had resulted in a prison sentence of only six years. For Mirtha and the activists, this direct comparison revealed the arbitrariness of the local judicial authorities' jurisdiction and the unpredictability of legal processes. Furthermore, it again pointed to the misuse of law in the criminalization cases.

De-constructing the criminal subject

On the third day of the juicio oral *of the Sorochuco case, the defendants who could not previously attend the trial are questioned. In addition, a local journalist is summoned and interrogated as witness, and the admission of different pieces of evidence to the trial is discussed. Then the prosecutor and the defense lawyer make their closing argument. It is the moment when the two sides are again given time to present their legal argumentations. The statements made during the* juicio oral *by the defendants, the complainants, and the witnesses are used to underline these positions. The prosecutor insists that the trial has proven that the accused held the two governors captive for about two hours and that they consequently kidnapped them. He maintains the demand for a prison sentence of more than thirty years.*

*Mirtha, by contrast, does not again go into the discussion of what happened in Sorochuco on that day in April 2013, but focuses her summation on the trial and the results that have come to light during the hearings. She relies exclusively on procedural arguments and declares: "I want to start by saying that, basically, if there is not sufficient and adequate evidence in a given process, we cannot declare the guilt of any person. This violates fundamental principles." She continues, saying that no evidence has been presented during the trial which proved the defendants' involvement in the alleged crimes and that the evidence presented to the court "has ended up losing all evidentiary value." With regard to the formal procedural rules of a criminal proceeding, Mirtha explains that "we all know that the evidence must meet the requirements of existence, validity, and evidentiary effectiveness [*existencia, validez y eficacia probatoria*]." In her view, the evidence presented by the prosecutor did not meet these requirements. Therefore, Mirtha concludes by saying that "it would be a complete absurdity for justice to declare the guilt of my* patrocinados *for any crime that is imputed here" because the "jurisprudence speaks of sufficient evidentiary material to preserve the presence of innocence. If we do not have sufficient evidentiary material [...] this does not have accrediting force."*

In addition, Mirtha claims that after the validity of the evidence and the witnesses had been refuted, only the statements of the complainants remained and that, therefore, the question arose regarding whether a conviction for a criminal offense could be given based only on the statements of the aggrieved parties. "The doctrine, the jurisprudence says yes," Mirtha admits. However, she continues, explaining that the jurisprudence asks certain "guarantees of certainty" to be provided, for example "the absence of subjective incredibility, the verisimilitude, the persistence of incrimination." She points out that these requirements were not fulfilled and concludes by saying, "In that sense, I ask your honorable office to value these means of evidence and to declare the acquittal of all my patrocinados*."*

Then everything happens very quickly. The bench's speaker asks everyone to leave the room. We go into the small courtyard and wait. Mirtha says that the judgment will now be rendered. We all maintain a tense silence. After a few minutes, we are invited back in. The bench's speaker announces the judgment: "The court considers that the public prosecutor's office has not complied with its constitutional function, which is to provide evidence to support a conviction against the accused." The judge states that the accusation was "weak" and could not identify any illegal behavior on the part of the accused. He follows Mirtha's argumentation in saying that the only pieces of evidence available to support the allegations were the statements of the complainants. In the trial, however, it had become evident "that they are surrounded by a certain subjective incredibility." The spokesperson concludes that "with these considerations, the Collegiate Court of Cajamarca decides to acquit the accused." He announces that the official judgment will be read twelve days later and closes the session.

Immediately after the judgment, the situation in the courtroom remains calm. Nobody speaks out loudly; nobody cheers. We inform the defendants of their acquittal via WhatsApp. Mirtha packs her files and we leave the courtroom. About twenty police officers in full gear with helmets and shields are standing in front of the courthouse's entrance. Apparently, it had not been clear what the judgment would be today, and the police was requested to be ready to intervene in case of any protest against a conviction.

We return to Grufides' *office for a short evaluation of the judgment. The news about the acquittal has instantly spread to Celendín and Lima. Mirtha is constantly receiving calls from people who congratulate her on her success. Like the defendants who had to join the hearing today, the lawyer also seems relieved. She tells us that she woke up at four in the morning and went through her summation again. She had also felt very nervous in recent weeks, she admits, because she felt that the lives of others depended on her work.*

The activists prosecuted in the Sorochuco case coped in different ways with law's domination and with the threat of criminalization. Some activists found support in religious beliefs, which became apparent, for example, in the way and to whom the defendants manifested their gratitude for support after the acquittal was reached. After the *lectura de la sentencia*, the judgment's official reading, we met again in the office of *Grufides* to discuss the judgment and to celebrate the activists' victory. Almost all sixteen prosecuted activists were present that day, and many of them rose to speak and to individually express their gratitude. Many thanked, "first and foremost, God for guiding them through this process." Cecilia from Sorochuco, for example, thanked God for "touching the hearts of the judges." A man thanked God for "giving *doctora* Mirtha the knowledge and strength" that led to the acquittal.

For others, the success in the criminal case depended on secular strategies. The support of national and international networks, for example, was perceived as important by many of the criminalized activists. In the Sorochuco case, various national and international NGOs reported on the trial. NGOs sent a joint letter to the judicial authorities in Cajamarca expressing their concern about the case. The aim of this letter was to discursively de-construct the image of the criminal subject and to counter the hegemonic narrative of the violent activists as depicted by the complainants. In addition, the aim was to highlight that the protest in Sorochuco had been a legitimate political intervention. As I discuss later in this book, this kind of influence on the judicial authorities is an attempt by human rights organizations to challenge the hegemonic discourse of criminalization. It is difficult to assess to what extent this strategy was ultimately successful in the Sorochuco case because other strategies played a significant role in the acquittal, as well. However, for the activists themselves, the support they received from outside was an important source of strength, at least emotionally.

What seems much more important to me was Mirtha's legal reasoning. In one of the first meetings, she explained that her aim was to challenge the strategy of criminalizing social protest by invoking law and legality herself. "We have to *legally* deconstruct the discourse of criminalization," Mirtha announced. The prosecutor's strategy had been to indict a large group of people. Mirtha took advantage of this by asking witnesses and complainants repeatedly during the trial whether they could ascribe a specific act to the individual defendants. In doing so, she relied on the principle in criminal law that a person can only be convicted if an act can be directly attributed to him or her. Neither the complainants nor the witnesses were able to make such an attribution and to specify who of the sixteen prosecuted had actually committed the alleged crimes of abduction or coercion.

Two witnesses were questioned in the criminal trial, a police officer, and a journalist. Both testified that they had been in Sorochuco when the alleged events took place, but neither of them could give a precise description of the incident. Their statements were contradictory and inaccurate. The journalist even said during his interrogation that he did not want to accuse anyone of anything, but what he wanted was "peace for his village." In addition, a police report (*acta de constatación policial*) was presented as evidence in which the events were recorded by the police. During the trial, however, it turned out that the document's author described the events based on information given by a third person and not based on own observations. Mirtha argued that the presented *acta* therefore lacked veracity and validity as a piece of evidence.

In the trial, Mirtha based her argumentation on judicial norms and on the Peruvian legal framework. She strictly applied the written word of the Peruvian criminal code and on the exact text of the criminal procedure code. While the prosecutor and the ex-governors mobilized the law *from above* in order to intimidate the activists and to restrict them in their political mobilization and in their daily life, Mirtha also succeeded in using judicial mechanisms to get the activists acquitted. She also "enacted" (Welker 2014) the law, its written norms, and its procedures and thereby wanted to overcome the misuse of law through the prosecutor. Thereby, Mirtha took advantage of law's intrinsic procedural nature, as described by Rodríguez-Garavito (2011b, 273), i.e. the characteristic and the ability of law to establish and impose social rules and a lingua franca for negotiation between otherwise opposing parties.

The defendants did not oppose the law either. As Milton recalled to the group in one of the first meetings, it was important "to follow the instructions given by the lawyers," that is, to participate in the trial according to the rules endorsed by the judicial experts such as the lawyers, prosecutors, and judges. They did not involve themselves in "a resistance understanding of legality" and did not "enact a resistant consciousness of legality" (Ewick and Silbey 1998, 188–9), but rather followed the rule of law, although many of them had little to no confidence in the system of justice. This again reveals the domination *of* law and the hegemonic power judicial institutions impose on the individuals standing before the law.

Conclusion

Criminalization of social protest does not stop at the doorstep of the courthouse but enters the political sphere as well as the communal and family domain. Criminalization arises from the power to define a certain behavior as illegal and to define who is prosecuted as a criminal subject and sanctioned for his or her actions. Ewick and Silbey described how people who perceive legal means as unreliable "turn to other means, such as acts of resistance" (1998, 238). What I found in the Sorochuco case, however, was people being confronted with an attempt to misuse and manipulate the law. Their strategy was not to turn to other means, but to recapture law and legality in order to win in court. Their counterhegemonic act was not to defy the law or to take a stance against it, but rather to invoke it against those who attempted to misuse it.

At the same time, however, legal mobilization *from above* in these criminalization cases stands in sharp contrast to the impunity of state and corporate actors for human rights violations, which I describe in Chapter 3. In the perspective of many activists in Cajamarca, the system of justice is hardly accessible to them. "If we file a complaint against the *mineros*, the public prosecutor's office will immediately dismiss it. But if they report us, we are prosecuted and we face long prison sentences," one activist told me. These differences in the official treatment of rights violations have led social movement activists to adopt a negative attitude toward legal processes. They perceive law as an instrument used by "groups of power" (*grupos de poder*) – be it powerful economic or political actors – to repress dissent and to criminalize social protest. As this chapter has demonstrated, criminal proceedings are a major hurdle for the persons concerned, restricting them in their everyday lives, but also in their social relations and political activities. In the Sorochuco case, Mirtha was able to obtain an acquittal, but other cases, such as the case of the *ronderos* from Oxamarca, demonstrated that trials can also end in convictions.[11] It is this indeterminacy of law and the unpredictability of legal processes that makes the criminalization of protest particularly dangerous for social movements.

11 The two *ronderos* appealed against the ruling and were later, in May 2019, acquitted of all charges.

In the Sorochuco case this unpredictability of legal processes became apparent once more after the acquittal. When I returned to Cajamarca for the second round of fieldwork in 2018, I was surprised to hear that the lawsuit had been reopened and sent to the Court of Appeals in Cajamarca. When I had left Cajamarca some months before, the activists had told me that the deadline to appeal had elapsed without any further actions by the opposing party. As it turned out, however, the activists had misinterpreted this deadline because it did not begin on the day when the official reading of the judgment took place, but when the complainants and the prosecutor's office were notified in written form about the court order. The appeal was therefore lodged within the prescribed time. According to the activists, the two governors, the prosecutor's office, and the *procurador* had all appealed the first judgment.

Thus, we went back to the courtroom in May 2018 – about fourteen months after the first acquittal had been granted. For me it was a nice opportunity to meet the people from Sorochuco again, but for them it was frustrating to appear once more before court. The hearing can be summarized very briefly as it was suspended from the outset. We waited in the courtroom. The ex-governors were also present. After waiting a short time, a court clerk appeared and informed us that the hearing would be postponed because the judges had changed recently and had not had enough time to prepare for the hearing. For the defendants this meant, once more, that they had traveled in vain to Cajamarca. Later, the activists told me that the hearing was finally scheduled to take place in August 2018. However, it was then postponed again because one of the judges was unable to attend, and the magistrate appointed to replace him was busy with other proceedings. Ultimately, the hearing on the appeal took place at the beginning of September 2018. The court rejected the objections of the opposing party and confirmed the acquittal of the sixteen activists. After five and a half years of criminal proceedings and about more than a dozen court hearings, their acquittal was final.

Chapter 5. Transnational advocacy campaigns

Wednesday, 3 May 2017

Delivery of judgment in the case of Máxima Acuña and her family.

I arrive at the Palacio de la Justicia *shortly before eight in the morning. As usual at this time of the year, thick gray clouds hang over Lima. The traffic in front of the Supreme Court is not yet as crowded and noisy as it will be a few hours later. On Facebook, Amnesty International and several national NGOs have called for a* plantón, *a rally, to which about seventy people announced their participation and about 260 people showed their "interest." However, at 8 a.m. only two members of Amnesty International are there. They brought signs with them that say,* "Máxima no está sola – *Máxima is not alone," and positioned themselves by the fountain across the street from the courthouse. A few reporters are standing on the other side of the street and wait with cameras. They immediately start filming when a taxi stops at the sidewalk and Máxima Acuña, her husband Jaime Chaupe, and Elías, their son-in-law, arrive. The three quickly get out of the taxi and enter the courthouse through a side entrance. I enter the building through the visitors' entrance. Via a narrow staircase I reach the upper floor and cross a populous hall with a high ceiling.*

In front of the entrance to the actual courtroom, there are already many people standing around, mostly elegantly dressed people over fifty – men in dark suits and women in two-pieces. The Chaupe family sits on a wooden bench to the right of the entrance to the courtroom, somewhat separated from the crowd of other people. María Elena Foronda, a Member of Parliament of the leftist party Frente Amplio, *is with them, later joined by Mirtha, the lawyer working with* Grufides, *and Hugo Blanco, the icon of the Peruvian* campesino *movement. Rocío Silva Santisteban, the former executive secretary of the* Coordinadora, *and Marco Arana, the former priest and founder of* Grufides, *who is now a member of Congress for the Cajamarca region, appear and talk to the family. Juliana from EarthRights International also arrives and joins the group. The Peruvian human rights movement seems to have sent its most important figures to the court hearing. Several reporters and photographers stay with the group constantly, taking pictures and filming.*

Shortly after 8:30 a.m. the crowd becomes restless as the entrance to the hall is opened. A few people, primarily those directly involved in the court case and their lawyers, are called up and let in. The remaining people start following them; a crowd develops because the entrance is narrow, and space – and especially places to sit – in the courtroom is limited. I make it in and get a seat on the right side of the hall in one of the back rows. The Chaupe family and their supporters sit on the left side. Reporters with cameras have taken up position between the two rows of chairs, completely blocking the view to the left and to the front.

A judge opens the hearings and begins to make a statement in the most complicated official language. I hardly understand anything, only that the trial or the decision has been postponed again. The young woman sitting next to me and I look at each other confused. "¿Otra vez?" *we wonder. Is the decision seriously being postponed again? Did Máxima and her family travel to Lima again in vain? Suddenly, however, it becomes clear that this first pronouncement concerns a different court case. The judge then moves on to the Chaupe family's case and asks the lawyers of the two parties to introduce themselves. Mirtha steps forward, takes a seat, and states her name and her registration number as a lawyer at the* Colegio de Abogados *in Cajamarca. The judge announces that the court has reached a decision and asks the clerk to read it out loud. The clerk presents the decision of the court and reads the ruling so quickly that I again hardly understand anything. However, my neighbor confirms that the decision is positive: Máxima and her family have definitively won the legal battle against Minera Yanacocha.*

As with the sentencing in Cajamarca in the Sorochuco case, the uncertainty in the courtroom as to whether to applaud or not is noticeable. The room is filled with beaming faces, but no one dares to cheer or applaud in this formal and disciplined courtroom environment. The judge ends the hearing with the ringing of a bell. Then the hustle and bustle at the door starts again but now in the other direction. Reporters with cameras surround the family and accompany them outside into the hall of the courthouse. Máxima and Mirtha are being interviewed, they are hardly visible behind all the media people. Jaime and Elías stand next to them; congressmen Marco Arana and María Elena Foronda remain next to them to be in the picture as well. From outside, chants and slogans come floating into the building. Apparently, more people have joined the rally. I notice a man in a suit standing around in the hall, who I believe I recognize from newspaper photos as a lawyer of Minera Yanacocha. He looks lost, and when none of the reporters turn to him, he walks away quickly.

I go down to the ground floor to be outside in front of the courthouse when Máxima and the others leave the court via the main staircase. However, I get hopelessly lost in the many corridors and rush past the many offices, which all look the same, up and down the corridors without finding the right exit. By the time I finally hurry out of the door, the others have already left the courthouse and have joined the supporters of the plantón *on the other side of the street. The crowd has grown to about thirty or forty people. Other members of Amnesty International, activists from the women's organization FENMUCARINAP*[1] *and from other NGOs and grassroots organizations have joined them. Many carry signs, posters, or flags. Milton is*

1 *Federación Nacional de Mujeres Campesinas, Artesanas, Indígenas, Nativas y Asalariadas del Perú*, National Federation of Peasant, Artisan, Indigenous, Native and Wage-Earning Women of Peru.

also there, who traveled from Celendín to Lima for another event and came to show his support with the Chaupe family.

Further interviews by the reporters with Máxima, Mirtha, but also with Marco Arana follow. Photos are taken with the different support groups, with the women's organization, and with Amnesty International. The activists and members of the NGOs take photos with their mobile phones. Everyone talks loudly and is excited. Using a megaphone, Máxima turns to the crowd and thanks them for the support. An NGO lawyer holds a mobile phone to her ear so that she can receive congratulations from afar. Amidst all this excitement, Máxima seems confused and probably cannot fully realize her victory yet. Amidst all the happy, beaming faces, she continues to look worried, and the whole scene just seems to be too much for her.

Introduction

With the pronouncement of the Supreme Court's judgment in Lima, a long-lasting legal dispute ended on May 3, 2017. The court case concerned the accusation by the mining company Minera Yanacocha that the *campesino* family of Máxima Acuña and Jaime Chaupe and their adult children had illegally occupied a plot of land in the Cajamarca region. At the local level, the family had initially been found guilty of this alleged crime and was sentenced in a local court. Later, an appeal body in Cajamarca had acquitted them. The company did not accept this judgment and took the case to the Supreme Court in the capital, where it was then finally concluded with a decision about the cassation appeal. The court case was part of a larger legal dispute that had been going on between the family and the mining company since 2011, and which has long been about much more than a simple land dispute. As I mentioned in the introduction, the disputed land is located in the area of the planned Conga Mine. In order for Minera Yanacocha to be able to realize this mining project, the family would need to leave the land. However, the Chaupes have argued that they never sold their land and that they will not leave it. On several occasions, the mining company attempted to evict the family from the land and allegedly committed human rights violations in doing so.

Within the Conga conflict, the Chaupe family, and in particular Máxima Acuña, became central figures of resistance against Minera Yanacocha's mining project. Various national and international NGOs, but also local social movements and grassroots organizations ran solidarity campaigns to support them (Hoffman 2017, 59). In these campaigns, a recurring picture emerged relatively quickly, juxtaposing the *campesino* family, whose modest livelihood in subsistence agriculture is threatened, to the company Minera Yanacocha, which is attempting to deprive them of their *tierra*, their land. The resulting image was that of David against Goliath, an image that is well suited to publicly denounce transnational mining companies for human rights violations and environmental damages.

Furthermore, the support campaigns by national and international NGOs followed the typical patterns used by transnational advocacy networks to support local political struggles through international attention and external pressure. As mentioned in the introduction, such transnational advocacy networks are a frequently used means of accompanying legal struggles arising from social conflicts. Various authors have discussed this phenomenon in recent years in their research on transnational social movements, including, for example, Kirsch (2007, 2014, 2016), Rajagopal (2003), Nash (2012), and Santos (2005) and Rodríguez-Garavito (2005, Santos and Rodríguez-Garavito 2005). In their well-known book on "activists beyond borders," Keck and Sikkink (1998) described the efforts of transnational advocacy networks as an attempt to create a "boomerang effect" by relying on allies abroad. Others described this phenomenon of transnational networking and alliance building as "counterglobalization" (Kirsch 2007), "globalization from below" (Santos 2015, 11), or "subaltern cosmopolitanism" (Nash 2012). Basically it is about local protest movements networking internationally and thereby strengthening their scope of action and their bargaining power.

This chapter is aimed at contributing to these discussions and seeks to analyze the example of the Chaupe family to shed light on how such transnational advocacy networks evolved in the Peruvian context. In doing so, I am interested in analyzing the relations between the support campaigns and the legal disputes at stake. In the first part, the chapter traces the land dispute between Minera Yanacocha and the Chaupe family and outlines the main points of the conflict and its judicialization into a legal dispute. In the second part, I then reflect on the transnational support campaigns in favor of the family and illustrate how these manifested themselves and had an impact at the local level. In doing so, I focus in particular on the campaign of Amnesty International and reflect on possible impacts of such a campaign on the legal proceedings that the family and Minera Yanacocha went through.

These considerations are linked to my analysis of legal mobilization *from below* and *from above*, respectively, and thus build on the discussions in the previous chapters. I am particularly interested in how hegemonic discourses are negotiated in a legal dispute at the local level in the face of the campaign of a transnational advocacy network. The "juridification of protests," as Eckert *et al.* (2012a) called it, and the reference to international human rights discourses offer an ideal starting point for mobilizing international support.

From a land dispute to legal disputes

The piece of land around which the conflict between Minera Yanacocha and the Chaupe family evolved is locally referred to as Tragadero Grande and belongs to the *comunidad campesina* of Sorochuco in the province of Celendín, Cajamarca. Jaime

Chaupe and Máxima Acuña acquired possessory rights to Tragadero Grande from a relative of Jaime in 1994 and have, as they claim, been using it for subsistence farming ever since (RESOLVE 2016, vii, 31–2, Hoffman 2017, 59).[2] With the purchase of the land, Jaime Chaupe and Máxima Acuña became members of the peasant community of Sorochuco (Vásquez 2016, 8).

In the late nineties, the company Minas Conga acquired land from the *comunidad campesina* to develop a mining project in the area. As I discussed earlier (see Chapter 1), there are particular legal requirements to purchase land owned by a *comunidad campesina*, which the mining corporation claimed to have fulfilled at that time. According to the Chaupes' view, the community, however, did not decide to sell all the land requested by the mining company, but only individual plots of land, the owners of which had agreed to sell. Jaime Chaupe and Máxima Acuña were not among those who had agreed to sell (Vásquez 2016, 8). In 2001, Minera Yanacocha acquired Minas Conga and all its assets, including the land titles, which, according to the company, also included the area of Tragadero Grande (RESOLVE 2016, 8, Vásquez 2016, 8). However, members of the Chaupe family insisted that they never sold their land (RESOLVE 2016, 18). Consequently, both the company and the Chaupe family claimed Tragadero Grande for themselves, and both sides claimed to have documents proving their ownership of the land.

In 2011, the mining company carried out infrastructure work in the area, which led to the first confrontations between corporate employees and family members. The conflict escalated in May 2011 when employees of Minera Yanacocha attempted to evict members of the family from the disputed land, burning down a hut they had built and destroying their potato fields (Li and Paredes Peñafiel 2019, 229). Three months later, the company made another attempt to clear the land. The family accused the company employees as well as the security forces accompanying the mine workers of threats and the use of physical violence (RESOLVE 2016, 22–3). In the years that followed, a number of other such clashes occurred, in which company employees allegedly threatened family members, used violence, destroyed the plantations in their fields, and tore down huts and animal shelters. In the early years, the

2 In 2015 and 2016, the Washington-based U.S. NGO RESOLVE conducted what it claims was an "Independent Fact Finding Mission" in Cajamarca and summarized its observations on the conflict between the Chaupe family and Minera Yanacocha in a report (RESOLVE 2016). RESOLVE was commissioned and paid for by Minera Yanacocha's parent company, Newmont Mining. Although the mission's report was commissioned by the mining company itself, it recognized that in the context of the land rights dispute the mining company repeatedly violated human rights and internal corporate rules. The report provides an important basis for the description of the events in this chapter and was supplemented by data I collected during my field research in Cajamarca and information from other literature, NGO reports, and newspaper articles.

mine workers were accompanied by police officers who were later replaced by personnel from the private security company Securitas commissioned by the mining company.

In these interventions, the company argued that it was the legal owner of the land and therefore had a right to vacate it on its own. In doing so, Minera Yanacocha invoked its right to conduct an "*extrajudicial* defense of the property" (*defensa posesoria extrajudicial,* Minera Yanacocha 2015a, 2015b, 2016). Under the Peruvian Civil Code, a *defensa posesoria extrajudicial* constitutes a legal mechanism that allows an owner to evict another party which is unlawfully appropriating his or her property.[3] The addition of "extrajudicial" does not refer to the fact that the defense of property would take place outside the law, but only states that the action is taken without the involvement of judges and courts. In the land dispute, Minera Yanacocha explicitly invoked this fact to act in accordance with legal norms. It argued to have the right to protect its property and claimed that this right is encoded in Peruvian civil law. The Chaupe family, in turn, maintained that Tragadero Grande is their land and that they have a right to live there without being attacked by mine workers or security forces. By challenging the company's property claims, they argued that the eviction attempts were a violation of law. The dispute about the piece of land consequently turned into a dispute about who has the law, and thus the truth, on their side.

The disputes over the land underwent a process of judicialization as confrontations between family members and corporate actors occurring in Tragadero Grande resulted in various criminal charges, which the family and the company filed against each other. In these legal cases, the Chaupe family received legal assistance from *Grufides*, the local NGO from Cajamarca. Mirtha, the NGO lawyer involved in the Sorochuco case, which I analyzed in the previous chapter, became the family's main attorney. In addition, the family was represented by at least two other lawyers who worked in *Grufides*' legal team.

The Chaupe family's mobilization "from below"

The Chaupe family contributed to the judicialization of the land dispute by filing criminal charges after every "extrajudicial defense of property" that the company undertook. Most of these complaints concerned usurpation, damage to property, or offenses such as physical and psychological violence and threats against family members. As Mirtha and another *Grufides* lawyer with whom I discussed the case told me, the complaints were filed against the security forces and corporate employees directly involved, but also against the superiors of the latter, who had presumably ordered the interventions. At the time of writing, only a few of the criminal charges lodged by the family have led to the opening of a criminal investigation, and none

3 Article 920, Peruvian Civil Code.

of these investigations have resulted in an indictment, as the lawyers told me (see also: Amnesty International 2018, 30–1). Thus, from a legal point of view, efforts to pursue human rights litigation have been unsuccessful in this case.

Reasons for this failure include several of the aspects I have already described in Chapter 3 regarding the hurdles and difficulties faced by complainants in the Peruvian judicial system. These include the difficulty of gathering evidence of the abuses that were accepted by the judicial authorities as well as the lack of will on the part of the prosecutorial authorities to investigate allegations. In some cases, the complaints lodged by the Chaupe family were disregarded right away; in others, the public prosecutor's office initiated preparatory investigations, but later discontinued them, mostly because of a lack of evidence, as the authorities argued. On several occasions, the Chaupe family recorded the abuses with a mobile phone. However, these video recordings were not admitted as evidence by the public prosecutor's office (Li and Paredes Peñafiel 2019, 229). In our conversations, the *Grufides* lawyers argued that the accusations were not investigated with the necessary care because the authorities lack the political will to take action against a economic actor such as Minera Yanacocha. In this context, there have been repeated accusations that the public prosecutor's office has been corrupted by the company and would therefore protect it from criminal proceedings. However, these allegations could not be substantiated in the past.

In addition to all these hurdles, the legal work on behalf of the family was obstructed by defamation and harassment from mine supporters and other local actors. The family and the staff of the NGO *Grufides* have been repeatedly insulted in public by local journalists and have been called "troublemakers" and "radicals" who would prevent the region's economic development with their opposition to the Conga project (Li and Paredes Peñafiel 2019, 229). Mirtha and her own family were repeatedly threatened by unknown persons, which she explained as a response to her work as the Chaupes' attorney. Mirtha's house was broken into without anything valuable being stolen, and there were signs that she was being shadowed (Silva Santisteban 2017, 93).[4] For several years, Mirtha lived under police protection and was accom-

4 By 2006, in the context of an earlier mining conflict, *Grufides* had already been affected by a systematic surveillance campaign allegedly ordered by Minera Yanacocha to infiltrate and intimidate the civil society organization and its staff. Under the code name *Operación Diablo*, Operation Devil, members of *Grufides* were observed by the private security company Forza; the NGO's telephones were tapped and its members were harassed, threatened, and intimidated. When the operation came to light and *Grufides* filed a criminal complaint, the prosecutorial authorities only reluctantly followed up on the allegations. Later, the investigation was dropped. Thus, it could not be legally proven that Minera Yanacocha had commissioned the operation from the security company Forza, with which it had worked closely for years. For a detailed discussion of the *Operación Diablo*, see the work by Charis Kamphuis (2011, 79–80, 2012b, 233–9, 2012a, 550–1).

panied by a police officer in her daily life. At the end of 2017, she decided that the situation was no longer bearable for her family and that there was no other option but to move to Lima, where she continued her work as attorney of the Chaupe family.[5]

Because the filing of criminal charges did not lead to the judicial authorities taking action and intervening in the dispute, *Grufides* searched for other legal actions that could provide relief and access to justice for the family. Mirtha filed two *habeas corpus* actions with the judicial authorities in Celendín, i.e. she invoked constitutional mechanisms that require the state to guarantee certain fundamental rights (Silva Santisteban 2017, 161).[6] With these lawsuits the family's attorney demanded that Minera Yanacocha grant them access (*libre tránsito*) to their own property. Both claims were rejected by the judicial authorities in Celendín (Newmont Mining Corporation 2015, Fransciscans International and Grufides 2017, 4, 9, 22). In addition, *Grufides*, together with the women's rights organization DEMUS[7], demanded the protection of Máxima from violent attacks by Minera Yanacocha on the basis of a specific law regarding protection against gendered violence in social conflicts. However, this complaint was rejected by the judicial authorities as well (DEMUS, 2017). As the mechanisms of the national judicial system had thereby been exhausted, the NGOs referred the case to the IACHR, where a final decision was still pending at the time of writing (Machacuay 2017, Wayka.pe (online) 2020).

In earlier years, the legal NGOs had already approached international bodies and, in particular, the IACHR in search of support of Máxima and her family. In May 2014, the IACHR issued a so-called *medida cautelar*, a precautionary measure for the Chaupe family, along with more than fifty leaders, activists, and other key figures of the social movements against the Conga project (de la Puente 2014).[8] The group of beneficiaries also included both Milton and Mirtha. In December 2011, several na-

5 After moving to Lima, Mirtha initially worked as a lawyer for the national legal NGO APRODEH. At the beginning of 2020, she was elected to the national congress for the left-wing party *Frente Amplio* as representative of the Cajamarca region. From October 2021 to the end of January 2022 she served as the country's prime minister under President Pedro Castillo. Thus, during the time of my research, Mirtha was still a lawyer who was known only in human rights circles in the Cajamarca region. Afterwards, she became a nationally known political figure.

6 Article 200, Peruvian Political Constitution of 1993; article 25, Peruvian Code of Constitutional Procedure.

7 *Estudio para la Defensa de los Derechos de la Mujer*, Study for the Defense of Women's Rights, a national NGO based in Lima.

8 *Comisión Interamericana de Derechos Humanos, Resolución 9/2014, Líderes y Lideresas de Comunidades Campesinas y Rondas Campesinas de Cajamarca respecto de la República de Perú, Medida Cautelar No.* 452–11, May 5, 2014, document on file with author.

tional NGOs had submitted an application to the IACHR requesting this action.[9] The IACHR's resolution obliged the Peruvian state to take action to guarantee the safety and personal integrity of the beneficiaries (RESOLVE 2016, 2, 30–1). The measure was thus directly aimed at the state's responsibility to protect and guarantee the rights of its citizens. As with other decisions by international bodies, the difficulty lay in the fact that the resolution's implementation depended on the Peruvian state itself. Although the Ministry of Justice took initial steps to implement the resolution, in many cases it did not meet the demands of the involved beneficiaries.[10] In the case of Máxima, the action was found to be insufficient in protecting her from further attacks by the mining company, which continued after the IACHR's resolution. Thus, neither the use of domestic criminal or constitutional law, nor the invocation of international organizations could improve the situation of the Chaupe family through legal mobilization from below.

Minera Yanacocha's legal mobilization "from above"

In recent years, several cases have revealed that corporations involved in extractive industries seem especially eager to strategically use legal means to counter criticism. The oil and gas company Chevron, for example, prominently used the Racketeer Influenced Corrupt Organizations (RICO) Act in the United States to sue those individuals and their attorneys who had filed a lawsuit against the corporation for environmental damages in Ecuador (Skinner 2014, 234). In a similar way, the corporation Ross Mining took legal action before the High Court of Solomon Islands against an Australian law firm for its involvement in a claim against the mining

9 Formally, the application was submitted by the *Asociación Interétnica de la Selva Peruana* (AIDESEP), the *Confederación Campesina del Perú* (CCP) and other indigenous and *campesino* organizations. However, as several activists in Celendín told me, the driving force behind the application was the *Instituto Internacional de Derecho y Sociedad* (IIDS, International Institute on Law and Society). IIDS is a national NGO based in Lima that works closely with several *rondas campesinas* in the Cajamarca region and supports them through legal assistance. The NGO has a rather dubious reputation within the Peruvian human rights movement. During fieldwork, I repeatedly heard the accusation that the NGO is obsessively attempting to persuade the *campesino* population in Cajamarca to identify as "indigenous," convincing them of their indigeneity to demand internationally recognized rights (see also: Santiago 2017, 65–6). In connection with the application to the IACHR, various activists in Celendín and Cajamarca argued that the members of IIDS, due to a lack of knowledge of local conditions, had requested protection measures for people who did not need or require them, while forgetting others who were actually threatened by the conflict.

10 One of the beneficiaries told me, for example, that as a result of the *medidas cautelares*, the Peruvian state offered to provide him with police protection. For this man, however, it was no option to be constantly accompanied by a police officer, because it was in his opinion the state itself that posed a danger to him.

company, as Kirsch (2018, 126) reported. In May 2017, mining corporation Glencore threatened the German NGO Facing Finance with a lawsuit because it had called, in a press release, for the cessation of credit and investment transactions with the mining company (Facing Finance 2017, *heute journal* 2017). This corporate use of law is often described as what Penelope Canan and George William Pring (1988, 1996) have called *Strategic Lawsuits Against Public Participation* (SLAPP).

Minera Yanacocha has also actively used the existing criminal law to enforce its interests. In contrast to the legal actions filed by the Chaupe family, the company's criminal charges led to proceedings that lasted several years. In August 2011, the company lodged a criminal charge against Máxima and her family for "aggravated usurpation" (Hoffman 2017, 59). In this complaint, the Chaupes were alleged to have illegally invaded and occupied Tragadero Grande. According to the company, the "aggravation" of the crime was asserted because members of the family had allegedly used violence against police officers and mine workers during the eviction attempts (Amnesty International 2018, 30).

In October 2012, only fourteen months after the complaint was filed, the family was found guilty of "aggravated usurpation" and sentenced to a conditional prison term of three years and a compensation payment (RESOLVE 2016, 27). The family appealed this judgment, whereupon the first judgment was overturned and a new criminal trial was ordered. The court in the second instance, however, confirmed the conviction in August 2014. In its ruling, the court reduced the prison sentence to two years and eight months of suspended imprisonment, but increased the compensation payment to 5,500 Nuevo Soles (approximately US$ 1,900, El Comercio (online) 2014, Vásquez 2016, 10). The family again appealed this ruling and finally won in December 2014 when the Cajamarca High Court acquitted them and overturned the judgment of the lower court (Panorama Cajamarquino 2014a). As in the Sorochuco case, which I discussed in the previous chapter, Mirtha and her colleagues had thus succeeded in finally obtaining an acquittal in the case of the Chaupe family.

With the acquittal, the case would normally have been closed, as the highest court level had been reached. However, Minera Yanacocha managed to have the case transferred to the Supreme Court in Lima, where a judgment of cassation was handed down to decide on the ruling of the regional court. This transfer to the Supreme Court under the *recurso de casación*, the cassation appeal, is only allowed under restricted conditions in Peru. The New Criminal Procedure Code limits appeals in cassation to cases in which a superior court or the Supreme Court itself has given a judgment that is procedurally or substantively contrary to the constitution, to other legal norms, or to the existing jurisprudence.[11] Mirtha told me that in her view the Chaupe cases did not fulfill these requirements and alleged that Minera Yanacocha had exerted pressure on the judicial authorities to admit its appeal. In this way, the

11 Article 429, New Peruvian Criminal Procedure Code.

legal dispute reached the Supreme Court of Lima, where the Chaupe family was finally acquitted in May 2017, as I described at the beginning of this chapter (see also: Romero 2017). However, the legal dispute has not yet been concluded, as Minera Yanacocha also filed a civil suit parallel to the criminal proceedings. This civil case is intended to clarify whether the Chaupe family or the mining company holds rightful possession documents proving ownership of Tragadero Grande. At the time of writing, this civil case is still ongoing.

The criminal trial and the almost six-year-long procedure caused great psychological strain for the Chaupes. Criminalization means a great loss of time and money for those concerned, but also a psychological burden that they have had to bear through law's domination. Máxima and her family had to live for a long time with the fear of having to leave their piece of land due to the first two court rulings. In addition, the court proceedings themselves were a great burden because they necessitated many trips to the regional courts and later to the Supreme Court in Lima. One example of this was a court hearing in April 2017, for which the family traveled from Tragadero Grande to Lima for the pronouncement of the ruling on the cassation appeal. They only found out while being in the courtroom that, due to the absence of individual judges, no decision had yet been made on their case. The family and the attorneys had not been informed about the suspension of the appointment beforehand and had therefore made the long journey in vain (Observatorio de Conflictos Mineros en el Perú 2017). For Máxima and her relatives, such experiences led to resignation and a feeling of not being taken seriously by the judicial authorities. In this situation, their lawyers had the task of convincing them to continue to believe in the law.

When standing in front of the courthouse in May 2017, Mirtha said to a group of journalists that the decision of the Supreme Court was a great satisfaction for her because it confirmed the innocence of Máxima and her family. In Mirtha's view, the acquittal put an end to the misuse of the criminal law by the mining company. She noted that the acquittal was "legally speaking, the logical thing to do (*que era lo lógico, jurídicamente hablando*)." Furthermore, she added that the acquittal confirmed that "the poor and the weak also have rights that must be respected". Mirtha had thus succeeded in putting an end to the misuse of the law and the criminalization of mining opponents by invoking the law. Whether she was thereby able to restore the faith in the law of the persons she represented in court remains uncertain, however. Immediately after the judgment was pronounced, Máxima said in front of her supporters that she was happy that "justice had been done here in the capital, too," and she thanked the authorities for ruling in her favor. She added that she was now asking the company to let her and her family live in peace in Tragadero Grande and not to make any further attempts to evict her from the land.

With this demand, Máxima responded to the fact that even during the court proceedings the company had not relied solely on the strategy of legal mobilization.

When we take a closer look at the trajectory of the criminal case, the chronology of the events reveals that there was a sharp increase in the company's interventions in Tragadero Grande following the acquittal of the family by the Cajamarca High Court in December 2014. Between February 2015 and October 2016, there were at least twelve "extrajudicial defenses of property" by the company.[12] Eviction attempts occurred almost monthly, and the family's agricultural fields were repeatedly destroyed. For the Chaupe family, this meant that although they were acquitted in court, they could not live in peace.

Furthermore, as the company was defeated in court, Minera Yanacocha subsequently adopted other strategies, which critics of the company described as intimidation attempts. In 2015, Minera Yanacocha built a pasture for alpacas next to Tragadero Grande, which was guarded by ten police officers and secured with a fence that also restricted the family's freedom of movement (RESOLVE 2016, 17). As activists in Celendín told me, the police officers were obviously not present to guard the alpacas, but to control the family. These allegations were strengthened when a drone flew over the Chaupes' house at the beginning of 2016, probably also to monitor them, as the activists told me. In the perspective of the family and their supporters, these were clear indications that the mining company sought to intimidate and harass them after losing in court. Thus, as soon as the law offered no or limited possibilities for Minera Yanacocha to obtain the land, the company resorted to other means.

With regard to Minera Yanacocha's legal mobilization from above, we can conclude that although the company finally did not succeed before court, the proceedings became a great burden for the Chaupe family. Even though Máxima and her family remained in Tragadero Grande, the price they paid during the legal dispute was extremely high. The support they received from national and international solidarity networks and NGOs could only offer limited mitigation, as I argue in the following sections.

Advocacy campaigns at home and abroad

"We stand with Máxima!"

I have a clear memory of the time when the Superior Court in Cajamarca pronounced its judgment on the criminal case against the Chaupe family in December 2014. About eight months before, I had been in Cajamarca doing fieldwork for an earlier

12 This counting is based on Minera Yanacocha's press releases published on the company's website for each its interventions in Tragadero Grande (see, for example: Minera Yanacocha 2015a, 2015b, 2016, see also: RESOLVE 2016, 28).

research. On the day when the judgment was passed, activists in Lima set up an online radio program, in which the judicial decision was transmitted to the capital and, from there, broadcasted worldwide. Giovanni, an Italian volunteer in development cooperation who worked in Cajamarca at that time, reported from the courtroom via telephone and informed about the family's acquittal. In the background, a large crowd of people, who had gone to the courtroom to express their solidarity with the family, could be heard. Mirtha, Milton, and other activists were brought to the phone and shared their joy at the victory over Minera Yanacocha. The next day, the front page of the local newspaper *Panorama Cajamarquino* featured the headline "*Absuelven a Familia Chaupe*" (Panorama Cajamarquino 2014b). A full-page photo showed the crowded courtroom, the defendants and complainants sitting with their lawyers in the front row; behind them, the room was filled with reporters, activists, European volunteers, and NGO staff. The national and international campaigns in support of Máxima and her family reached a first peak at that time. A transnational community euphorically celebrated the legal victory over the mining company.

The strategy of publicly demonstrating support for the Chaupe family's case to strengthen their position in the legal dispute was thus not only applied in the Supreme Court in Lima in May 2017. Since the conflict with the mining company started being carried out in the courtrooms, the family has been closely accompanied by various NGOs and grassroots organizations. International and foreign NGOs such as EarthRights International, Amnesty International, Front Line Defenders, Oxfam International, Earthworks, the Latin American Women Union (*Unión Latinoamericana de Mujeres*, ULAM), CATAPA, and the Society for Threatened Peoples launched campaigns that addressed the family's dispute with the mining company. At the national level, Máxima and her family received support from the PIC, the *Coordinadora*, the national women's rights organization DEMUS, the Peruvian section of Amnesty International, and especially from *Grufides*, the NGO in Cajamarca, which provided them with long-term legal assistance. These campaigns resulted in a great wave of solidarity for the Chaupes at home, as well as abroad. As soon as Minera Yanacocha again intervened in Tragadero Grande, the news spread quickly through social and traditional media and triggered a wave of public protest.

In an early phase of the dispute, Máxima traveled abroad as part of these advocacy campaigns. She went to the United States and France, for example, where she met with NGOs and other allies. Various documentaries dealt with her unequal fight against the transnational mining company. NGOs launched online petitions and protest letters in her favor directed at the Peruvian government, prosecutors, judges, and other state authorities, as well as to Minera Yanacocha and its U.S. parent company, Newmont Mining. The case was presented to the IACHR, and Máxima met with the commission's representatives several times. Furthermore, during its visit to Peru, a delegation of the United Nations Working Group on Business and Human Rights paid special attention to the family's case (United Nations Working

Group on Business and Human Rights 2017). In addition, as I describe in Chapter 6, EarthRights International filed a transnational lawsuit against the parent company Newmont Mining on behalf of the Chaupe family in 2017. The case thus exemplified how the NGO community directed all the spotlights on a specific, emblematic case thereby seeking to influence the underlying legal dispute.

The international NGOs' campaigns addressed the issue of criminalization but also the issue of corporate impunity. The human rights violations that the Chaupes had suffered, both through criminalization and through the attacks on their property, were the center of attention. This reference to human rights discourses was particularly well suited for advocacy campaigns aimed at an international audience. The NGOs exploited a "global human rights consciousness" (Chimni 2007, 207) and invoked the "universal logic of rights" (Brinks *et al.* 2015, 290). This universal logic of rights enables transnational social movements to advance rights-based claims. The fact that the land dispute had turned into a legal dispute benefited the NGO campaigns because through being framed within a human rights discourse, the claims of the Chaupe family became generally comprehensible. In this sense, human rights discourses create a common language that is understood both at the local level as well as transnationally and thus transcends spatial boundaries (Merry 2006b, 42). The juridification of the dispute was a crucial precondition in this respect (see also: Eckert *et al.* 2012a).

With regard to the political mobilization against the Ok Tedi mine in Papua New Guinea, Kirsch (2006, 17, 2007, 2014, 2016, 2018) described the development of a similar transnational solidarity campaign. Kirsch concluded that the "strategy of counterglobalization has both advantages and disadvantages" (2007, 304) for local movements. In his view, transnational campaigns can, on the one hand, "replicate the geographic distribution of capital" (*ibid.*) and allow pressure to be put on the different entities of a transnational corporation. We can observe several of these aspects in the Chaupe case, too. Because the parent company, Newmont Mining, is based in Denver, various NGOs supporting the Chaupe family have targeted their campaigns toward a U.S. audience. Protest meetings were held outside the U.S. headquarters. The campaign by the Society for Threatened Peoples in Switzerland, in turn, was directed at the locally based refinery Valcambi, which processed gold mined by Minera Yanacocha (GfbV 2016). The different NGOs thus highlighted and made use of the global entanglement inherent in the conflict. In doing so, they addressed the "chains of action" or "*Handlungsketten*," as Eckert (2016, 253) framed it, on which the dispute between the mine and the family was based.

Furthermore, to bring political claims abroad also allows for the production of external pressure on the domestic actors. This is what Keck and Sikkink (1998, 12) described as the "boomerang effect" of transnational advocacy networks. They wrote that in cases of human rights struggles in which channels to negotiate with state authorities are blocked, "domestic NGOs bypass their state and directly search out international allies to try to bring pressure on their states from outside" (*ibid.*). Keck and Sikkink (1998, 16) define different types of activities applied by transnational advocacy networks, which include rapid and broad dissemination of information, symbolic and leveraged politics, and a clear attribution of accountability. We can observe a variety of these aspects in the transnational campaign in favor of Máxima as well.

From the perspective of the Peruvian human rights lawyers who represented the Chaupe family, the pressure from abroad was aimed at supporting their position and argumentation in the courtroom. As I pointed out above, regarding the criminalization of protest, criminal trials discursively revolve around what behavior is permissible or criminal in a society. In the courtroom, Mirtha sought to deconstruct, through legal arguments, the hegemonic image with which the activists and the Chaupe family were portrayed as criminals. The transnational advocacy campaigns sought to foster them discursively and to strengthen Mirtha's counterhegemonic argumentation. Thus the campaigns were aimed at strengthening the Chaupe family's legal opportunity structure. By using the campaign of Amnesty International as an example, I discuss the prospects of this approach in the following section.

Amnesty International's campaign "Máxima is not alone!"

Samuel Moyn wrote that, within the global human rights movement, Amnesty International is the organization that "almost alone [...] invented grassroots human rights advocacy" (2010, 129). Various authors have described the organization's leading role in the evolvement of a global human rights movement (see, for example: Moyn 2010, 129–33, 146–9, Sikkink 2011, 36–41). In Peru, the organization contributed significantly to the establishment of a national human rights movement during the internal armed conflict (Youngers 2003, 89–90, Gonzáles-Ocantos 2017, 145). To date, Amnesty International has remained an important force within the national human rights movement, being an important political ally and a close partner of the *Coordinadora* and of other national NGOs and grassroots organizations.

The Peruvian section of Amnesty International has accompanied Máxima and her family since 2011, i.e. since the very beginning of the dispute with Minera Yanacocha. The NGO's campaign was developed by the national office in Lima and disseminated internationally by other country sections. As part of its global campaign, Amnesty International carried out at least six so-called *Urgent Actions*, in which activists of the worldwide network wrote protest letters in favor of the family to the Peruvian Ministry of the Interior, the responsible police chief, and the public prosecutor's office. The authorities were urged to initiate a judicial investigation into the intimidation and eviction attempts that the mining company had made against the family and to bring the persons responsible to justice. In this way, Amnesty International attempted to strengthen the Chaupe family's counterhegemonic struggles in court. The campaign's goal was to urge the Peruvian State to guarantee that the family will not be forcibly evicted nor further harassed as long as there is no judicial decision determining who is legally entitled to Tragadero Grande, as one of Amnesty International's representatives told me. Arguably, the campaign was thus directed at the state as the guarantor of rights and not at the company as the perpetrators of the alleged abuses. The campaign clearly focused on the responsibility of the state.

Later, Máxima and her family became beneficiaries of Amnesty International's annual campaign *Write for Rights*. Every year on International Human Rights Day, the organization brings attention to ten cases of human rights defenders with this campaign (Amnesty International 2016, 17). The NGO's followers are invited to write letters of solidarity to these ten personalities and to strengthen them in their fight for human rights. The campaign builds on the worldwide "juridification of social protests" (Eckert *et al.* 2012a) and is based on universally understandable human rights discourses. As I discussed above, this is an approach often used in transnational advocacy campaigns. In spring 2017, as a result of Amnesty International's global appeal, Máxima received more than 150,000 letters and cards (Amnesty International 2017). People from all over the world expressed their solidarity with their claims for justice. As part of the same campaign, several thousand letters were also directed to Marisol Pérez Tello, Peru's then Minister of Justice. In these letters, the minister was asked to become active in protecting the Chaupes' rights. Amnesty International Peru also arranged for Marisol Pérez Tello to visit Tragadero Grande, where she publicly promised to support the family (Andina (online) 2017).

Thus, Amnesty International sought to directly influence the Peruvian authorities and how they dealt with the Chaupe case. The NGO's broad international network of supporters served as a kind of threatening backdrop to make the judicial authorities understand that a global audience is closely watching how they deal with this one court case. The rally in front of the Supreme Court in Lima was also part of this strategy. As mentioned at the beginning of this chapter, during the court hearings in 2017, when the Supreme Court in Lima ruled on the cassation appeal, activists from Amnesty International Peru and other national NGOs gathered in front of the court building. Using the slogan "*¡Máxima no está sola!*" ("Máxima is not alone!"), they publicly demonstrated their solidarity with the family.

However, the organization not only exerted public pressure on the Peruvian judicial authorities, but was also active behind the scenes. As a representative of the Peruvian section told me, the NGO repeatedly demanded meetings with the Ministry of the Interior, the correspondent prosecutorial authorities, and the Ministry of Justice to discuss Máxima's case. At this point, Amnesty International benefited from the fact that it is both an international and a national organization. When I asked a U.S. lawyer involved in EarthRights International's campaign in favor of the Chaupes if she had intervened with the Peruvian judicial authorities, she replied that she could not afford to do so. As a lawyer from abroad, she did not feel entitled to make such demands of foreign judicial authorities. For the members of the Peruvian section of Amnesty International, however, such interventions are an important part of their national campaign. As an organization that plays a leading role in national civil society, they clearly feel entitled to intervene directly with their authorities and to make demands.

Although the Ministry of the Interior refused to discuss the matter, Minister of Justice, Marisol Pérez Tello initiated a dialogue and visited the family in Tragadero Grande. Within the social movement in Celendín, the story circulated afterward that the Minister of Justice had been severely reprimanded by the government, especially by representatives of the Ministry of Finance, for her visit to Tragadero Grande. It also remains questionable to what extent the visit actually impacted the legal dispute between the family and the mine. However, the symbolic effect of the visit to Tragadero Grande was enormous. It exemplified how the NGO campaigns attempted to deconstruct the image of Máxima as the "criminal occupier" of Tragadero Grande. As a result of a member of government visiting the disputed plot of land and declaring her support for the family, the hegemonic picture drawn by the mining company in the criminal proceeding was challenged. Amnesty International's campaign thus sought to underline the counterhegemonic discourse of the Chaupe family's lawyers and their use of law from below.

Amnesty International Peru staff, activists on the ground, and lawyers of *Grufides* involved in the family's legal defense all told me that, in their opinion, the campaign was a success for Máxima and her family. Many believe that without the international attention the family would have been effectively evicted from Tragadero Grande long ago. The acquittal before the Supreme Court in Lima confirmed them in their stance. In addition, several people who were in close contact with the family also told me that, for example, Amnesty International's letter campaign had the effect of strengthening Máxima emotionally in her struggle by showing her that she was "not alone," as the campaign slogan read. This emotional support was particularly relevant because, as I point out below, the transnational advocacy campaigns also entailed severe social costs for Máxima and her family.

Moreover, on closer inspection it also becomes clear that the support campaigns, by Amnesty International, but also by other NGOs, may have had a positive influence on the criminal case against the Chaupe family. Thus, international attention provided them with a certain protection against criminalization. At the same time, such an effect was largely absent from the criminal charges filed by the family for the abuses they experienced. These alleged abuses remained unpunished, and the attribution of legal responsibility to state and corporate actors failed. With regard to the question of whether transnational advocacy campaigns are able to support counterhegemonic discourse in legal mobilization from below, the Chaupe case therefore reveals clear limitations. It was possible to counteract criminalization but not to persuade the prosecutorial and judicial authorities to take action against powerful actors. Moreover, the transnational advocacy campaigns also led to negative social impacts on the family, as I describe in the remaining part of this chapter.

Effects of counterglobalization

As mentioned above, Kirsch has identified both advantages and disadvantages when considering the effects of counterglobalization. With regard to disadvantages, he argued that transnational advocacy campaigns on behalf of indigenous movements often rely on an "essentialist representation" (2007, 310) of the actors concerned. We can observe the same tendency in the case of Máxima. The personality and figure of Máxima was extraordinarily well suited for transnational campaigns: As a woman, a *campesina*, a mother and grandmother, a poor subsistence farmer living with and from nature, she represented an ideal image to appeal to an international audience. Strong images could be created with her clothes, the wide-brimmed hat and colorful skirts – typical for the *campesino* population of the Cajamarca region – and with her combative appearance. The fact that she is illiterate and lives in humble living conditions in a simple house in the middle of the *jalca*, the rough eco-zone of the Peruvian highlands, also suited the idea to be conveyed. Although the other members of the Chaupe family also actively opposed Minera Yanacocha, Máxima was given more exposure by various NGOs, in particular those directed toward a foreign audience.

Kirsch observed that international NGOs pursue their own political agendas with which they attempt to address their "constituencies" (2007, 304), i.e. their donors and supporters. In his view, this gives rise to the risk that demands and expectations will be made on partners in the Global South that cannot be fulfilled, for example in terms of the discourses on which social movements are supposed to rely. In the case of the Chaupe family, for example, this tendency became evident when foreign NGOs describe them as "indigenous,"[13] although the Chaupes, like the majority of the rural population in Cajamarca, define themselves as *campesinos* and *campesinas* (Bebbington, Humphreys Bebbington, *et al.* 2008, 2903). EarthRights International (2018a) called her a "matriarch" in its campaign, thereby referring to her role as a mother who defends her rights, her family, her plot of land, and the nature around her. Amnesty International, in turn, used the description of Máxima as a *campesina* and a "human rights defender." The first label corresponded to Máxima's self-perception and the latter to a definition used by Amnesty International to describe human rights activists regardless of their cultural or social background.

As a staff member of the Peruvian section of Amnesty International explained to me, his NGO was very careful in defining how the Chaupe family was portrayed

---

13 See, for example: Earthworks (2015) or EarthRights International in the civil complaint on behalf of the Chaupe family to the District Court of Delaware (U.S. District Court for the District of Delaware 2017).

within the campaign. Through direct contact with Máxima, her family, and the team of lawyers and activists supporting them, Amnesty International tried to achieve a representation in the campaign that was as close as possible to their own ideas. Since the research for the actual campaign was done by its Peruvian section, Amnesty International held a considerable advantage in meeting these demands. According to my observations, NGOs whose campaigns were planned abroad were much more likely to resort to essentialist stereotypes. Thus, the question of representation, as raised by Kirsch, also played a role in the transnational advocacy campaigns on behalf of the Chaupe family. As the example of Amnesty International reveals, however, it is possible to overcome these risks by ensuring a close cooperation with those directly affected.

Far more serious, however, were the negative effects of the transnational advocacy campaigns which the Chaupes experienced at the local level in the form of social envy and public defamation. As mentioned above, Máxima, her family, and their lawyers have long been publicly defamed by mining advocates and local journalists. Critics discredited them as "obstructers of economic development," thereby referring to a discourse that the Peruvian human rights movement in general has long been confronted with. Other activists who have publicly spoken out against the Conga mining project have also been publicly defamed, as I discussed with regard to the criminalization case from Sorochuco (see Chapter 4).

In the case of the Chaupe family, however, this public criticism was further reinforced by the transnational advocacy campaigns. Critics complained that the family acted out of pure self-interest, that they received large sums of money from foreign organizations, and that they could thus enrich themselves personally. The trips abroad that members of the family made as part of the NGO campaigns were critically assessed and interpreted as for personal profit, too. In addition, rumors arose that the family would own other plots of land and would actually not be dependent on Tragadero Grande. These rumors were discussed and spread in the local media (see, for example: Uceda 2015, El Montonero (online) 2016). This criticism reached a climax when Máxima received the *Goldman Environmental Prize* for South and Central America in 2016. With this award, also known as the "Nobel Prize for Environmental Protection," a U.S. philanthropic foundation honors environmental activists.[14] The large sum of prize money that accompanies this honor was proof for the critics that the Chaupe family was only interested in making a personal profit from the international campaigns.

At the local level, this award led to fierce controversy. People who had previously been critical of the Conga mining project began to be hostile toward Máxima. Even

---

14 The two U.S.-based NGOs EarthRights International and Earthworks both belong to the group of organizations conducting the nominations for the Goldman Environmental Prizes (Goldman Environmental Foundation 2020).

within the social movement against the Conga project, people claimed that Máxima would only stand up for her own interests, that "she is not a real activist" and is "only committed to her own piece of land," but is not active in the local *comunidad campesina,* for example. For these people it was not understandable why an individual was honored for a resistance in which, in their opinion, the population of the entire region had participated. During my stays in Cajamarca, these accusations were initially made sporadically by individuals and in private conversations. However, over time, they began being voiced in assemblies and meetings. Personal envy probably played a major role in these hostilities; many people felt left out and could not understand how foreign organizations could select and honor an individual. The boomerang of transnational advocacy networks thus returned with full force against the Chaupe family.

In this way, the NGO campaigns led to unintended consequences, while, at the same time, the company carried out further attempts to evict the family. Within the national human rights movement, the development of the case triggered discussions. Doubts arose regarding the extent to which visibility and international attention for a particular case could actually constitute protection for the persons concerned. Many activists became aware that the family and especially Máxima had been over-exposed. One example of this is the critique raised by a Lima-based lawyer who was not directly involved in the Chaupes' case, but who knew the case quite well because of her close contact with *Grufides*. In a conversation I had with this lawyer, she argued that many national and foreign NGOs seemed to be unaware of how much they demand from the people they work with. She told me, "It is [they], the members of the Chaupe family, who persevere day after day under adverse circumstances and maintain their resistance to a powerful company. And it is [they] who must constantly fear interventions by the company." One day, however, the campaigns of the international NGOs would come to an end, and the Chaupe family would then be at odds with all its neighbors and would remain socially isolated, as the lawyer told me.

This is the other "boomerang effect" a transnational advocacy campaign may involve. In Keck and Sikkink's (1998, 12) use of the term, transnational advocacy campaigns lead to favorable effects on the ground. In communication psychology, however, the term "boomerang effect" has a different meaning, and this use describes the outcomes we observed in the Chaupe case. Psychologists use the term to describe an effect in a "direction opposite to the intention of the sender" (Wirtz 2014, 312, own translation). Launching a boomerang thus results in unintended, often negative consequences. Keck and Sikkink suggest that the senders of the boomerang, i.e. the local NGOs that rely on transnational advocacy networks, are able to achieve a positive effect with their collaboration with organizations from abroad. The impression is created that in transnational advocacy campaigns everything follows a fixed strategy and a clear plan. The consequences achieved are thus intended and positive from the point of view of the sender. However, the case of the Chaupe family shows us that transnational advocacy campaigns can also have unintended, negative consequences on the ground.

Conclusion

Pistor wrote that "[l]egal dispute settlement offers an alternative and perhaps more peaceful way to clarify priority rights, although the results can be as brutal as physical conquest" (2019, 24–5). In the case of the Chaupe family, legal NGOs sought to ease the land conflict with Minera Yanacocha through the judicialization of the dispute. By filing criminal complaints against the company, the aim was to protect the family from further eviction attempts. As I have pointed out in this chapter, however, this legal mobilization from below largely failed. *Grufides'* lawyers did succeed in obtaining an acquittal in favor of Máxima and her family, freeing them from charges of illegal occupation of land. At the same time, however, the alleged human rights violations against family members went unpunished. Furthermore, after the company failed to get a conviction against the family in court, the attacks in Tragadero Grande increased considerably. This calls into question the extent to which the use of law has been effective in this specific case. In a similar sense, Pistor also acknowledged that "indeed, legal battles over land have often gone hand in hand with the battles on the ground" (2019, 25).

In addition to the question of the effectiveness of law in this specific example, this chapter focused above all on the role of transnational advocacy campaigns for such legal disputes. In May 2017, the Peruvian human rights movement celebrated the acquittal of the Chaupe family and their legal victory before the Supreme Court. At the same time, amidst all the hustle and bustle, Máxima demanded only one thing: to be able to live in peace with her family in Tragadero Grande. This chapter confirmed that transnational advocacy networks are particularly well suited to address the issue of TNCs' responsibility and to put the spotlight on emblematic court cases dealing with human rights violations committed by TNCs. At the same time, the Chaupe case revealed that campaigns on behalf of an individual family can trigger unintended dynamics and that they can also be a burden for those concerned.

Chapter 6. Human rights litigation abroad

Introduction[1]

In March 2019, the United States Court of Appeals for the Third Circuit in Philadelphia remanded a lawsuit to the District Court of Delaware and instructed the lower court to reevaluate whether Peru, in light of various corruption scandals, is an "adequate alternative forum" for dealing with corporate abuses.[2] The previous year, the District Court dismissed a civil complaint of Peruvian plaintiffs on the grounds that access to the justice system is provided in their home country.[3] Why would judges in Delaware care about the ability of their colleagues in Peru? And what prompts a U.S. appellate court to order an evaluation of foreign judicial institutions? In the context of the debates on TNCs' responsibility, several judges in the Global North evaluated the capability of courts abroad in recent years. They were asked to hear lawsuits on parent companies' responsibility for human rights violations and environmental damage committed in the context of the subsidiaries' activities abroad.

There are various reasons for bringing such cases before a court in the Global North. Difficulties in suing corporate actors in Peru is, in global comparison, the rule rather than an exception. Thus, the obstacles in accessing the domestic justice system are one reason for human rights litigation abroad. Another reason arises from the conviction of civil society organizations that global business activities should lead to global chains of responsibility, thus the idea that parent companies bear legal responsibility for their subsidiaries' conduct. Behind this is the moral claim that companies should not be able to evade responsibility for activities from which they profit economically. Courtrooms in the Global North are considered an appropriate

1 Parts of the material on which this chapter is based were previously published in an article entitled "Transnational Human Rights Litigation: A Means of Obtaining Effective Remedy Abroad?", *Journal of Legal Anthropology* 4, 2 (2020).

2 U.S. Court of Appeals for the Third Circuit 2019.

3 U.S. District Court for the District of Delaware 2018a, 2018b.

forum to transform this moral claim into a legal claim of responsibility. Finally, a further reason is the aim of supporting legal mobilization at home by bringing a claim abroad, for instance by obtaining evidence in foreign courts or by exerting pressure on domestic authorities through a judgment in another country. This chapter examines how Peruvian human rights lawyers perceive and evaluate this particular form of legal mobilization and how transnational complaints contribute to their struggles in Peru. The chapter provides insights into the question of (transnational) corporate responsibility, which adds an important dimension to the judicalization of local mining conflicts.

Several of the human rights violations that emerged from the mining conflicts in Cajamarca and Piura became transnational court cases. The claim in the District Court of Delaware mentioned previously was filed by Máxima Acuña and her family, who live in the area of Minera Yanacocha's planned Conga mine. Another example is a lawsuit against the parent company Monterrico Metals in the United Kingdom, which resulted from the torture case in the context of the Río Blanco project in Piura. Third, EarthRights International took legal action abroad in favor of Elmer Campos, the *campesino* from Cajamarca who was shot during the Conga protests. Based on these three transnational court cases, this chapter discusses possible reasons and motivations for transnational human rights litigation. In particular, it provides an analysis of what expectations members of the Peruvian human rights movement placed on the law in such cases.

In all three lawsuits discussed in this chapter, Peruvian human rights lawyers decisively contributed to bringing the cases abroad. However, they were not the only actors involved. As I will show in this chapter, the various actors involved in such human rights litigation have different objectives and legal expectations of what should and could be achieved. Transnational human rights litigation, like other forms of legal mobilization, takes place in specific social contexts and is characterized by power asymmetries and shaped by the actors' different interests and political objectives. In many cases, we can observe discrepancies in the actors' perception of legal processes. I am interested in the implications of these discrepancies. In this sense, transnational lawsuits not only exemplify the legal mechanisms encountered and the judicial obstacles faced when trying to get justice abroad. My aim is to understand the "risks and benefits of [transnational] legal activism" (Kirsch 2018, 17) but also to explore its effects on the legal proceedings and the actors in Peru.

Like the rest of this book, this chapter is primarily based on my field research with the Peruvian human rights movement. In addition, information was gathered during a shorter stay in London, where I conducted interviews with British lawyers and NGO representatives. Unfortunately, a lawyer from the law firm Leigh Day later retracted his statements and prohibited me from using the interview. With regard to the lawsuits in the United States discussed in the chapter, an interview was conducted via Skype with a lawyer from EarthRights International based in Washington.

In Peru, I had several conversations with representatives of this same office. Finally, this chapter also makes use of a wide range of court documents. In the U.S. courts, the prevailing transparency strategy and the payment of a small fee allowed me detailed access to digital court files. In the case of the High Court in London, access was more restrictive and limited to the courts' judgments.

Suing transnational parent companies at home

Suing parent companies in the countries where they are headquartered, thus in their *home states*, for abuses committed by subsidiaries in *host states* involves what Liesbeth Enneking (2014) defines as "foreign direct liability cases" (see also: Zerk 2006, 198). Criminal law has been applied in some of these cases, but more often they are based on civil or tort law (Zerk 2014, 43). Plaintiffs have sued parent companies either directly for human rights violations committed by subsidiaries or for negligence in preventing such abuses (Schrempf-Stirling and Wettstein 2017, 545–6).

Complaints filed under the Alien Tort Claims Act (ATCA) in the United States played a pioneering role in transnational human rights litigation. This statute grants U.S. district courts jurisdiction over "any civil action by an alien for a tort only, committed in violation of the law of nations or a treaty of the United States."[4] Originally, ATCA was legislated as part of the First Judiciary Act in 1789 and then, for nearly 200 years, fell into oblivion (Skinner *et al.* 2013, 19). In the eighties, the Center for Constitutional Rights in New York "(re-)discovered" the act and applied it before a U.S. court against a Paraguayan police officer for acts of torture and kidnapping during the Stroessner regime (Kaleck 2008, 285, Brett 2018, 54).[5] Since the mid-nineties, U.S. NGOs used ATCA to claim compensation for corporate abuses committed in third countries (Shamir 2004, 638). Thus, the legal activism in the ATCA claims can be historically related to cases of human rights violations committed under authoritarian regimes. Like in Peru, the U.S. human rights movement has thus over time extended its experiences to new areas, from litigation against state actors to lawsuits against corporations.

Legal NGOs based the ATCA claims on the principle of universal jurisdiction and argued that, following this principle, U.S. courts also have jurisdiction over corporations, even if they are headquartered abroad. For several years, the strategy seemed promising: Until 2014, around 150 claims were filed against TNCs on the basis of ATCA, and a considerable number resulted in settlements and thus in financial compensation (Enneking 2014, 44). As the statute was thought to be "truly extraterritorial in its reach" (Shamir 2004, 639), it seemed to be an ideal instrument for redressing

4 28 U.S. Code §1350. Alien's action for tort.

5 Filartiga v. Pena-Irala, 577 F. Supp. 860 (E.D.N.Y. 1984).

abuses committed abroad. However, the question about whether the United States was an appropriate site to hear such cases or rather a so-called *forum non conveniens* remained the central issue over the years (Deva 2012, 69). Based on the *forum non conveniens* doctrine, corporate defendants have argued that such actions should be heard in the countries where the aggrieved parties reside and where the alleged offenses were committed. The home states are said to be an unsuitable forum for this, as the courts there have no jurisdiction and therefore no competence, according to the doctrine.

Corporate actors persisted in this jurisdictional question and finally succeeded when, in April 2013, the Supreme Court handed down a landmark decision in *Kiobel v Royal Dutch Petroleum Co* by restricting the possibilities for using ATCA to only when the claims "touch and concern" the United States with "sufficient force."[6] In 2018, the Supreme Court held, in another case, "that foreign corporations may not be defendants in suits brought under" ATCA.[7] As a consequence of this precedent ruling, access to U.S. courts has since been largely restricted (Skinner *et al.* 2013, 5, 19–20, Enneking 2014, 51, Zerk 2014, 95–6).

As mentioned above, the ATCA experience exemplified how lawyers strategically searched for new legal routes to hold TNCs liable at home. At the same time, however, it also revealed the fierce controversy surrounding access to courts in the Global North, which became evident in other countries, too. The question of whether home state courts can and should have jurisdiction over extraterritorial cases was key in many lawsuits. Following a landmark decision by the European Court of Justice in 2005,[8] the *forum non conveniens* doctrine is no longer an obstacle for transnational lawsuits in the European Union, but it is an issue in many other non-EU Anglo-Saxon countries (Kamphuis 2012a, 560, Blackburn 2017, 38–9). In addition, corporations have relied on a wide range of procedural and legal strategies to keep themselves out of court. A central legal issue, for example, is the so-called "corporate veil," an argument by which parent companies contest being liable for the misconduct of subsidiaries, which they seek to describe as "separate" corporate entities (Kaleck and Saage-Maaß 2010, 716, Müller-Hoff 2011, 25). Thereby, the corporations seek to achieve a "fragmentation of responsibility" (Eckert 2016, 246, own translation). In the United Kingdom, this obstacle could be circumvented by claiming a TNC's duty of care, which means that a parent company is not sued for being directly involved in the abuses but for acting with negligence (Zerk 2014, 44, Blackburn 2017, 44).

In addition, depending on the jurisdiction, plaintiffs face formal obstacles, such as the lack of class actions or contingency fee arrangements, which makes claims financially unviable (Taylor *et al.* 2010, 21, Zerk 2014, 80–1). Other obstacles include

---

6 Kiobel v. Royal Dutch Petroleum Co., 569 U.S. 108 (2013).

7 Jesner et. al. v. Arab Bank, PLC, 16–499, 584 U.S. ___ (2018).

8 Owusu v Jackson ([2005] ECR 1383).

strict statutes of limitation (Skinner 2014, 228, 231). Such transnational lawsuits require considerable time and human resources to be brought to court and can often not meet the time limits set in procedural law for ordinary domestic claims. Obtaining companies' internal documents as evidence is complex, whereas, on the other hand, the burden of proof is high and a claim is likely to be dismissed if the parent company's direct influence on its subsidiary cannot be proven (Zerk 2014, 44, Blackburn 2017, 54–5).

People who become plaintiffs in such lawsuits often belong to marginalized groups living in remote areas. They often lack litigation experience and are thus what Galanter (1974, 97) titled "one-shotters" (see also: Kirsch 2014, 85). These circumstances demonstrate the importance of willing lawyers in the Global North who have the knowledge and the resources to bring forth such claims. Such attorneys often work for international human rights NGOs or for *pro bono* law firms. These lawyers are rare, especially those who dare to face the proverbial "army of corporate lawyers" and who risk being involved in costly litigation for many years without knowing whether their expenses will ever be recovered (Taylor *et al.* 2010, 17–8).

As a result of the legal barriers and procedural hurdles, litigation against parent companies has repeatedly failed, and claims against TNCs rarely have made it to trial. Procedural issues often remain at the core of lawsuits against TNCs, whereas the question of whether a corporation actually holds responsibility remains untouched. In addition, those cases that are not dismissed for procedural reasons are often settled out of court, meaning that a trial is avoided in these cases, as well (Kamphuis 2011, 87). Thus, despite years of transnational efforts to overcome the global accountability gap and to fight corporate impunity in courtrooms abroad, it has so far hardly been possible to actually attribute legal liability to a parent company. These examples show that in cases involving the responsibility of corporations, even in the Global North there are still considerable hurdles in accessing the justice system.

While in countries like Peru corruption and weak state institutions are blamed for corporate impunity, in countries of the Global North "procedural" or "formal" reasons are advanced to dismiss claims and to avoid dealing with the sensitive issue of corporate responsibility. In reality, however, there are political reasons in both the Global South and North that prevent corporations from being held accountable because they are "too big to jail," as Brandon Garrett (2014) boldly framed it in relation to the United States.

Case studies: an overview

Guerrero & Ors v. Monterrico Metals Plc & Anor

Despite these difficulties, efforts for transnational human rights litigation have continued worldwide in recent years and have also reached Peru. From a Peruvian perspective, the case against Monterrico Metals in the United Kingdom was a pioneer in this regard. It was one of the first cases of human rights violations occurring in the extractive sector that later reached a foreign justice system. As described in Chapter 3, *Fedepaz* has worked for years to obtain justice in Peru for the twenty-eight individuals who suffered acts of torture when protesting against the Río Blanco project in August 2005. Progress in criminal proceedings in Peru has been slow, and the difficulties in including corporate actors in the investigation became evident over time. For this reason, *Fedepaz*' team, along with lawyers from the *Coordinadora*, looked at their transnational networks and their partner organizations for ways to bring the case forward with foreign assistance. In this way, they contacted the U.S. Environmental Defender Law Center (EDLC),[9] which then introduced them to the British law firm Leigh Day. In 2009, Leigh Day filed a civil complaint at the High Court in London against Monterrico Metals and its Peruvian subsidiary Río Blanco.[10]

Leigh Day is a private law firm that, since its founding in 1987, has led several court cases against UK-based TNCs. It has attempted to establish the principle in English law that parent companies owe a direct "duty of care" to those affected by subsidiaries' activities abroad (Brett 2018, 55–6). Leigh Day's lawyers are convinced that the British judicial system offers legal opportunities, which they attempt to exhaust. In the law firm's own words, its lawyers "represent people all over the world fighting for justice and challenging powerful corporate and government interests" (Leigh Day 2018, 2). They "push the boundaries of the law to hold the powerful to account" (*ibid.*), and they "are not afraid to take on daunting challenges" since they "believe passionately that every individual and community, no matter who they are or where they live, is entitled to defend their human rights, including their right to justice" (*ibid*, 4). Working on a *pro bono* basis, the law firm was involved in litigation against corporations such as Thor Chemicals, Rio Tinto, Cape plc, BP, Trafigura, Xstrata, Unilever, Shell, and Vedanta Resources. Some of these lawsuits have been settled, meaning that plaintiffs received compensation and that Leigh Day could cover its litigation costs. However, as a consequence of these settlements, no judgment

9 EDLC is a type of gatekeeper for transnational litigation. The NGO based in the United States supports local communities in suing TNCs by establishing contact with lawyers in the Global North.

10 *Guerrero v Monterrico*, [2009] EWHC 2475 (QB).

was ever made as to whether parent companies actually owe a duty of care for the activities of their subsidiaries.[11]

Compared to other transnational lawsuits, the Monterrico claim made relatively rapid progress. Leigh Day's lawyers argued that "officers of Rio Blanco or of Monterrico ought to have intervened so as to have prevented the abuse of the Claimants' human rights and/or are otherwise responsible for the injuries which they suffered."[12] The lawsuit was based on "the fact that [Monterrico Metals] exercised effective control over the management of [Río Blanco S.A.]."[13] The detention of demonstrators in the mine camp in Piura was described as "a joint operation"[14] between Monterrico Metals, the private security firm Forza, and the Peruvian National Police. The corporation and its subsidiary were alleged to have "authorized the police and their security guards to detain the Claimants on the Defendants' property over the course of three days."[15] The claim mentioned that the corporation had "provided the police with the materials that were used in the torture of the Claimants including ropes, heavy metal objects, black bags and sticks."[16]

The lawsuit was, in this sense, closely tied to the Peruvian criminal case and the legal argumentation brought forth by the Peruvian human rights lawyers. By becoming a transnational claim, the torture case was, however, translated into a tort law case of negligence.[17] According to a British lawyer familiar with the claim, this was "not ideal" because "to characterize [...] torture as negligence, breach of a duty of care, that seems to be minimizing the significance of what happened." It was, however, the only access point in English law and the only legal basis for presenting the case in London. This reveals that, as a consequence of the process of judicialization, compromises must be made in order to comply with the categories of the law.

Leigh Day's lawyers traveled to Peru several times to meet with the plaintiffs and the local NGO lawyers. In addition, the law firm employed a Spanish-speaking assistant, who stayed in Peru and who established confidence and helped maintain contact with the plaintiffs in Piura. *Fedepaz'* team, along with lawyers working with the *Coordinadora*, had collected evidence and information that served as a basis for drafting the claim. They introduced the British lawyers to the context in Peru, shared

11 An exception was the case against Cape Plc, where a court ruled that the parent company has a duty of care for its subsidiary's employees (*Chandler v Cape Plc* [2012] EWCA Civ 525). Leigh Day has sought to extend this principle to the people affected by business activities who are not employed.

12 *Guerrero v Monterrico*, [2009] EWHC 2475 (QB), para. 8, (see also: Meeran 2011, 40).

13 *Guerrero v Monterrico*, [2009] EWHC 2475 (QB), para. 8.

14 Cited in: *Guerrero v Monterrico*, [2009] EWHC 2475 (QB), para. 10.

15 *Guerrero v Monterrico*, [2009] EWHC 2475 (QB), para. 10.

16 Cited in: *Guerrero v Monterrico*, [2009] EWHC 2475 (QB), para. 10.

17 This translation from torture to tort is emblematic for transnational human rights litigation and has been discussed by various authors (see, for example: Scott 2001, Augenstein 2018).

their material relating to the criminal investigation with them, introduced them to the Peruvian legal framework,[18] and established contact with the plaintiffs. In retrospect, *Fedepaz*' team recounted that video conferencing and Internet calls were still unusual at that time and communication was challenging, also because of language barriers.

The legal proceedings in London initially looked promising. Shortly after they began, the court ordered a worldwide injunction, freezing over £5 million of Monterrico's assets.[19] The judges declared that the plaintiffs demonstrated "a good arguable case."[20] The corporation thus came under considerable pressure. Later, the High Court scheduled a ten-week trial starting in October 2011 (Meeran 2011, 41, 2013, 385). About eighty witnesses were prepared to participate in the trial on the plaintiffs' side, including some of Monterrico's employees (Leigh Day & Co. 2011). However, the trial ultimately did not take place as an out-of-court settlement was reached in July 2011, three months before the trial date (Skinner *et al.* 2013, 96). Monterrico did not admit any liability but agreed to pay an undisclosed sum as compensation to thirty-three victims (Meeran 2012, 19, Velazco Rondón and Quedena Zambrano 2015, 40, 52).[21] In return, the plaintiffs withdrew the claim by accepting the compensation and waived the need for a judgment on the corporation's responsibility (Kamphuis 2012a, 548). This closed the case.

Campos-Alvarez v. Newmont Mining Corporation et al

This chapter's second case example is a lawsuit in the United States on behalf of Elmer Campos, the *campesino* who was injured during the Conga protests in 2011. As described in Chapter 3, Elmer became complainant in a criminal lawsuit in Cajamarca, in which the presentation of corporate internal documents led to Minera Yanacocha being included in the proceedings as a civilly liable third party. These pieces of evidence were obtained through a legal action that EarthRights International's team in Washington D.C. filed in January 2014 under the so-called Foreign Legal

18 The complaint to the High Court in London was formulated on the basis of both Peruvian and English law. The High Court had to determine whether Peruvian or English law would be applied. Knowing the relevant Peruvian legal norms was thus crucial for bringing the claim.

19 *Guerrero v Monterrico*, [2009] EWHC 2475 (QB), para. 41 (see also: Jahncke 2011, 52, Kamphuis 2012a, 547, Skinner *et al.* 2013, 66, 95).

20 *Guerrero v Monterrico*, [2009] EWHC 2475 (QB), para. 26 (see also: Kamphuis 2011, 77, Leigh Day & Co. 2011).

21 The compensation payments not only included the 28 detainees, but also the relatives of the man who died during the conflict in August 2005 and the relatives of another person who died one year before in another violent clash in the context of protests against the Río Blanco project.

Assistance (FLA) statute in the United States.[22] The U.S. NGO attempted to obtain evidence that substantiated the relationship between Minera Yanacocha and Peru's National Police. To this end, it filed an application with the District Court of Colorado, which sought discovery from Newmont Mining, Minera Yanacocha's major shareholder.

The FLA statute allows parties involved in foreign court cases to request disclosure of documents located in the United States. Initially, TNCs used the statute to obtain documentation about competitors or critics. Chevron Corporation, for example, gained access in this way to raw footage from a company critical documentary produced in the United States, which served as evidence in a well-known lawsuit in Ecuador. EarthRights International recognized the statute's potential and began using it to assist human rights lawyers in the Global South in claims against TNCs, among them the Peruvian human rights movement.

At least two of the U.S. lawyers involved in this legal action had lived and worked for a longer period of time in Peru and knew the local context well. In addition, they received assistance from EarthRights International's team in Lima, who supported them in establishing contact with Elmer and with his Peruvian attorneys. As I mentioned in the previous chapters, EarthRights International's Peruvian team worked for several years with national NGOs such as the *Coordinadora* and with regional grassroots organizations, in Cajamarca in particular, with *Grufides* and the PIC. The FLA application in the United States resulted from this collaboration and was aimed at supporting EarthRights International's Peruvian allies in their struggles within the Conga conflict.

The NGO's lawyers filed the application for discovery to the District Court of Colorado in order to pursue documents – including videos, photos, security reports, and internal company communication – from Newmont Mining Corporation and two of its affiliates (Newmont Peru SRL and Newmont USA LTD). They argued that the Peruvian National Police officers who shot Elmer Campos had acted under a contract with Minera Yanacocha. Furthermore, they claimed that Newmont USA LTD controlled and managed Minera Yanacocha and that there was an "unusually close relationship between and among the Newmont entities."[23] EarthRights International stated that "there is every reason to believe that Newmont, as manager of Minera Yanacocha and its operations, possess [...] critical evidence" relevant to the legal proceedings in Peru.[24] *Coordinadora* lawyer Mar, Elmer's Peruvian attorney, submitted declarations to the U.S. court underlining the application's necessity. She explained

22 28 U.S.C. § 1782.

23 As an indicator of this "unusually close relationship," EarthRights International mentioned that several individuals simultaneously worked for the management of Minera Yanacocha and for Newmont Mining (U.S. District Court for the District of Colorado 2014a, 5).

24 U.S. District Court for the District of Colorado 2014a, 5.

that, theoretically, Peru's Public Ministry is responsible for gathering evidence in criminal investigation, but that, in practice, prosecutors are overworked and under pressure to not investigate corporate or state actors.[25] Thus, the difficulties in suing corporate actors in Peru, which I discussed in Chapter 3, served as a justification for Mar bringing the FLA application in the United States.

Newmont Mining opposed the application and submitted various motions to the court. The corporation argued that, from a legal point of view, discovery of documents should be demanded from Minera Yanacocha in Peru and not from Newmont Mining in the United States. The second argument to oppose the application was political. Newmont Mining claimed that the lawsuit was motivated in bad faith and argued that "the background of [the] request is complex and involves a deep and longstanding social and political controversy in the Republic of Peru."[26] According to the corporation, the discovery request was "extremely broad and not at all limited to the incident" in which Elmer was shot.[27] To question the legitimacy of the application, the corporation sought to discredit Elmer's lawyers and portrayed them as political actors and "anti-mining" activists. For instance, Newmont Mining called into question the role of Mar by stating the following:

> Ms. Perez appears to be an NGO advocate actively involved in a national political debate in Peru regarding the role of the National Police in anti-mining protests. No evidence has been submitted showing that [...] her testimony in the [declaration to the U.S. court] is unbiased, reliable, or accurate. – *Respondents Newmont Mining Corporation et al., Motion to the U.S. District Court for the District of Colorado*[28]

As Ronen Shamir (2004, 649) wrote, this strategy of discrediting opponents' lawyers is often used by TNCs in lawsuits in the United States. Newmont Mining also attacked EarthRights International and accused the NGO of trying to obtain internal company information not for the purpose of the criminal investigation in Peru but for "some other political or activist purpose."[29] The company stated that both the *Coordinadora* and EarthRights International "appear to be players in the on-going political and social controversy in Peru about the role of the public security forces."[30] The involvement of the two human rights organizations in the case was, according to Newmont Mining, "suspicious."[31] Questioning the credibility of human rights lawyers by accusing them of pursuing "political" intentions is a strategy also pursued

25 U.S. District Court for the District of Colorado 2014b, 3.
26 U.S. District Court for the District of Colorado 2014c, 1.
27 U.S. District Court for the District of Colorado 2014d, 2.
28 U.S. District Court for the District of Colorado 2014c, 4.
29 U.S. District Court for the District of Colorado 2014e, 4.
30 U.S. District Court for the District of Colorado 2014e, 5.
31 U.S. District Court for the District of Colorado 2014d, 10.

in Peru by corporate and state actors. Behind this is the accusation that a politically motivated lawsuit would constitute an abuse of the legal system.

Elmer's U.S. attorneys responded to these allegations by stating that Newmont Mining did not present any evidence of the applicant's bad faith.[32] They argued that neither Mar's nor EarthRights International's political convictions were relevant to the lawsuit and stated,

> Even if Newmont were to show that Mr. Campos' U.S. or Peruvian counsel agreed to represent him because of their advocacy interests in challenging police violence against those who protest environmentally destructive mining projects in Peru, that would have no effect on the merits of his Application – just as it makes no difference why Newmont Mining's counsel agreed to represent Respondents. – *Applicant Elmer Eduardo Campos-Alvarez, Opposition to Respondent's Motion to Conduct Discovery*[33]

Newmont Mining's motion to dismiss the case on these grounds delayed the progress of the proceedings. EarthRights International feared that the corporation was intentionally delaying it so that the obtained evidence could ultimately not be used in Peru.[34] The NGO therefore submitted a Motion to Expedite Consideration of the application in November 2014.[35] In March 2015, Judge Robert E. Blackburn finally issued an order in Elmer's case and approved the application for discovery, but limited to the district of Colorado and to a specific time frame.[36] Newmont Mining had to disclose over 1,600 documents. However, the court's decision did not bring the dispute to an end but simply concluded the first of several stages.

In July 2015, Newmont Mining submitted a Motion for Protective Order and demanded eight documents to be declared confidential.[37] The company complained that shortly after the first court ruling, EarthRights International had issued several press releases suggesting that the company was linked to police repression in Peru. Newmont Mining stated that its fear that the NGO would misuse the documents for political purposes had been confirmed.[38] In March 2016, Judge Blackburn granted the TNC's motion.[39] Already in November 2015, Elmer's attorney had returned to

32 U.S. District Court for the District of Colorado 2014f, 8.

33 U.S. District Court for the District of Colorado 2014g, 8.

34 U.S. District Court for the District of Colorado 2014h, 6.

35 U.S. District Court for the District of Colorado 2014h.

36 U.S. District Court for the District of Colorado 2015a.

37 U.S. District Court for the District of Colorado 2015b. On the basis of public court documents, I understand that the eight documents concerned are internal company reports providing information on the deployment of private and public security forces to protect the mine site in Peru in November 2011.

38 U.S. District Court for the District of Colorado 2015b, 6.

39 U.S. District Court for the District of Colorado 2016a.

court and submitted a Motion for Supplemental Discovery to disclose further documents located in the United States, but outside of the District of Colorado. Newmont Mining's security office for the Americas is based in Nevada and the corporation, by strictly insisting on the wording of the court's first order, refused to disclose documents located outside of Colorado. In September 2016, this motion was granted.[40]

After losing in U.S. courts, the corporation then attempted to impede the submission of evidence in Peru. When two documents were filed in the criminal proceedings in Cajamarca, Minera Yanacocha questioned their authenticity because a certification of origin was lacking. EarthRights International returned to the U.S. courts with an Emergency Motion requiring the corporation to certify the documents' authenticity.[41] The NGO argued that the mining company "refuses to simply certify that the documents it produced are the documents it actually produced. It does so because it knows that without such certification, the Peruvian court [...] is unlikely to accept the documents."[42] Judge Blackburn granted the motion in March 2018 and ordered Newmont Mining to certify the documents they had submitted almost three years earlier.[43] With this order, the court case on behalf of Elmer Campos was closed in the United States.

Acuna-Atalaya et al v. Newmont Mining Corporation et al

The FLA application on behalf of Elmer Campos was an attempt to use foreign courts in support of domestic litigation. However, similar to Leigh Day, EarthRights International is also convinced by the idea of suing TNCs in U.S. courts and holding corporations liable at home. As part of its efforts in this regard, the NGO filed a civil complaint for damages and equitable relief on behalf of Máxima Acuña and her family before the District Court of Delaware in September 2017. The claim was brought against Newmont Mining Corporation, Minera Yanacocha's parent company, and three of its entities.[44] As I mentioned in Chapter 5, the Chaupe family had made

40 U.S. District Court for the District of Colorado 2016b.

41 The mail correspondence published as exhibits in the U.S. case file indicate that the NGO first tried to obtain the documents' certification directly from the corporation. Newmont Mining refused to issue these certificates, therefore EarthRights International returned to court (U.S. District Court for the District of Colorado 2017).

42 U.S. District Court for the District of Colorado 2017, 1–2.

43 U.S. District Court for the District of Colorado 2018.

44 The complaint was on behalf of Máxima Acuña, her four children, two of her children's spouses, and one minor grandchild. Jaime Chaupe, Máxima's husband, was not involved in the lawsuit. When I asked why Jaime was not involved in the court case, I did not receive any information from EarthRights International's U.S. team.
The three corporate defendant entities included Newmont Second Capital Corporation, Newmont USA Limited, and Newmont Peru Limited (U.S. District Court for the District of Delaware 2017).

several attempts to take criminal action before local courts against Minera Yanacocha and its employees but had not been able to find relief or justice for the human rights abuses they suffered. In order to improve their situation, EarthRights International brought their legal claims to the United States.

In the transnational lawsuit, the Chaupe family demanded financial compensation for the emotional and physical harms and the damages to property they had suffered. The complaint listed more than fifty incidents in which employees of Minera Yanacocha, employees of the private security company Securitas, and police officers supposedly contracted by the mining company intervened in Tragadero Grande and harassed family members. The allegations included, *inter alia*, battery, assault, verbal threats, destruction of property and crops, surveillance, harming of livestock and pets, detention, and obstruction of access to Tragadero Grande. These incidents had occurred between 2011 and 2017.[45] From a legal point of view, the claim's intended outcome was to attribute responsibility to the parent company for acts carried out in the context of a subsidiary's operations. Thus, the case was comparable to the lawsuit against Monterrico in the United Kingdom, although there was no explicit claim for the violation of a duty of care.

The complaint was based on evidence EarthRights International had obtained in the FLA on behalf of Elmer Campos. As a Peruvian lawyer explained to me, due to a statute of limitation, it had not been possible to use the obtained documents to file a civil lawsuit on behalf of Elmer himself. However, the documents provided general information on Newmont Mining's involvement in the Conga conflict and contained details related to the situation of the Chaupe family. Most importantly, the documents demonstrated Newmont Mining's control over security issues related to the Conga project, and, as one of EarthRights International's attorneys explained, the documents revealed that "Newmont is [...] the chain of command for security operations for Conga." Thus, based on the documents produced for Elmer, the NGO believed to have sufficient evidence to file the complaint on behalf of the Chaupe family.

Newmont Mining opposed the claim by arguing that the District Court in Delaware was not the appropriate forum to hear the case and submitted a motion to dismiss it on the grounds of the *forum non conveniens* doctrine. As I mentioned above, this is a legal argument widely used by companies in the United States to obtain a dismissal in a transnational lawsuit. In April 2018, the court followed this argumentation, granted Newmont Mining's motion, and dismissed the case.[46] The plaintiffs appealed against this order, and the case went to the Court of Appeals for the Third Circuit, where the appeal was granted, as I mentioned at the beginning of this chapter, in March 2019. The Court of Appeal argued that in the face of a corruption scandal

45 U.S. District Court for the District of Delaware 2017, 14–35.

46 U.S. District Court for the District of Delaware 2018a.

that shook the Peruvian judiciary to its core at the time, it was necessary to reassess whether Peru was indeed an adequate alternative forum for the plaintiffs to bring a claim.

The District Court in Delaware then addressed the case again, considering the aspects introduced by the Court of Appeal. In March 2020, Judge McHugh again decided that the plaintiffs had the opportunity to use the Peruvian judicial system and dismissed the case once more.[47] EarthRights International then filed another appeal.[48] However, in December 2020, the Court of Appeals for the Third Circuit upheld the lower court's ruling and dismissed the appeal by arguing that "the Peruvian forum is generally adequate despite the recent, serious allegations of corruption".[49] Based on this procedural argument that their case should be heard in Peru, the Chaupe family was denied access to the U.S. judicial system.

Interesting for this book's discussion is the fact that the U.S. judges' order to reject the Chaupes' claim were based on the reasoning that developments in Peru in recent years had demonstrated that the family did have access to the domestic legal system. In one of the orders of the U.S. district court, the responsible judge explicitly referred to the transnational advocacy campaigns in favor of the family and held that "Plaintiffs have generated intense interest in their cause, with all the salutary effects such public attention brings"[50] and that the "continued spotlight [placed on the Chaupes' case by the media and by human rights groups] makes it less likely that judicial proceeding in Peru will be subject to untoward influences."[51] The responsible judge thus indicated that transnational advocacy campaigns can positively support legal actions.

To underline this point, the U.S. judge noted that the family had been able to win a case against Minera Yanacocha in the Court of Cassation of Lima and in lower courts in Cajamarca. In doing so, he referenced the court case in which Minera Yanacocha had accused the family of illegally occupying Tragadero Grande, for which the family was first convicted and then acquitted by the Court of Appeal in Cajamarca and the Court of Cassation in Lima after several years of prosecution. The U.S. court thus interpreted this success of the family in evading criminalization and being acquitted as sufficient evidence that the Chaupe family "can be treated fairly by Peruvian courts."[52] The court thus concluded that Peru was an appropriate forum for the legal treatment of the complaints about the alleged abuses of the mining company. However, the U.S. court did not consider the fact that the Peruvian judicial system

47 U.S. District Court for the District of Delaware 2020a.

48 U.S. District Court for the District of Delaware 2020b.

49 U.S. Court of Appeals for the Third Circuit 2020.

50 U.S. District Court for the District of Delaware 2020a, 24.

51 U.S. District Court for the District of Delaware 2018b, 20.

52 U.S. District Court for the District of Delaware 2020a, 25.

has never followed up on any charges brought by the family and that no criminal investigations have been initiated against the company, even though the Chaupes had reported corporate abuses for years. Thus, being able to defend against legal mobilization *from above* was considered sufficient by the U.S. court to claim that access to the legal system was guaranteed in the plaintiffs' home country, even though all their attempts to mobilize the law *from below* had failed.

Expectations of law in litigation abroad

The three transnational lawsuits emerging from the Conga and the Río Blanco conflicts exemplify different aspects of legal mobilization that may emerge when turning to courts abroad. Several of these aspects are related to the Peruvian human rights movement's legal expectations and to the law's emancipatory force and thus link back to the discussion of Chapter 2. However, the transnational dimension of the court cases adds further aspects to this discussion and provides further insights into the perception of the Peruvian human rights movement regarding the use of law. The aspects I discuss in the following concern (1) financial compensation, (2) differences in legal culture, (3) the aim of having a deterrent effect on corporations, and (4) the aim of obtaining evidence or, more generally, having a supportive impact on domestic litigation.

Financial compensation

As I discussed in the previous chapters, human rights lawyers in Peru often rely on criminal or constitutional law. Civil claims are perceived as a less desirable option because the burden of proof is high, proceedings are even more lengthy than in criminal cases, and, most importantly, the state's role is less prominent because of its involvement as a mere mediator between disputing private parties. In consequence, indemnifying the injured parties often plays a subordinate role in domestic lawsuits, since criminal and constitutional cases are aimed at other legal outcomes, such as punishment or compliance with constitutionality. The issue of financial compensation has raised controversy within Peru's human rights movement, as I explained in the second chapter. However, at the same time, it is an integral part of the demand for justice, especially when it comes to dealing with human rights violations affecting marginalized groups. Bringing a civil case against a parent company abroad provides a way of obtaining such financial compensation, in particular because foreign direct liability cases based on tort law or cases claiming a parent company's negligence are aimed at obtaining this form of remedy. Financial compensation can therefore be a reason for filing a lawsuit abroad.

At the same time, the claim for compensation is sometimes a condition for filing a claim in a foreign court. Legal requirements in the United States, for example, set a minimum of at least US$75,000 to file a civil complaint before a federal court.[53] Claims for less money are heard in state courts, meaning that the amount of money in controversy sets the jurisdiction. In the case on behalf of the Chaupe family, this minimum sum was exactly the amount of money the plaintiffs demanded in compensation.[54] The U.S. legal system thus required them to demand money in order to gain access to federal courts, and the Chaupe family's legal representation fulfilled this requirement to be able to bring the case to a federal court, although the actual goal of bringing the claim to the United States was not financial compensation.

In the Cajamarca region, it is well known that Minera Yanacocha had offered the Chaupe family large sums of money to leave the disputed piece of land. Various people close to the family told me that the company had taken an aggressive approach with these sales offers and had also attempted to persuade individual family members to accept them, thus attempting to divide the family. However, Máxima Acuña repeatedly announced in public that their land was not for sale and that all she and her family wanted was to live in peace in Tragadero Grande. In this sense, Máxima continually declared that she did not want any money from the mining company. In the civil action in the United States, however, the foreign legal system expected her, as the plaintiff, to claim damages from the company in order to be admitted to court. Consequently, the transnational lawsuit caused concern among activists and lawyers in Peru.

During my fieldwork, several people shared their doubts with me as to whether a possible individual compensation payment by Newmont Mining may also have negative effects because it would provide grounds for criticism after the family had already been accused of enriching themselves by cooperating with international NGOs. They feared that the court case would lead to further exposure of the family. At the same time, these lawyers and activists immediately emphasized that the family is "of course entitled to financial compensation." Thus, they all stressed the family's right to reparations, but the question remained as to whether a civil lawsuit abroad potentially resulting in financial compensation involved risks that would outweigh the benefits for the plaintiffs.

This fear was, *inter alia*, based on the human rights movement's experience in previous transnational lawsuits, in particular in the Monterrico case. As I mentioned above, the plaintiffs in the Monterrico case had received compensation resulting from an out-of-court settlement reached with the parent company in the United Kingdom. The plaintiffs had agreed to this settlement after consultation with their British lawyers. Afterwards, they were harshly criticized for this decision, especially

53 28 U.S.C. § 1332(a).

54 U.S. District Court for the District of Delaware 2017, 93.

by other members of the local social movements, who accused them of being bought by the mining company when accepting the payments. The local protest movement subsequently experienced major internal disputes, as David and Rosa told me.

Mar, the *Coordinadora* lawyer involved in the case, recounted that some of the plaintiffs had been important leaders in the local resistance against Río Blanco. As a consequence of the settlement, they experienced hostility, since it "appeared as if they had been bought, that the company had covered their mouths, and that they were delegitimized before the community," as Mar explained. She told me that the mining company took advantage of these tensions and used the payments to discredit opponents and to weaken the social movement. This example thus illustrates that an individual financial compensation payment can in fact entail social costs and can therefore undermine the individual benefits.

In addition, the Monterrico case also illustrated problems arising from confidentiality agreements, which often form an integral part of out-of-court settlements. A group of plaintiffs is exposed in a transnational court case; the plaintiffs receive a compensation payment, but they are not allowed to talk about it. At the same time, however, it is publicly known that they accepted money from the company because the plaintiffs' lawyers also have an interest in disclosing that they have reached a settlement. Everyone knows that money has been paid, but the injured parties are not allowed to provide any information or clarification. Rumors arise and circulate, leading to accusations and social tension.

According to the Peruvian lawyers involved in the Monterrico case, one way to avoid friction within the social movement would have been to claim a communal compensation in London instead of, or in addition to, the individual compensation payment. These lawyers told me that the social tensions were, for the most part, not due to envy toward the individual claimants. Rather, the torture case was, from the perspective of the local protest movement, only one of several cases of human rights violations committed during the Río Blanco conflict. The lawyers of the *Coordinadora* and of *Fedepaz* argued that the torture case had to be understood in this larger context. Mar, for instance, told me that the acts of police violence had been a message to the *comunidades campesinas* and the protest movement as a whole, not only to the affected individuals. In her opinion, the case therefore had a clear "community dimension" (*dimensión comunitaria*), and the political context of the communities had to be considered when pursuing the claim abroad. This also refers to the expectation of the Peruvian human rights movement to support the *comunidades* in their political struggles through legal proceedings, as discussed in Chapter 2. Through the transnational lawsuit, however, the abuses the *comunidades* had suffered during the mining conflict were individualized and reduced to a single event.

Fedepaz lawyer David also understood the torture case as an act of violating individual and collective rights. As he explained, Leigh Day's lawyers, however, did not consider these aspects when bringing the claim because of a "different understanding of collectivism." David criticized that their "perception is the individualistic British perception, isn't it? For them, collectivism doesn't exist, nor do they even have a way of knowing what it is." Mar argued along the same lines and told me that, in her opinion, in the form of individual compensation, "money cannot in itself be the end" of such a lawsuit but that "English lawyers, I mean, they don't understand that. They don't understand it!" She told me that they had tried to explain to the English lawyers that, according to Peruvian law, a *comunidad campesina* has a legal personality, and that it should therefore be possible to "include the community as a victim" in the claim. However, this concept ultimately did not come up in the claim, as the British lawyers only considered the individual plaintiffs. The action was brought under both English and Peruvian law, and the court would have decided which law would have been applicable in a later stage of the proceedings. Thus, in theory, it would have been possible to introduce the alternative approach of collective compensation. However, the British lawyers did not accept this proposal, and since it was ultimately them and not the Peruvian lawyers who controlled the lawsuit, the community dimension was not included in the claim.

Apart from this question of collective compensation, the financial compensation also led to social tensions in the communities because of the lack of follow up regarding the local dynamics following the settlement. Rosa told me that, in retrospect, it might have been better if *Fedepaz* had done a follow up (*seguimiento*) on the case, since Leigh Day did not do it. However, Rosa and her colleagues did not want to interfere in the case after the settlement. She told me that they had been heavily involved in the case in the beginning and had spent much time and effort to help bring the claim. Leigh Day had used them to establish contact and to gain the plaintiffs' trust. When it came to the settlement, however, the English lawyers traveled directly to Piura and no longer met with the NGO staff in Lima. In the logic of Leigh Day's lawyers, this was the only reasonable approach because they "take instructions" from "their clients," not from local NGOs (Leigh Day 2018, 5).

In addition, the plaintiffs had signed a confidentiality agreement, and *Fedepaz*' team was reluctant to approach them because they did not want the plaintiffs to feel like they were interfering. For Leigh Day, the case was closed after the settlement, and, consequently, no one was there to ensure that the case would not result in tensions in the *comunidades* and in allegations against the plaintiffs. Thus, the transnational lawsuit in London resulted in the opposite of what *Fedepaz* anticipated with the use of law – namely, the empowerment of local communities in their political struggle – and, in contrast, weakened the protest movement.

Differences in "legal ideologies"

As I have discussed in detail elsewhere (Lindt 2020), the Peruvian lawyers attributed the social tensions in the communities primarily to the fact that the Monterrico case was settled out of court. The out-of-court settlement led to major disagreements between the British and Peruvian lawyers, which was mainly related to the legal expectations the different actors had placed in the claim. For Leigh Day's attorneys, out-of-court settlements are a part of common court practice and legal culture. They see them as a reasonable way to secure financial compensation for plaintiffs without having to engage in lengthy and risky trials. In general, settlements offer *pro bono* lawyers "the best business option," as Kamphuis (2012a, 561) argued, and a safe means to recover costs.[55] Richard Meeran, Leigh Day's leading lawyer in the Monterrico case, wrote that settling a case against a parent company is "undoubtedly frustrating for academic lawyers and campaigners" but that it "reflects the financial realities and risks to [TNCs], the claimants and the claimants' lawyers of not settling" (2011, 10). In his opinion, "the risk of going to trial usually makes little commercial sense" (*ibid.*).

In transnational lawsuits against TNCs, going to trial poses a high risk for plaintiffs because such cases are often dismissed due to procedural hurdles or practical obstacles, as I explained above. On the one hand, this is because corporate defendants do all they can to avoid having their responsibility heard in court rooms in the Global North. At the same time, it is also because judges in the North attempt to evade the politically sensitive issue of parent companies' liability. In terms of procedural law, the Monterrico case, for example, entailed the risk of being dismissed as it had not yet been decided whether the court would apply English or Peruvian law, and the claims were time-barred under Peruvian law.[56] Leigh Day's concerns about a trial were therefore not unfounded.

The Peruvian human rights lawyers also acknowledged this risk of a trial, as they told me, not only because of the statute of limitations. Rosa recounted that they also feared a possible trial in London because the plaintiffs from Piura might have had to testify. From her work with the *comunidades*, Rosa repeatedly witnessed the difficulties people from rural areas faced while giving declarations before a local prosecutor or judge. She doubted that appearing before a court in another country, in a completely alien environment, would have had a positive effect on the plaintiffs. Veena Das argued that the settlement in the Bhopal case in India had negative impacts on the plaintiffs because they were deprived of their "day in court" and their "right to be

55 Lawsuits against corporate actors that resulted in out-of-court settlements have been critically assessed by various authors. See, for example, the work by Li (2017a, 185–7), Kamphuis (2012a, 561–2), and Kirsch (2006, 21–2, 2007, 308). Particularly detailed discussions were held on the settlement reached in relation to the Bhopal disaster (see, for example: Cassels 1991, Das 1995, Fortun 2001). For a more detailed discussion of this literature see: Lindt 2020.

56 This is exactly what happened to Leigh Day's lawyers some years later. They brought a similar case to the High Court in London against the mining company Xstrata. The lawsuit was on behalf of a group of Peruvians who had been maltreated in the context of protests against the corporation's project in Espinar, Peru (Vilca & Ors v Xstrata Ltd & Anor [2018] EWHC 27 (QB). This case was dismissed on the grounds of the Peruvian statute of limitations.

heard" (1995, 146). However, Rosa's view questions whether "to have a day in court" has a healing effect on plaintiffs in a transnational court case, given that it can be intimidating to "stand before the law" (Ewick and Silbey 1998). Rosa feared that a trial could become a re-traumatizing event for the plaintiffs if they had to testify about the abuses they had suffered.

In addition, Rosa was also concerned about whether the plaintiffs, under the difficult conditions of having to testify before a court in a completely foreign setting, would have been able to fulfill the expectations placed on them as "victims" of human rights violations. In doing so, Rosa referred to the difficulty of translating personal suffering into legal terms and of making experienced abuses understandable for judicial authorities. Several legal anthropologists have discussed this aspect in recent years. Jonah Rubin (2008), for instance, used the example of a U.S. court case in favor of a torture victim from El Salvador to illustrate how challenging this translation process can be for plaintiffs. As Rubin described, plaintiffs are required to translate the traumatic experience of a personally suffered human rights violation into the language of the law and face the challenge that their testimonies are limited to a "legally-acceptable form" (2008, 275). In a similar way, Rosa had been worried that the injured parties in the torture case from Piura would not have been able to provide the narratives that were expected and the translation into the language of law, especially in a foreign country.

In face of these challenges of going to trial abroad, *Fedepaz'* lawyers stressed their support for the plaintiffs' decision to settle the case, although they had hoped for a different outcome. Furthermore, David stressed that the payment of compensation was "also a manifestation of justice" for the plaintiffs. The lawyers in Peru hoped that it would allow the plaintiffs to "change their life" and "to compensate them for the acts of violence they had suffered." David rhetorically asked, "Who are we to take from them this opportunity?" Thus, he was also careful in stressing that the plaintiffs had a right to financial compensation.

In addition, David told me that Monterrico's concession to pay compensation can and should be interpreted as an admission of guilt. *Fedepaz* published a press release about the settlement that underlined this argumentation (Fedepaz 2011). For David, the compensation payment was a clear acknowledgment by the corporation of having committed mistakes, although it officially denied any moral or legal responsibility. He told me,

> I mean, the company didn't pay compensation because it occurred to them, right? The company paid compensation because it knew that its employees had acted badly, on behalf of the company. So, that's why it paid compensation. Beyond the fact that in the out-of-court settlement it is said that the company does not recognize responsibility, if it does not recognize responsibility, why does it pay? – *David, lawyer with* Fedepaz*, May 2017, Lima (interview transcript)*

In this way, *Fedepaz* attempted to interpret the out-of-court settlement as a kind of attribution of responsibility. In retrospect, though, David admitted that this attempt had achieved little success. He referred to the fact that the settlement avoided a trial; in consequence, the actual process of adjudicating did not occur, the question of the parent company's responsibility was not addressed, and no judgment was passed.[57] Therefore, *Fedepaz'* expectation of the law to create public recognition for a crime and to establish the truth, as I discussed in Chapter 2, remained unfulfilled. In our conversations, the Peruvian lawyers assessed the Monterrico case critically, not only because of the negative consequences of the compensation payments but, above all, because the settlement prevented the actual use of the "force of law" (Bourdieu 1987). Their expectation of law is to establish the truth and create public recognition for the harm the plaintiffs had suffered. However, in the lawyers' opinion, this can only be achieved with a trial and a judgment.

In cases that are settled out of court, the absence of a trial means that there is no adjudication and no judgment on the legal issue underlying the claim, i.e. the question of the parent company's responsibility. In this sense, I propose to compare out-of-court settlements to the form of "alternative dispute resolution" that Laura Nader (1999, 305, 308) has discussed in detail. In her analysis of "harmony law models," Nader claimed that alternative dispute resolution is aimed at achieving consensus between the parties about a conflict rather than being aimed at adjudication. She also states that it is based on negotiation in the private space rather than in a courtroom (see also: Mattei and Nader 2008, 18–9, 77). This is very similar to what we can observe when transnational lawsuits against parent companies are settled out of court (see also: Lindt 2020). In transnational lawsuits, access to justice is not equal for all, and corporations often "come out ahead" (Galanter 1974), as I demonstrated in the previous discussion on the hurdles and barriers in accessing foreign courts. However, the *Fedepaz* team believes in the counterhegemonic use of law, as we have seen in the previous chapters. The NGO's lawyers had hoped that litigating the case in London would support their struggle against state and corporate impunity in Peru and would help attribute legal responsibility to the corporation. This testifies to different expectations of the law than those that have been pursued by the lawyers working with Leigh Day.[58] The legal ideology of the Peruvian lawyers was in this regard very different from that of their British counterparts.

David expressed his disappointment by telling me, "We are not very much convinced of the extrajudicial agreement because we, as human rights defenders, what we want is that the truth is publicly known and that justice is established by official

57 For a more detailed discussion of out-of-court settlements and how they avoid adjudication, see: Lindt 2020.

58 These differences in expectations of the law became apparent in the interview I conducted with Richard Meeran, which, as mentioned above, I am unfortunately not allowed to quote.

acts. [*Queremos que se conozca públicamente la verdad y que se haga justicia de medida pública.*]" *Fedepaz* as an institution has a clear understanding of the role that litigation should play in the struggle against corporate impunity. Its strategy is to bring cases to trial and to provoke a response by the state. For *Fedepaz*, the trial holds great significance as a central space where responsibility is negotiated and determined. "Justice is to know the truth! [*Justicia es que se conozca la verdad*]," David told me. Bringing a claim abroad is a "subsidiary option" to the Peruvian lawyers' struggles in the domestic system of justice. They had hoped that litigating in the United Kingdom would contribute to the legal reconditioning of alleged corporate abuses in Peru. However, this was not the case.

Strengthening social struggles on the ground

The central aim of the Chaupe family's transnational lawsuit, in turn, was to ensure that "the family will finally be able to live in peace at Tragadero Grande," as one of the attorneys working with EarthRights International explained to me. The underlying purpose was to urge Newmont Mining to use its control over Minera Yanacocha and to put an end to the harassment against the family. This expectation relies on the assumption that legal proceedings, in particular a conviction for human rights violations, will cause major damage to a company's image, which will consequently change the corporation's behavior in the future. A lawsuit may result in a "litigation threat" (Schrempf-Stirling and Wettstein 2017, 556) when TNCs acknowledge the possibility of being held accountable in their home states for abuses committed abroad.

For EarthRights International, as a legal NGO, a lawsuit does not need to be financially viable, but politically relevant. They do not rely on winning cases to cover their costs – as Leigh Day, for example, does – because as an NGO they are funded by donors. In turn, the selection of cases that EarthRights International brings to court is guided by the organization's broader agenda and is aimed at supporting the social movements and grassroots organizations that the NGO collaborates with. In this sense, EarthRights International understands Máxima Acuña's lawsuit as an "emblematic" case to demonstrate the imbalance of power between marginalized people in the Global South and TNCs headquartered in the United States. One of EarthRights International's U.S. attorneys told me that the lawsuit on behalf of the Chaupe family is aimed at "giving a message to companies that they cannot act beyond the law, they cannot act with impunity, [and that] there should be consequences." Similar to the Peruvian human rights organizations, EarthRights International thus views the law as an emancipatory means for strengthening the rights of marginalized population groups. The U.S. NGO's aim is to "combine [...] the power of law and the power of people in defense of human rights and the environment" (EarthRights International 2006, 77).

"I think it's fine that they try to sue Newmont Mining in their own home [*en su propia casa*]," an activist in Celendín commented when we talked about Máxima Acuña's lawsuit in the United States. This activist, however, did not know much more about the court case and about the legal strategies EarthRights International and the family pursued with this legal action, although he, as an active member of the PIC, was in constant exchange with lawyers of the international NGO. In general, the Chaupe family's lawsuit in the United States was hardly discussed in Cajamarca or Lima during my fieldwork. Only a few activists and human rights lawyers actually knew about the case, and those who did – for example, EarthRights International's team in Lima – were reluctant to discuss the case with me. They told me that this is an "issue dealt with by the NGO's main office in Washington D.C." and that lawyers in the United States would lead the case. Therefore, they did not want to comment further on it. Other lawyers and activists I talked to in Peru, however, were more direct in expressing concerns that, as mentioned above, the lawsuit or a possible compensation payment would lead to adverse effects for the family.

In a manual on transnational human rights litigation, EarthRights International acknowledged this danger that a court case could lead to social conflicts on the ground. There, the NGO stated that a "lawsuit may create tensions and jealousy, especially if a few plaintiffs stand to gain from it and their neighbors do not" (EarthRights International 2006, 39). Additionally, one of the NGO's U.S. lawyers explained to me that "[...] in general, when we evaluate a case, we don't only look at the facts [...] but also what the case means in the politics of the region." Hence, EarthRights International seems aware of the risks of legal activism on the ground. But what did this mean in practice? How would the U.S. NGO staff prevent negative impacts from occurring on the ground?

A U.S. lawyer working at that time with the NGO explained to me that communication was key to avoiding such negative social outcomes in the plaintiffs' local communities. For her, it is important to, first, "just really listen and ask" the plaintiffs what they want, thus to have a close relationship with the affected people and to personally develop legal strategies in close collaboration with them. This approach is fully in line with the recommendations made in EarthRights International's manual on transnational lawsuits, which states that "victims and affected communities should take the lead in any transnational lawsuit. [...] The victims should make the decision whether to file a case freely and with as much information as possible" (EarthRights International 2006, 7). A second important point the U.S. attorney referenced in the lawsuit of the Chaupe family was informing the wider population in Cajamarca about the ongoing U.S. lawsuit in order to avoid social tensions and a negative outcome of the court case. In her opinion, this could happen, for example, "by informing the local communities and the social movements via social media."

From the perspective of Peruvian human rights activists I talked to, the Chaupe family's lawsuit in the United States did not meet the requirements to be considered an example of how bringing a claim abroad could strengthen the political struggles on the ground. Although EarthRights International pursues similar ideas about what can be achieved through legal mobilization as many of Peru's human rights NGOs, the example of this lawsuit nevertheless reveals how the risks of legal activism may be assessed differently from the perspective of human rights lawyers in the Global North and their colleagues in the South.

Producing evidence in foreign courts

While the lawsuit against Newmont Mining in the United States was thus viewed cautiously to very critically from a Peruvian perspective, the FLA application on behalf of Elmer Campos was received much more positively. In contrast to the Monterrico and Chaupe case, this lawsuit was an attempt at using a foreign jurisdiction not to seek compensation or justice but to obtain evidence that would help to bring forward local lawsuits. In this sense, the approach represents a sort of paradigm shift in transnational human rights litigation.

The FLA application was based on close cooperation between EarthRights International's U.S. lawyers, their Peruvian colleagues and the *Coordinadora* lawyers, in particular Mar, who represented Elmer in the criminal case in Cajamarca. The fact that the central legal proceedings, i.e. the criminal proceedings on behalf of Elmer, occurred before domestic courts was of great importance for the Peruvian human rights lawyers. Litigating the case domestically contributed to their feeling of maintaining control over the case. The lawsuit abroad was, in contrast, only aimed at supporting this domestic claim. This allowed the Peruvian lawyers "to maintain the power to decide about the course of the lawsuits," as Mar told me.

Moreover, by focusing their efforts on the domestic proceedings, the Peruvian lawyers were able to pursue their expectations of the law to bring about institutional change. Mar told me that "in this way, it is possible to get things moving here [in Peru]," although she stressed that they did not yet have a favorable judgment in Elmer Campos' case in Peru and that, therefore, they could not yet "talk of a success." However, as I pointed out in Chapter 3, the Elmer's case has advanced further than other cases of police violence in mining conflicts. Even more importantly, the fact that the company Minera Yanacocha has been included in the proceedings as a civilly liable third party is already a great achievement for the Peruvian human rights movement, which the lawyers explicitly attribute to the FLA application in the United States.

The innovation of the FLA statute lies in its focus on disclosure of corporate documents that can then be used in domestic lawsuits. Thus, the legal action is directly aimed at supporting legal struggles on the ground. Access to evidence is key in litigation against TNCs. *Coordinadora* lawyer Mar explained to me that the FLA application's most significant outcome was to prove that important decisions concerning the collaboration between Minera Yanacocha and the police during the Conga protests were made in the United States.[59] Peru's human rights movement had known for a long time that a contract for extraordinary services existed between Minera Yanacocha and the police, and they had also assumed that Newmont Mining was well informed about its subsidiaries' activities on the ground. However, evidence backing up these assumptions had always been lacking.

As I described in Chapter 3, although obtaining and presenting evidence in a court case should be the responsibility of the prosecutor, in practice, the complainants' side often takes up this task in order to prevent a case from being closed because of a lack of evidence. In Elmer's criminal proceeding, important evidence was eventually obtained thanks to EarthRights International's efforts to bring the FLA application abroad. In this sense, the legal action in Colorado had a direct influence on the legal proceedings in the courts in Cajamarca and supported the human rights movement's struggles.

In addition, the FLA application also differed from the other two examples since it required the U.S. judge to conduct a different legal analysis than the two lawsuits on parent companies' liability. This made a crucial difference and helped the case to be successful. In the FLA application, the question at stake was not whether the parent company bears a legal responsibility for the committed crimes. Rather, the lawsuit was limited to the question of whether Newmont Mining had a certain degree of control over the operation in Peru and was therefore in possession of relevant documents. This helped EarthRights International claim a link between Newmont Mining's headquarter in Colorado and the police intervention in Cajamarca.

If we look at lawsuits in which plaintiffs seek to attribute legal responsibility to a parent company – for example, in the Monterrico case or in the lawsuit on behalf of the Chaupe family – courts in the Global North take a much more restrictive approach to establishing this link of control between different corporate entities.[60] In contrast, the question of parent liability was not at stake in the U.S. legal proceedings

59 The documents demonstrated that employees of Minera Yanacocha sent reports to the U.S. headquarters on a daily basis commenting about where protests in the Cajamarca region occurred.

60 A striking example of this is the civil lawsuit in the United Kingdom against Royal Dutch Shell plc (RDS) and Shell Petroleum Development Company of Nigeria Ltd (SPDC) for environmental pollution caused by the subsidiary in Nigeria. The parent company's level of control over its Nigerian subsidiary was the central issue discussed during a three-day hearing at the Court of Appeal that I attended in London in November 2017. Appellants used corporate documents such as RDS's annual and sustainability reports to convince the Court of Appeal that control was "exercised through mandatory policies" and that, as a result, the parent company had, in fact, a duty of care. Two of the three responsible judges did not follow this argumentation, and the court consequently dismissed the appeal, stating that the claimants failed to prove a relationship of proximity between the parent company and its subsidiary (Okpabi and others v Royal Dutch Shell Plc and another, [2018] EWCA Civ 191).

on behalf of Elmer. As I mentioned above, it is not only judges from the Global South but also their colleagues from the Global North who attempt to circumvent this political issue. In Elmer's claim, however, the elephant in the room went untouched, and the Court of Colorado accepted that there exists the necessary relationship between the corporation's headquarter in Colorado and the Peruvian mine site.[61]

Conclusion

Although transnational court cases are often aimed at attributing legal responsibility to the parent company, the example discussed in this chapter illustrates that this question is ultimately left out in such lawsuits. Furthermore, Elmer's case in the United States revealed that it is precisely the exclusion of the political question of parent companies' responsibility that can lead to the courts in the Global North granting a claim. If a lawsuit in a home state is based on the question of parent responsibility, it ends with a dismissal in most cases, as in the Chaupe case, or with an out-of-court settlement, as in the Monterrico case. This points to the political sensitivity of corporate responsibility, not only in countries like Peru, but also in the Global North. As a consequence of these circumstances, it was possible in the lawsuit on behalf of Elmer to obtain important documents in the United States that, in turn, had a positive effect on the legal struggles in Peru.

The Monterrico case, in contrast, had no impact on the Peruvian criminal proceedings. Moreover, ten years after the settlement, the *comunidades* in Piura faced new attempts by the state and the corporation to develop the Río Blanco project, while the local protest movement had been weakened as a result of the out-of-court settlement. All Peruvian lawyers with whom I discussed this lawsuit told me that they had learned much from the case. The major reason for the negative outcome of such lawsuits is, in their view, that their counterparts in the Global North were able to dictate the collaboration and that, as one lawyer said, "all the rules of the game [were] set from there." She expressed the hope for the future that "maybe at some point, we can count on a counterpart in the North who is more open" to the needs and aspirations of the social movements and the legal NGOs on the ground. In this sense, she hoped that international NGOs and *pro bono* law firms would learn from past experience and adapt their cooperation with partners in the South "in such a way that the decisions are taken in the South, the priorities continue to be taken in the South, and [the lawyers in the North] are simply operators."

61 The court's order was based on the fact that there were several managers working for both corporate entities, which, in comparison with other cases, is a rather simple way of proving parent control over a subsidiary.

David told me that their lack of experience in transnational lawsuits had been one of the principal obstacles. If members of *Fedepaz* were ever involved in such a case again, they would approach it differently in order to be able to maintain control over how a lawsuit evolves. The Peruvian lawyers' understanding of achieving justice entails determining who is responsible for the offenses and not just achieving individual financial compensation. Mar told me that the lawyers from the Global North are "super-efficient in their work, but their logic is only one of cost and benefit." For the Peruvian human rights lawyers, lawsuits do not need to make "commercial sense," but they do need to have a positive impact on the ground – for individuals and for the communities. Only in this way can such legal processes be seen as an emancipatory means to support the social struggles on the ground and to fulfill the expectations people place on law.

Chapter 7. Law's limitations

Introduction

I started this book by referencing the legal anthropological debate on law's ambiguity, thus on the observation that law is "simultaneously a maker of hegemony and a means of resistance" (Hirsch and Lazarus-Black 2012, 9). Throughout the book, I discussed the differences between Peruvian human rights lawyers – especially those from Lima – and activists from grassroots organizations in the provinces when it comes to hopes and expectations placed on law. I have argued that it is the ambiguity of law that leads to the different experiences and that shape the actors' legal consciousness. Human rights advocates have much more faith in the force of law as a counterhegemonic means than the activists do. As I highlighted in the preceding chapters, this is not only related to the lawyers' professional relationship with the law. Rather, it is also related to their experience with successfully applying legal means as an emancipatory tool in their political struggles. Activists on the ground, in turn, are confronted with the law primarily in connection with the issue of criminalization. Thus, they mainly experience the "dark side of judicialization" (see also: Lindt 2023). In addition, they often witness the mobilization of law from below against human rights violations going unpunished. The task of the human rights lawyers in this context is to convince the people at the margins of the state that it makes sense to mobilize the judicial system as an ally.

The human rights lawyers I worked with in the field have remained firm in their belief in law despite the limitations imposed by the lack of implementation or abuse of the law. But, as I illustrate in this final chapter, even among themselves, this belief in the law is far from being beyond all doubt. Doubts were not caused by the practical and jurisdictional hurdles mentioned in the discussion on the difficulties of litigating human rights from below. These lawyers have learned that courtrooms are a battlefield in which conflicts of interest exist. They have also learned that their opponents are powerful actors who have the resources and power to "come out ahead" (Galanter 1974) in court. They have become aware that corruption, a lack of political will on the part of the judicial authorities, and the influence of companies on the judiciary are integral parts of the Peruvian justice system. Rather, doubts were caused by limitations inherent in the law and the legal mechanisms themselves. These doubts usually surfaced in the direct negotiation processes with the persons the lawyers represented in court. First, they emerged in situations where it became apparent that it is not enough to only have a "right to have rights" (Arendt 1998 [1951], 614, Dagnino 2003, 213). Second, there are also several controversies arising from the relationships in law – that is, the relationships between lawyers and plaintiffs, which is shaped and predetermined by law's proceedings. I discuss these two limitations of law in this chapter.

Beyond the right to have rights

During my fieldwork, law's limitations mostly became apparent in unexpected situations. Such a situation occurred during a trip to a *comunidad nativa*, which I made with the team of *Fedepaz* in March 2018. Lawyer Rosa, anthropologist Ingrid, and I traveled to the province of San Ignacio, in the northernmost part of Cajamarca, where we visited the Awajún *comunidad* of Supayaku. *Fedepaz* has been working with this *comunidad* since 2013, providing the community members with legal assistance and representing them in a legal dispute with the mining company Exploraciones Águila Dorada S.A.C. (Sanca Vega 2017, 8). In 2013, *Fedepaz* had filed a constitutional complaint, a so-called *amparo*, demanding the suspension of the mining project Yaku Entsa that threatened the community and its natural resources (Servindi (online) 2013, Sanca Vega 2017). In 2016, the corresponding constitutional court ruled in favor of the community, thereby ordering the mining project's suspension; two years later, this judgment was upheld during an appeal.[1] Consequently, the mining project was halted. With its legal work, *Fedepaz* had thus significantly supported Supayaku's resistance against mining.

In addition, *Fedepaz* formed part of a coalition of NGOs that supported the *comunidad* in the defense of its territory and livelihood. This collaboration resulted in a so-called *Plan de Vida*, a "life plan," which community members had elaborated with *Fedepaz*, *Grufides*, the Catalan association *Ingeniería Sin Fronteras*, and the Peruvian NGO *Soluciones Prácticas* (Comunidad Nativa Awajún de Supayaku *et al.* 2015, see also: Sanca Vega 2017, 194, 223). Based on a long-term participatory process, this plan set out the joint projects that the *comunidad* wanted to pursue in order to achieve their vision of the *tajimat pujut* (*buen vivir* or the "good life" in Awajún). It contained proposals and visions of how the community wanted to develop in terms of economic,

1 *Corte Superior de Justicia de Lima, Quinto Juzgado Constitucional de Lima, Sentencia, Resolución 26,* 10.12.2018, court order on file with author (see also: Fedepaz 2018a).

cultural, and social aspects over a fixed period of ten years. During the elaboration of this plan and beyond, *Fedepaz* focused primarily on legal capacity training with the community. The legal assistance provided by the NGO thus went beyond the actual defense of the *comunidad* in the courtrooms.

Several times a year, members of *Fedepaz* traveled to Supayaku and conducted workshops: for example, on the rights of indigenous communities, on women's rights, or on other topics that were determined in dialogue with the community. During the trip on which I accompanied the team, Rosa and Ingrid conducted a workshop on domestic violence with the women of Supayaku. In addition, they worked with the community members on revising the community's statutes. This was a long-term project on which the *comunidad* and the NGO had been focusing for several months. According to the national legislation, every *comunidad nativa* and *campesina* in Peru needs such a set of rules that defines the local customs and regulates the most important aspects of community life. The statutes usually include points such as the regulation of membership in the *comunidad*, political decision-making, the use of communal land and forest resources, and the organization of community work. In many cases, however, these statutes are outdated and no longer correspond to everyday practice in the communities. *Fedepaz* considered it a key issue to revise the community's own norms together with its members. The revision of the statutes was aimed at strengthening the community members in their collective and individual rights, as Rosa told me. In this sense, the workshops that she and Ingrid conducted in Supayaku illustrated what *Fedepaz* understood by the premise of initiating empowerment processes in the communities through legal advocacy training.

The days in Supayaku were intense, especially because Rosa and Ingrid were seen by many community members as much more than external advisors in legal matters. Rather, the *comuneros* and *comuneras* who participated in the workshops also brought their personal concerns to the NGO staff. Women talked about conflicts with their husbands, parents discussed problems at school, and many others asked Rosa and Ingrid for advice on internal family problems or issues with state authorities. The workshops had hardly been completed when people were already standing at the door of the community house, waiting to discuss their personal concerns with the two NGO employees. This demonstrated the close relationship and the mutual trust that *Fedepaz*' team has built over the years with individual members of the *comunidad*. Rosa and Ingrid's intention in taking me to the field was precisely to demonstrate this relationship and their way of working with the *comunidad*. The two wanted to make sure I understood that their human rights work was not only being completed in the office in Lima, but rather took place in the communities as well.

The day we left the community to travel back to San Ignacio, we were picked up by a private driver as there are no bus or *colectivo* connections to Supayaku. There is only an unpaved road connecting the *comunidad* to the next settlements. The drive takes several hours and is only possible with a 4x4 off-road vehicle; in case of rain, the road quickly becomes impassable. For this reason, vehicles leaving from Supayaku to the city are always full. Among the group of people who shared our trip to the city was Hernán, a young, timid man from the *comunidad*, who worked in San Ignacio. Hernán was employed by the provincial authority as special representative for the *comunidades nativas*.[2] In this function, he had participated in the workshops of *Fedepaz*. In spite of his official position, however, he had been rather reserved during the workshops and had hardly participated in the discussions.

However, as soon as we left Supayaku behind us, Hernán overcame his shyness and did not stop talking. He recounted that there was a contract between the community and a lumber company allowing for cutting timber within the communal territory. Hernán seemed nervous when he talked about this issue. I later suspected that he had been told by other community members to address the matter with the NGO staff on the way back to the city. Rosa and Ingrid were surprised since they had never heard about such a contract. At first, they directly questioned what Hernán had told them. They argued that if this were the case, the members of the *comunidad* would certainly have told them about it. Just the day before, they said, during the revision of the statutes, the issue of extracting timber from community forests had been discussed, and participants of the workshop had not mentioned anything along these lines. Instead, they had reaffirmed their position that the community does not want to have such collaboration with external companies, Ingrid and Rosa argued. However, Hernán insisted that the contract existed. He said that he himself had been involved in the negotiations. In this way, it came to light that the *comunidad* had begun negotiations with a timber company and had not talked with *Fedepaz* about this collaboration. Rosa and Ingrid later spoke, by phone, with community representatives, who confirmed the negotiations with the company. During our stay in Supayaku, the same members of the *comunidad* had not said a word about it.

"Después de la resistencia, después de la victoria, ¿qué?"

The episode on the way back from Supayaku revealed a dilemma that Peruvian human rights lawyers and legal NGOs have often been confronted with in recent years. The point here is that, in view of their difficult economic situation, it is often no longer sufficient for many local communities to simply have rights and defend these

---

2 The official name of the authority for which Hernán worked was the so-called *Oficina de Enlace de Asuntos Indígenas*, the "Liaison office on Indigenous Affairs." In his position, Hernán was responsible for ensuring that, within the provincial municipality of San Ignacio, the interests of the *comunidades nativas* were adequately represented. For *Fedepaz*, this office has been an important partner in its work of strengthening the indigenous community.

rights against unwelcome extractive industry projects but that alternatives for economic development must also be offered. This raises the question of what should follow the victory over a major industrial project like a mine, for example. What comes after the victory, after the successful resistance against the undesirable economic development? For the human rights NGOs, the questions arise regarding what they can offer to the *comunidades* as alternatives to the economic development promised by the companies. This situation is particularly striking because mining projects are often located in Peru's highland regions, which are marginalized areas characterized by high poverty rates and a poorly functioning local economy. Under these circumstances, NGOs are quickly accused of having prevented the economic development of a region – whatever this economic development may have meant in practice and whatever negative side effects it may have had.

In the capacity-building workshops of various NGOs that I attended in Lima, Celendín, and San Ignacio, the term *fortalecer* appeared repeatedly. NGO representatives said that it was about "strengthening" the *comunidades* and empowering them in their rights and in their resistance against the mining projects. This discourse also included discussions with the community about alternatives for a different kind of economic development, development that was not based on extractivism and the exploitation of natural resources. What this alternative development should look like in practice, however, often went unanswered. NGO representatives and grassroots activists likewise talked about encouraging the development of *microempresas* (micro-enterprises) or the promotion of agriculture, ecotourism, and handicraft products. As human rights organizations, however, the NGOs were not in a position to provide the knowledge and resources to build such alternatives. Their area of expertise is the legal sphere, not the promotion of local economic development.

Regarding the issue with the timber company in Supayaku, it later became clear that the representatives of the community had not yet signed a contract but that negotiations were ongoing. Back in Lima, *Fedepaz*' team had various conversations with the community's leaders via phone, and Ingrid traveled back to Supayaku shortly later to discuss the issue with the *comunidad*. *Fedepaz* offered to review the contract to make sure the *comunidad* was not being ripped off by the company. At the same time, the NGO employees did not want to force themselves on the community with this offer so that they did not get the feeling that *Fedepaz* wanted to interfere and dictate to them how they should decide to proceed in this case. Furthermore, the opportunities offered to them by law, as the most important of their allies, were simply insufficient for this situation. Their role as a human rights organization repeatedly threw them back into the pattern of being unable to do more than promote rights, while people on the ground had the expectation to be able to enjoy the substance of these rights (see also: Mukherjee 2019, 72).

In this regard, Rosa told me that she and her colleagues were fully aware that it is not enough to only have rights and to be able to claim these rights if people, at the same time, do not have the opportunity to sustain themselves (*sustentarse*). Pure legal assistance is not enough, Rosa said; rather, they must look for cooperation with organizations that can work with the *comunidades* in the "productive" sector (for example, in agriculture) and thus offer them practical support for economic development. With the elaboration of the *Plan de Vida*, *Fedepaz* and the other NGOs had taken steps in this direction with the community of Supayaku. However, it had become clear that these efforts were not enough.

To only have rights is not enough

At the heart of this dilemma is the limitation of law, especially that of international human rights law. This limitation was discussed by Moyn (2018), who claimed that human rights are "not enough" to demand distributive justice. His key message was that human rights discourses are not an appropriate way to fight for social justice, because they rely on the concept of *sufficiency* rather than *equality.* In his book *Not Enough*, Moyn lamented that in the post-Cold War era of human rights, the "egalitarian aspiration" (*ibid.*, 5) of political struggles has been lost and that human rights have become a "worldwide slogan in a time of downsized ambition" (*ibid.*, 6). "The call for a modicum of distributive equality" (*ibid.*, 3) had, in his view, increasingly fallen silent in the course of human rights discourses because "[h]uman rights guarantee status equality but not distributive equality" (*ibid.*, 213).

When applied to communities such as Supayaku, Moyn's theory means that while it is all well and good to invoke the right to live in a healthy and clean environment, free from damage caused by mining, it is, however, not enough to lift marginalized communities out of poverty. This means that while it is desirable for the community to be granted the right, as an indigenous group, to be consulted on major development projects, these rights are not enough to overcome the daily economic hardship the people experience. Human rights discourses and the juridification of social protests are suitable for preventing a mining project, as I have made clear in the previous chapters. At the same time, however, legal discourses, especially human rights discourses, do not provide marginalized population groups with a sufficient basis to demand distributive justice – neither from the state nor from other actors. Large-scale projects may be prevented by human rights discourses, but, at the same time, the marginalization remains.

These limitations of human rights law in relation to poverty issues have been discussed in recent years by various other authors. James Ferguson, for instance, described this dilemma using the example of an NGO workshop on housing rights in Cape Town. At the end of the legal capacity training, a man raised his hand and said that he did not want the *right to a house*, but that he wanted a *house* (Ferguson 2015, 48). As in Supayaku, the promises of justice alone were not enough for this

South African; he was not content with only knowing that he had a right to a home but demanded the enforcement of this right.

In addition, Harri Englund (2006) observed that human rights activism in Malawi was primarily driven by the country's elites. Among the impoverished population, in turn, the concept of human rights had acquired a strongly negative connotation. As Englund described, due to the poor translation of human rights concepts to local contexts, the local population considered these concepts insufficient to actually meet their concrete needs. Thus, the human rights discourse was seen as something foreign, something brought in from the outside. However, this does not correspond to the situation as we can observe it in Peru. The concept of human rights, or the right to have rights in general, plays a major role in social movements as well as for the marginalized sections of the population who oppose industrial mining projects. As I have discussed elsewhere (Lindt 2015), they actively invoke their rights, not only in capacity-building trainings with legal NGOs but also in their political struggles and in everyday life.

Rights talks and the demand for rights are therefore not only discourses that emanated from an elite of human rights lawyers from Lima. Rather, the juridification of protest also emerged from the local resistance itself. At the same time, however, it has become apparent over time that these demands for rights are not enough, especially when facing the promises of corporate development programs. Social movements and grassroots organizations were especially exposed to such criticism because they had fought against the mining projects even on the most demanding front, as the example of Cajamarca reveals.

Facing corporate anti-politics

> El agua no se vende, ni por mochilas ni cocinas.
> – *Protest poster carried by a group of young girls during the Conga conflict in Sorochuco, 2012*[3]

In the field, I observed that the limitations of human rights discourses are particularly evident in regions where transnational mining companies are active with CSR programs, such as in Cajamarca. Minera Yanacocha had learned from the social conflicts of the past and had made great efforts to address the criticism voiced in the region. Activists criticized that the company attempted to "buy" the "social license to operate" with gifts and donations to individuals, institutions, *comunidades*, and

---

3 "The water is not for sale, neither for backpacks nor for kitchens." Picture on the PIC's blog *Celendín libre* (https://celendinlibre.files.wordpress.com/2012/04/sorochuco-paro-regional.jpg).

municipalities. The protest poster cited above referred to precisely this kind of criticism. Donating "kitchens" – mostly gas stoves – and school supplies, including backpacks, to economically disadvantaged families in the mine's area of direct influence was regarded as one of the company's most infamous strategies for gaining support among the local population. Minera Yanacocha had already begun to implement development projects with the launch of the Conga project; after its suspension, it kept them going.

"The water is not for sale (*el agua no se vende*)" because "water is worth more than gold (*el agua vale más que el oro*)," was one of the slogans with which the protest movement opposed the Conga project. In its resistance, the right to water was at the center of the movement's demands and united the rural and the urban population. The political mobilization on the streets proved to be particularly effective. Through strikes, roadblocks, and demonstrations, the social movement was able to build up the necessary pressure to assert their interests from below. Thereby, they challenged the nation state's hegemonic development discourses. In the end, the Conga mine project was stopped because of the local population's broad political mobilization. The demand for rights and the resulting juridification of the protests played a major role in this. As I have argued elsewhere (Lindt 2015), it was precisely the reference to the "right to have rights" that provided an important basis for making demands on the nation state and urging the government to stop the mining project. Legal discourses thus served as a key justification for resistance. Furthermore, the juridification of its protest also helped the local social movement build coalitions with national human rights organizations and foreign supporters. In this way, the rights discourse provided a common ground to link the local demands to a broader political context. The juridification thus strengthened the movement in several ways.

At the same time, however, the judicialization of the social conflict – i.e. the struggle in the courtrooms – had been much less successful. Legal NGOs had tried to have the Conga project declared inadmissible through constitutional complaints, but the claims were dismissed. With criminal charges, the NGOs could at best take retroactive action against human rights violations, but the legal mobilization from below could not prevent these abuses. At the same time, activists on the ground were confronted with the increasing threat of criminalization and the use of law by their opponents. Therefore, it comes as no surprise that grassroots organizations such as the PIC, in retrospect, see political mobilization as much more effective than legal mobilization. The *juridification* of the protest bolstered their resistance and their political demands, while the *judicialization* had little effect in this regard.

In the phase that the social conflict had reached during my fieldwork, however, the situation in Cajamarca had become even more complicated. The Conga project was suspended, and political mobilization on the streets against it had ended. At the same time, the economic situation in the region had deteriorated, partially because mining activities had decreased, but for other reasons as well. As a consequence, the region had entered a severe recession. Minera Yanacocha and the other mining companies operating in the area, in turn, were still strongly present with CSR programs, which caused the social movements great concern. Members of the grassroots movements repeatedly expressed worries that these CSR projects would break the population's resistance against mining. Milton, for example, repeatedly said that the social movement must not lower its guard (*no bajar la guardia*) and must remain vigilant; otherwise the company would come back with the Conga project, and the social movement would lose the fight. He and other activists clearly saw, behind the corporate development projects, an attempt to break the political resistance; in the perception of the social movement, the CSR programs were a kind of "anti-politics machine" (Ferguson 1994) that they faced after the suspension of the actual mining project (see also: Sydow 2016).

During the *Escuela de Líderes y Lideresas* in Celendín, the corporations' activities in the rural areas were an important point of discussion. A woman from Sorochuco expressed her concerns by saying,

> Right now Yanacocha is entering through the *anexos*, [the peripheral settlements of the district]. The company arrives with gifts, for example, with water tanks for the people. Now they are going to have the neighborhoods with solar panels [of] Yanacocha. What do they say? What do the people of Sorochuco say? [They say to us,] "Yes, it's fine if you defend the water. But what do the people from the social movements give us? Yanacocha provides us with many things and with what do you provide us? None of you take care of us." That's the way people talk in Sorochuco these days. – *Women activist from Sorochuco,* Escuela de Líderes y Lideresas, *March 2017, Celendín (field notes, own translation)*

Within Sorochuco, a strong division of the population has taken place due to the Conga conflict. After the project's suspension, the members of the social movement suffered defamations and were presented as those who would have prevented economic progress. These accusations were often made by young people who hoped for employment in the mine and who demanded to see economic progress in the region. Older people, in turn, would have been much more committed to the resistance, as several activists told me. During the critical phase of the social conflict, it had been far easier for the social movement to counter the development discourses of the company. The CSR projects are based on so-called soft law, they are thus voluntary and dependent on the "moralization of responsibility," as Eckert (2016, 254–6) termed it. The social movements, on the other hand, demanded legally binding concessions from the state. They did not want to be dependent on the mercy and goodwill of the company, as I have argued earlier (Lindt 2015, 94–5), but they rather demanded their rights as citizens.

In the aftermath of the large protests, however, doubts arose as to the extent to which resistance based on this appeal for rights could be sustained. The activists became aware that it is good and right to have rights, but people must also remain convinced that their opposition to powerful actors such as transnational mining corporations is worthwhile. The company would supposedly offer something to the community, and would carry out projects, as the woman recounted during the *escuela*. The *ambientalistas*, the environmentalists, on the other hand, were accused of having nothing to offer. They themselves remained convinced in their resistance, but there were doubts that invoking rights in this phase of the social conflict would be a useful means of maintaining the broader population's resistance against mining. In this sense, it became clear that the human rights discourses exposed considerable limitations not only for the national legal NGOs, but also for the grassroots organizations. While human rights lawyers and activists on the ground may have different expectations of law and litigation, thus of the *judicialization* of social conflicts, both sides face the same limitations of such conflicts' *juridification*. This constitutes the first of law's limitations that the human rights movement has been confronted with.

Relationships in law

It is May 2018, a few days before the end of my fieldwork. The two legal NGOs IDL and EarthRights International – represented by its Peruvian team based in Lima – hold a press conference in the city of Cajamarca. Through the local media, the NGOs want to inform about a constitutional complaint they filed that morning in a court in Celendín. Thereby, they intend to make the background of the complaint known to the wider public. The legal action lodged concerns about Chadín 2, a planned hydroelectric dam project in the province of Celendín. With a so-called proceso de amparo, *an injunction, the human rights organizations seek to challenge the award of the concession for the dam project. In the lawsuit, they argue that the project violates fundamental rights of the local population, in particular the right to a "healthy and ecologically balanced environment"* (derecho a un medio ambiente sano y equilibrado).

The press conference is held at the Restaurant El Zarco, a traditional restaurant not far from Cajamarca's plaza de armas. *Among the representatives of NGOs from Lima are Juan Carlos, one of the leading constitutional lawyers and attorneys of IDL, Juliana, the head of the Peruvian office of EarthRights International, as well as Valentina, the communications officer of EarthRights International's headquarters in Washington. On behalf of the local organizations, Milton for the PIC, and Ula, the president of a* comunidad campesina *in the Río Marañón basin, are there to provide information. About ten media representatives came to hear the NGOs' announcements.*

The majority of the journalists seem to belong to those newspapers of Cajamarca that hold a rather critical position toward social movements. The most central question they ask concerns what conditions would need to be met for the social movements to be satisfied with a major eco-

nomic project for once. They thereby voice the accusation that the NGOs and grassroots organizations, as ambientalistas, *would always prevent any economic progress in the region from the outset. Juliana and Juan Carlos, for their part, are trying to steer the conversation toward the constitutional complaint. They explain its content and emphasize, time and again, that the Peruvian state has a duty to protect the rights of its citizens, even in the face of major economic projects. They place the constitutional complaint in a broader context and refer to similar lawsuits in Colombia and other countries, as well as to international human rights agreements. Milton and Ula hardly ever rise to speak during the press conference. Ula initially expresses his support for the lawsuit but then lets the lawyers speak. Milton gives a longer explanation of why the dam project poses a threat from the perspective of the social movements. Afterward, however, the questions and answers revolve mainly around legal aspects, and Milton gives the floor to the attorneys, who are experts in this field.*

Later that day we go to the studio of Radio Líder, *a private radio station in Cajamarca that has supported the resistance against Conga and has close ties to the social movements. Juliana, Juan Carlos, and Ula go into the recording studio and answer the moderator's questions. Meanwhile, the rest of us sit down in the studio's entrance area and wait. Suddenly, Milton receives a call from Wilmer, a* rondero *leader from Yagen. Yagen is one of the villages that will be most affected by Chadín 2. Consequently, parts its population have met the project with strong resistance. The local* rondas campesinas *have joined the PIC and its protest movement. Locally, Chadín 2 led to severe tensions between the project's supporters and opponents, resulting in several deaths in recent years. Furthermore, many of the activists from the village have been criminalized for their resistance. Among those criminalized was also Wilmer. Wilmer is a shy, reserved man in his thirties, an* agricultor *(a farmer) and father of two children. After the death of Hitler Rojas, he took a leading role within the* ronda campesina *in Yagen. This led to serious negative consequences for him; he has repeatedly received death threats. In the past few weeks, the psychological strain was increasingly visible in his worried face. When I had returned to Cajamarca for the second round of field research some months earlier, I was struck by how emaciated he had become. He had also become even quieter within a short period of time.*

During the phone call, Wilmer informs Milton that the ronderos *from Yagen decided to withdraw from the constitutional complaint. The day before, a group of* ronderos *came to Cajamarca, where they had a court hearing in a criminalization case. Afterward, a meeting was held with Maritza and Miguel, two Peruvian lawyers working with IDL and EarthRights International, respectively. The NGO representatives explained what exactly the constitutional complaint was about, and the* ronderos *signed it afterwards. Then the* ronderos *and the lawyers traveled to Celendín, where they filed the lawsuit this morning. Subsequently, Maritza and Miguel returned to Cajamarca.*

Now, a few hours later, the ronderos *inform Milton by phone that they want to withdraw from the case. At first, it is not entirely clear why they decided to take this step. Initially, Milton assumes that Wilmer and his people got the impression that the representatives from the other affected communities did not cosign the complaint and that they, from Yagen, were the only ones who supported the case. Milton tells Wilmer that this is not the case. Later, it becomes clear that the group from Yagen is afraid that the court case will expose them even more as individual opponents of the project. By signing the lawsuits, they could become the target of further attacks by supporters of Chadín 2.*

The NGO representatives from Lima and Washington are, at first, a little helpless and worried about how to proceed. After the radio interview, they discuss what they should do. They are afraid that the lawsuit might fail now, which would mean that the work of several years would be ruined, as some attorneys keep saying. Finally, the lawyers decide to travel to Celendín again. They want to discuss the situation once more with the ronderos *before they return to Yagen, where the phone connection is poor and communication to the outside world is therefore difficult. When they set off, the NGO lawyers are convinced that they will be able to persuade the* ronderos *that it was the right decision to take the legal route.*

Unfortunately, I was not able to find out afterward how the meeting between the lawyers and the *ronderos* ended because I left Cajamarca and Peru shortly after. Facebook is a reliable channel to follow how lawsuits are filed, court decisions are obtained, and appeals are lodged. However, it is not always easy, via social media, to keep track of what is happening on the ground, especially with regard to subtle social tensions between lawyers and plaintiffs going on behind the scenes. Shortly after filing the complaint, EarthRights International and IDL informed about the lawsuit via their online channels (EarthRights International 2018b). Apart from that, there was little public information about the complaint in the following months. Then, in May 2019, the corresponding court in Celendín declared the case to be inadmissible. In its order, it argued that the complaint failed to fulfill several formal requirements (IDL 2019). Thus, the legal action was formally unsuccessful.

Moreover, the incident in Cajamarca indicated that the lawsuit must also be considered a failure with regard to the underlying social processes. The episode points to a second limitation of the law that the Peruvian human rights movement is confronted with and that has led – even among human rights lawyers – to doubting the strategy of legal mobilization. This second limitation results from the relationship that human rights attorneys in Peru have developed with the plaintiffs they represent in court.

This relationship is determined, first, by judicial processes and by the very nature of litigation. Law and litigation require specific roles of lawyers and plaintiffs and define how these two parties relate to each other. At the same time, this social relation may lead to considerable difficulties on the ground. There is, on the one side, the plaintiff as the injured party, the "victim," or the object of a legal dispute; on the other side stands the lawyer as his or her "defender," as the actual litigant and expert in the law. Lawyers have "ready access to important symbols of political legitimacy," as Stuart A. Scheingold (2004 [1974], 134) noted. This includes access to the courts and thus to one of the most central institutions of power in a society. Moreover, lawyers are the "gatekeepers to legal institutions," and they "maintain the control over the course of litigation" (Felstiner *et al.* 1980, 645).

In Chapter 3, I used Kafka's parable to describe prosecutors' role as gatekeepers of the law. I now argue that human rights lawyers also hold considerable power in this regard. In comparison with corporate actors, they may appear relatively powerless. From the perspective of the plaintiffs, however, they also form part of an elite. Access to the knowledge of law and thus to the institutions of the state gives them an authority which in turn shapes their interaction with the people they represent *vis-à-vis* these institutions. The human rights attorneys decide which cases to bring to court and whom they provide with access to the legal system. The procedural circumstances and mechanisms of the law entail that lawyers have a decisive say in deciding who gets a voice in court cases. Like the "haves," they are also "repeat players," to return to Galanter's terminology (1974, 114). It is they who are able to question the hegemonic discourses of corporate and state actors through their legal knowledge and their expertise as lawyers. At the same time, this legal expertise gives them a dominant position *vis-à-vis* the plaintiffs.

Second, the relationship between lawyers and plaintiffs is characterized by the social positioning and the socio-economic background of the actors involved. In human rights litigation in Peru, the constellation is usually that of middle-class lawyers from Lima representing plaintiffs who belong to marginalized groups from the rural areas of the highlands. As I point out below, this constellation has specific consequences for the interaction with plaintiffs. Thus, the lawyer-plaintiff relationship is, on the one hand, foregrounded by the law and by legal requirements. However, on the other hand, it is also, to a large extent, marked by the socio-economic background of the persons involved. As I argue in the following section, the resulting relationship is perceived as problematic for different reasons and from different points of view.

Allegations of manipulation

The profession of lawyers is associated with specific social concepts. In many societies, there exist precise ideas of what a lawyer should and should not do, what expectations she should meet and what her relationship with the "clients" she represents should be like. These ideas are even more explicit when it comes to *human rights* lawyers. These attorneys are widely considered the "good guys," the "ethically superior lawyers," or even the "saviors," as Makau Mutua (2001) described it. According to this perception, human rights lawyers work for a low wage but under a high price of self-sacrifice. They uphold human rights and stand up for the protection of humanity; thus, they defend morally noble goals.[4]

These ideas of human rights lawyers can also be found in Peru, but only in a specific social sector and political camp. Within the left-liberal circles, the well-educated, upper middle-class segments in Lima and other large urban centers, human rights lawyers enjoy much support. Within Peru's grassroot movements, human rights lawyers hold a great deal of influence. This includes not only the NGOs and activists in Lima, but also the social movements in the highlands, including in the rural areas. The *doctoras* and *doctores* – as the human rights attorneys are mostly called – are treated with much appreciation and respect.

Beyond this social minority, however, human rights lawyers have a rather poor reputation in Peru. "Here, we are the *terrucos*, the terrorists," *Coordinadora* lawyer Mar told me. Since the time of Fujimori's regime, legal NGOs have often suffered public defamation for taking on the defense of suspected "terrorists" (see Chapter 1). There is a clear historical development in this respect. In the eighties and nineties, the human rights lawyers were accused of being "*los abogados de los terrucos,*" the terrorists' lawyers. Today, they are labeled the defenders of the *anti-mineros*, the radical anti-mining activists. These attempts to delegitimize human rights lawyers mainly come from the right-wing or conservative sections of the population who are close to the military and to Fujimori's political movement. Thus, they are the supporters of the groups of actors the legal NGOs had sought to bring to trial in the nineties for the abuses they had committed. Johana, a sociologist working with the *Coordinadora*, once told me that this was the greatest burden of the internal armed conflict for the human rights movement. In her opinion, it had been possible to put an end to Fujimori's regime and put him in prison for the crimes he had committed. However, the human rights movement had not managed to win the discursive struggles and to anchor human rights narratives in public discourse. In this counterhegemonic struggle, the movement had so far failed.

In the context of the social conflicts around mining, new accusations have been added to this outside perception. There is now the criticism that human rights lawyers and NGOs from Lima would manipulate parts of the impoverished population of the highlands to rebel against large-scale economic projects. Again, it is mainly actors from the politically conservative sector who uphold this position. These critics accuse human rights NGOs of being either agents of "foreign powers" or "radicals"

---

4 This is, at least, the common opinion on human rights lawyers, which is held by the political left-liberal camp. On the other side of the political spectrum, human rights lawyers in many countries are often seen as "traitors" who want to harm the nation state with their legal actions against authorities and government, as several NGO employees and lawyers in Berlin and London told me.

who, through their "extreme" political demands, seek to prevent any economic prosperity in the country. Furthermore, they are accused of inciting the local population to resist mining projects in affected regions and stirring up protests.

The fact that legal NGOs resort to the law only constitutes, in the logic of these critics, further proof that the human rights movement does not have the necessary political support and must therefore rely on other means to assert its allegedly dubious interests. One example of this kind of criticism is a question that a journalist asked during the press conference on the constitutional complaint against Chadín 2:

> *Journalist:* So, you have taken the legal route?
> *IDL lawyer Juan Carlos:* Yes, it's the legal route.
> *Journalist:* There is also [another] route; that is the social route. And the social route, whether we like it or not, is that many people are supporting the issue of Chadín 2. That is to say, we shouldn't close our eyes either, right? There is a group, yes, that will be affected [by Chadín 2], communities that will be affected; it's in the Marañón basin. But a large part of the population [of the region of Cajamarca] does want these projects to go ahead. You are taking the legal route because you do not have, let's say, the total support of the population. – *Press conference concerning the* amparo *claim against Chadín 2, May 2018, Cajamarca (field notes, own translation)*

On the one hand, this criticism is clearly directed at the lawyers, supposedly abusing the representation of their subordinates to pursue their own political interests. On the other hand, however, it also depicts an image of plaintiffs who are manipulated because they do not have the agency themselves to pursue their own political intentions. This criticism thus manifests a clear interpretation of the lawyer-plaintiff relationship as one marked by difference.

The fact that the plaintiffs come from the highlands plays a central role in this perception. In this sense, the accusations clearly include racist undertones. They are based on a discourse emanating mainly from the capital region, that the "uneducated" inhabitants of the highlands cannot represent themselves and are therefore susceptible to manipulation from NGOs and human rights lawyers from the coastal area, in particular from Lima. The local population's participation in social protests results, according to these critics, from the fact that they are either controlled, paid, or manipulated by the NGOs, not from their own political intentions. The plaintiffs' own rationality is thereby discursively denied.

In the context of transnational mining projects, these discourses were used even at the highest political level. For instance, former president Alan García invoked these stereotypes in a widely read series of newspaper columns to degrade the population of the Amazon and the Andean regions as second-class citizens who impeded the country's prosperity by opposing mining and other large-scale projects (García Pérez 2007a, 2007b, 2008, see also: Arellano-Yanguas 2011a, 107, Silva Santisteban

2013, 435). García saw the population's rejection of mining and other extractive projects as caused by "demagogy and fraud (*demagogia y engaño*)" from environmentalists. In his opinion, the "*medioambientalistas*" are, in reality, what he calls the disguised twenty-first century version of the "old, communist, anti-capitalist" who resists any investment (García Pérez 2007b, own translation).

In a similar way, a representative of the Swiss Embassy in Lima also referenced these same narratives and discourses when he wanted to make me understand the difficulties that transnational mining companies in Peru were facing. During an interview, he told me that when protests against a transnational mining project in the highland area occur it is often because the local population is "stirred up" by external individuals or organizations pursuing "political interests." He did not go into further detail about the extent to which he considered such political interests to be legitimate or not, but he underlined the difficulties this had caused for the mining companies. Quite directly, he mentioned that, in his perception, the local population was not actually against the mining projects but that they were, in most cases, simply misled by outsiders. This also conceals the discourse of denying the local population in the highlands their own agency in political debates.

Several authors have described these discourses in other political contexts in Latin America. Sergio Miguel Huarcaya (2015, 2019), for example, observed the same accusations in the Otavalo region in Ecuador. In the face of indigenous uprisings in the early nineties, Huarcaya wrote that "such a massive, well-organized, and countrywide mobilization did not fit the stereotype of the indio, which characterized indigenous Andeans as submissive and passive" (2019, 571). Convinced of the view that indigenous people were not in the position or condition to lead such protests, their opponents claimed that "leftist agitators were behind it," as Huarcaya further noted (*ibid.*, see also: Huarcaya 2015, 807). Similarly, Kregg Hetherington (2011, 39–40) described this phenomenon using examples from Paraguay. He showed how the *campesino* population there was accused of being easily manipulated by populist politicians because of their alleged inability to participate in rational political debates. Finally, Maruja Barrig (2008) noted how representatives of the Catholic Church have used the same discourse in relation with forced sterilizations in Peru. As Barrig described, women belonging to the indigenous or the *campesino* population have been labeled irrational beings in these debates. Old stereotypes have been used, which speak of the "indios" as "naive creatures, [who] do not reach the category of adults, are subject to manipulation, devoid of will, of the capacity to express themselves and to assume their own defense" (*ibid.*, 234, own translation).

The judicialized mining conflicts in Peru's highland region lent themselves particularly well to applying these discourses against human rights lawyers for three reasons. First, the human rights NGOs themselves have repeatedly argued that they represented the poor, the marginalized, and the disadvantaged, i.e. those who otherwise would not have the resources and opportunities to use the judicial system. Representing the weak is part of the human rights movement's actual *raison d'être*. In a way, the lawyers themselves have also reproduced the image of the disadvantaged highland population, even if they did not use the same racist stereotypes as their critics. Although human rights lawyers place great importance on the fact that court cases should not lead to a process of re-victimization of the persons concerned, the NGOs, through their narratives, convey specific ideas about the injured party or the "victim." As Mutua (2001) discussed, this is an integral part of the "savages-victims-saviors construction" with which the human rights movement struggles worldwide.

Second, there is clearly a relationship of dependence that binds the plaintiffs to the skills of the lawyers. As I have demonstrated in the previous chapters, human rights litigation in Peru requires specific expertise, which the general population lacks but which is made available to plaintiffs by lawyers. Furthermore, as I discussed at the beginning of this section, litigation is based on a specific form of access to the judicial system, which is provided by the lawyers as gatekeepers. It thus follows from the characteristics of law's relationships that plaintiffs rely on lawyers. However, this process-related dependency also entails social vulnerability for the plaintiffs, which can quickly lead to accusations of manipulation, whereas the complexity of law's processes renders it extremely difficult to overcome this dependency.

Third, the legal NGOs themselves postulated that they wanted to initiate political change with the legal processes. Their expectations of the law are precisely to conduct strategic litigation in order to change the prevailing circumstances, and they see legal processes as political struggles, as I discussed in the previous chapters. As a consequence, the human rights lawyers are especially vulnerable to the allegation of using the law for their own interests, or, as their critics claim, of having dubious or dark political motives. Along with the other two reasons, this explains why it is so difficult for the lawyers to negate the external accusations that they are manipulating the plaintiffs.

Speaking on behalf of whom?

In addition to these accusations of manipulation raised by outsiders, there are internal controversies that Peru's human rights lawyers are confronted with, which have arisen from the issue of representation. The incident in the constitutional complaint, in which the plaintiffs from Yagen suddenly wanted to withdraw from the lawsuit, is an example of how these internal controversies have manifested themselves on the ground.

During the press conference on the *amparo* claim, the NGO employees made great efforts to emphasize the support of the local population for the complaint. EarthRights International lawyer Juliana, for instance, stressed that the complaint had emerged from a long-term collaboration with the affected communities. Before the groups of journalists, she said, "Today, it is an act of filing the lawsuit, but in reality, the construction of this process has been a long process. It has been a serious, responsible process that the two organizations present here have worked on together with the communities. This has been a process of several years." A few days earlier, I had attended a public event at the Law Faculty of the *Universidad Católica* in Lima. On that occasion, EarthRights International, IDL, and some of the leaders of the protest movement against Chadín 2 had presented the constitutional complaint to the public. At this occasion, Juliana had already repeatedly pointed out that the lawsuit was a legal process that resulted from "joint work" or "joint efforts" (*un trabajo conjunto*) with the affected communities. She said that the lawsuit emerged from the *voluntad*, the wish or willingness of the *comunidades*.

This emphasis on long-term cooperation with the *comunidades* is an important cornerstone of the narrative invoked by the human rights lawyers in legitimizing their representation of plaintiffs. As I argued in the previous chapters, the legal NGO's aim is to "empower" the local communities and to strengthen their struggles through legal actions. In practice, this means that the affected communities or the individual plaintiffs should acquire the processes, that they become subjects in the court proceedings, and that they perceive a legal action as part of their own political struggle. This aspect was repeatedly raised in the legal capacity trainings that I attended during fieldwork. For example, Sonia, a lawyer working with a national NGO based in Lima, said, with regard to constitutional complaints, during a workshop in Celendín,

> So, one strategy... look, I'm not saying it's the only one, but one strategy is to demand your rights peacefully. Peacefully! Without exposing yourself, that's filing an *amparo*. But that doesn't mean that you give up the fight. No, it's just one more mechanism. [...] The *amparo* will go [...] accompanying your social struggle. At the same time that you fight, the *amparo* will also fight, right? – *Sonia*, Escuela de Líderes y Lideresas, *March 2017, Celendín (field notes, own translation)*

The idea behind this is that legal action can be used to steer social conflicts into institutional channels and thus prevent outbreaks of violence, as I mentioned in Chapter 2. In Sonia's opinion, legal action would reduce the exposure of the actors on the ground. In the case of Yagen, however, we could observe the opposite development. In this case, it was the lawsuit itself which the activists on the ground perceived as a danger to their own safety. Due to procedural requirements, the complaint's petitioners had to admit to the lawsuit by name and thus exposed themselves individually. Although constitutional complaints can be filed for the benefit of entire population groups, it is individual plaintiffs who put their name under the complaint. This individualization through the legal process can entail a great risk for the plaintiffs involved (see also: Santos 2005, 50, Kirsch 2018, 38).

In addition, during the workshop, Sonia underlined the importance of the plaintiffs actually becoming part of the legal proceedings. In that sense, she said, "We will contribute to the legal part, [but] you have to contribute to the social part" because "you are the protagonists of these lawsuits. Here, the lawyers are not the protagonists; we advise you, but you are the interested parties, [...] you are going to *build the process*. It's more *you* than *us*." To underline how much a lawsuit depends on the plaintiffs, Sonia added that a lawsuit is "a social construction; if you do not get involved, it is difficult (*es una construcción social; si no se involucran es difícil*)." From the point of view of the legal NGOs, this involvement of the plaintiffs in the litigation process is clearly aimed at the empowerment processes mentioned above on several occasions. The example from Yagen, as well as other cases, however, illustrates the limitations of this approach; this, too, is related to the relationships in law and to the requirements set by legal mechanisms.

One difficulty in the relationship between lawyers and plaintiffs is already evident in the geographical distance between the remote communities in the highlands and the NGO offices in Lima. As the example of *Grufides* demonstrated, there are individual NGOs working directly in the provinces. Most of the important legal NGOs are, however, based in Lima. Furthermore, the case of *Grufides* and, in particular, of its main lawyer Mirtha also highlighted the fact that human rights attorneys working directly in the mining regions are personally exposed and must live with reprisals when they take on politically sensitive cases. Attorneys working for national NGOs in Lima are better protected from these security risks.

From an office in Lima, however, it is more difficult to know and follow the local contexts and circumstances. With plaintiffs living in areas that are hours away from the nearest provincial capital and that often have inadequate road and communication networks, this is a major challenge. In the case of the constitutional complaint filed by IDL and EarthRights International on behalf of the communities in the Marañón basin, these aspects undoubtedly played a significant role. The geographical inaccessibility of the village of Yagen had obstructed close cooperation between the lawyers and the plaintiffs. Consequently, the attorneys did not succeed in overcoming the social distance that resulted in part from the geographical distance to the plaintiffs.

Furthermore, the example of Yagen also illustrates that the marginalized location of the communities is a major difficulty, not only geographically but also in terms of safety issues. As I mentioned above, the conflict over the Chadín 2 dam project led to social tensions within the village, which resulted in outbreaks of violence between community members. Under these circumstances, it had not been possible for the lawyers from IDL and EarthRights International to personally travel to Yagen. The ideal vision of these NGOs involves their cooperation with the communities taking place through the *asamblea*, the community assemblies. "The *asamblea* represents the door to a *comunidad*," an IDL lawyer told me, so any information concerning a lawsuit involving a community should be provided during these assemblies. As this lawyer further noted, the *asamblea* provides a familiar space for the *comuneros* and *comuneras*. It thereby helps to build trust and create transparency. Many human rights lawyers are convinced that the more openly a decision is discussed in the *asamblea*, the less danger there is of social tensions arising and camps forming within the *comunidad* due to a lawsuit.

In the case of the constitutional complaint against Chadín 2, however, such a negotiation through an assembly was not possible in the case of all the affected communities, in particular in the case of Yagen. Since the NGO staff could not travel to Yagen themselves, they could only negotiate with a small delegation of *ronderos* who occasionally traveled to Celendín to meet with social movement activists or to take part in events organized by the PIC. Therefore, the complaint did not have the necessary social backing. This clearly indicates how far removed the constitutional complaint against Chadín 2 was from the ideal that the NGO lawyers actually claim to pursue in their work with the communities.

Finally, to construct a process (*construir el proceso*), as Sonia framed it during the workshop in Celendín, in practice means to *technically* build a judicial case. This includes, first, writing a complaint and filing it with the judicial authorities. In doing so, however, not only the willingness – *voluntad*, as Juliana noted – is necessary, but also the resources and the knowledge about the judicial processes. In terms of this knowledge, the plaintiffs depend on the lawyers since they are the legal experts. This illustrates the specific role that legal processes impose on lawyers. David, who works with *Fedepaz*, considers his role as a lawyer to be primarily that of a "technical advisor (*un asesor técnico*)," as he told me. In our conversations, David repeatedly argued that human rights lawyers who call for protests and participate in them themselves do not understand what their role is.

At the same time, as I mentioned above, through their expertise and their access to the judicial system, lawyers hold a great deal of power in their relations with the plaintiffs. On the one hand, they are thus, in their self-perception, only the implementing force – the technicians who have the necessary knowledge, "take instructions,"[5] and execute the decisions of the plaintiffs. On the other hand, however, it is this expertise that gives them the power to act as gatekeepers, to influence decisions, and to set strategies within the legal actions. Although the human rights lawyers seek to adopt a participatory approach and to ensure that the plaintiffs are involved in the proceedings, the role established by the law continually throws them back into these power relations. This raises questions of representation, such as, for example,

5 Using the example of transnational lawsuits against parent companies, I discussed elsewhere (Lindt 2020) how Peruvian human rights lawyers view this issue of taking instructions from the plaintiffs and how they distinguish themselves in this respect from *pro bono* lawyers in the Global North.

who has a say in these legal processes, who speaks for whom, and to whom do the lawyers provide access to the legal system. It is precisely these aspects of the legal relationship, which are evoked in litigation and promoted by legal processes, that demonstrate to human rights lawyers a further limitation of the law. In particular, these circumstances raise questions of whether legal mobilization can actually be an emancipatory means not only *on behalf of* "the weak," but also an actual "weapon *of* the weak," to refer to James Scott's (1985) term.

Beyond law and litigation

The relationship between lawyers and plaintiffs as well as the above-mentioned debates that having rights is often not enough illustrate the limitations of the law that Peruvian human rights lawyers face. As I have argued, these limitations are inherent to the law. Therefore, these limitations of law cannot be circumvented or overcome by the human rights lawyers; or if they can, it would be difficult. In the last section of this chapter, I discuss a third limitation of the law, not from the perspective of human rights lawyers, but from that of corporate actors. These limitations, which are also inherent to the law, explain why human rights lawyers still hold on to their belief in the law despite the limitations I have pointed out in the previous sections.

Setting limits to corporate power

> I think all of us in this room, we've had the opportunity to make a mistake along the way, and I think what is really important is to not get defensive and actually take the opportunity and learn from that issue or whatever caused it. – *Gary Goldberg, CEO Newmont Mining Corporation, UN Forum on Business and Human Rights, November 2018, Geneva*

In November 2018, representatives of TNCs, states, and civil society organizations met in Geneva for the seventh UN Forum on Business and Human Rights. The forum began with an opening plenary in the pompous Assembly Hall of the *Palais des Nations*. Part of this plenary was a "conversation with business leaders." The then chairman of the UN Working Group on Business and Human Rights, Dante Pesce, discussed, with CEOs of various TNCs, "experiences with human rights issues along their corporations' journey" in recent years. Gary Goldberg, who was the CEO of Newmont Mining Corporation at the time, was one of the corporate managers participating in this discussion. When Dante Pesce asked him to share his experience with human rights issues, Goldberg admitted that his company had made mistakes "along the way." Moreover, he replied,

> I'll point to an issue in Peru where we have had ... actually an ongoing issue where ... / it is a land rights issue around a mine next to our Yanacocha mine, at Conga, where we acquired the land from ... essentially a family back in the early nineties, and in 2011 the land was occupied by the descendants of this family. [...] And at that time a decision was made to go through a legal process, which is quite an extensive legal process to address the landownership. We have now gone through the courts, both in the U.S. and Peru, and... they have come out with decisions that we follow the right process for acquiring that land. Yet that hasn't yet resolved the issue. [...]
>
> You know, at the end of the day for me, I am not happy with the situation at all. I think we took a very legalistic approach to try to resolve it, and it is still not resolved today. And I think, had that situation posed itself today, we'd have taken a different approach based on what we have learned so far. [...] [Newmont Mining's experience in Cajamarca] just shows that the different approach [of] listening and actually not taking the legal approach – I think it has been mentioned by several people here today: Don't depend on the law. Get down, and listen to the people, and understand what their concerns are. That is critical. – *Gary Goldberg, CEO Newmont Mining Corporation, UN Forum on Business and Human Rights, November 2018, Geneva*

In his remarks, Goldberg referred to the land dispute that Newmont Mining's subsidiary Minera Yanacocha had been having with the Chaupe family for several years. Goldberg admitted that in this case it was not possible to use the law to obtain the land of the Chaupe family. The "legalistic approach" had not led to success from the point of view of the corporation. Goldberg did not specifically mention that the company had failed in the criminal case against the Chaupe family. In his opinion, the court cases had confirmed that the company had taken the "right process" for acquiring the disputed land, which is a rather surprising interpretation of the outcome of the criminalization case and the judicial process in the United States. As we have seen in Chapter 5, the Chaupe family was acquitted of the charge of illegal occupation of land. Furthermore, the U.S. courts had not even dealt materially with the conflict between the mining company and the family but had dismissed the case on jurisdictional grounds. Whether the Chaupe family or the company are the legally entitled owners of Tragadero Grande would only be decided in a civil case in Peru, which has not yet been concluded. Therefore, it comes as no surprise that Goldberg is dissatisfied with the strategy of relying on the law, although he claims that the judiciary has proven the company right.

From Goldberg's point of view, the legalistic approach had failed. The judicial system in Perú had set limitations to the corporation's power by acquitting the Chaupe family from the allegation of having illegally occupied the disputed plot of land. I have already discussed at length how this court order was obtained. What is interesting to note in this case, in addition, are the alternatives that Gary Goldberg suggests in the face of these limitations the corporations faced because of the law. Instead of taking disputes to the court, he proposes that one should "get down, and listen to the people, and understand what their concerns are." Thereby he referred to the CSR programs that Minera Yanacocha has been conducting for years in its direct sphere of influence in Cajamarca. As I mentioned in the second section of this chapter, mine opponents in the region argue that with these programs the company is attempting to buy the support of the population by profiting from their disadvantaged economic situation. From the company's point of view, however, it is a matter of clarifying needs and of thereby preventing or eliminating disputes. In retrospect, Goldberg believed that this "direct dialogue" with the local population is a far better approach than relying on the law and negotiating conflicts in court.

This indicates that even corporate managers such as Goldberg recognize the emancipatory power of law. With his comment, Goldberg acknowledged that legal action can also lead to companies not always "[coming] out ahead" in court (Galanter 1974), and the law may not always be on the side of the "haves" (*ibid.*). Law and litigation thus set limits for the powerful. As Goldberg's statement further illustrates, if corporate actors are unable to use legal means to defend their interests, they turn away from legality and rely on approaches outside the law. Thereby, they attempt to maintain their hegemonic position.

Alternative dispute resolution

This turn away from law is what Laura Nader coined "alternative dispute resolution" (Nader 1999, 304–9). Along with Ugo Mattei, Nader observed how powerful actors search for alternatives to the law as soon as judicial authorities decide against their hegemonic positions (Mattei and Nader 2008, 18–9, 76–7). In doing so, the powerful resort to extrajudicial alternatives, which ostensibly aim at harmony rather than adjudication and are intended to create a consensus between the parties to the conflict (Nader 1999, 309). According to Mattei and Nader, this strategy is aimed at suppressing resistance, "by socializing them toward conformity by means of consensus-building mechanisms, by valorizing consensus, cooperation, passivity, and docility, and by silencing people who speak out angrily" (2008, 77).

In a similar way, Pistor (2019, 139–40) described corporations' turn away from law by using the example of pharmaceutical companies defending patent rights. As soon as they are defeated in court, companies turn to the mechanisms of investor-state dispute settlements (ISDS) and attempt to have their privileges defended before this private institution. A third example of corporations' search for alternative routes involves the out-of-court settlements that I mentioned in the discussion of transnational lawsuits in Chapter 6. These settlements are aimed at reaching an agreement in the private sphere rather than in the public space of a court. They are, in this sense, "removed from public view," as Eckert (2021) put it. Furthermore, out-of-court settlements are based on private negotiation and not on adjudication, which is an external evaluation by judicial authorities according to binding norms. As I have discussed with regard to the Monterrico case, this leads to situations in which the political demands and moral claims underlying a lawsuit go unaddressed (see also: Lindt 2020).

As these examples discussed by Nader, Pistor, and myself have revealed, corporate actors seek extrajudicial solutions as soon as they believe themselves to be on the defensive in the courtroom. The Comaroffs (2006) criticized the juridification of conflicts as a tendency toward depoliticization. Based on the analysis in the previous chapters, I argue, in turn, that it is precisely the recourse to such alternative dispute resolutions or other extrajudicial mechanisms that depoliticizes disputes and social conflicts. Extrajudicial dispute resolution serves as a sort of "corporate antipolitics," to use Suzana Sawyer's (2004, 118) wording. In this sense, I follow the position of Eckert *et al.* (2012a, 5–6), who questioned the Comaroffs' depoliticization claim. To "[g]et down, and listen to the people, and understand what their concerns are," as Goldberg framed it, allows companies to use their power in private negotiation processes, thereby "silencing people who speak or act angrily" (Nader 1999, 308). This is what may contribute to a depoliticization of the claims from below.

Conclusion

As I have discussed in the previous chapters, due to various obstacles and hurdles, the idea in legal liberalism that everyone is equal before the law is often illusory in everyday judicial practices in Peru. In my case studies, corruption and undue influence on the side of corporate actors prevented access to the legal system; and the abuse or manipulation of the law led to inappropriate proceedings that did not comply with legal standards. These mechanisms set limits on the use of law by marginalized groups. At the same time, the criminalization cases in Cajamarca, for example, demonstrated that, if social movements succeed in using the "indeterminacy of law" to their advantage, counterhegemonic positions can also be enforced in the courtroom (see also: Marks 2007). The judicialization of social protests and the reliance on legal mobilization offers social movements opportunities to use institutional mechanisms; it allows them to make themselves heard by state authorities, to prevent outbreaks of violence, and to question and challenge differences in power *vis-à-vis*, for example, corporate actors. So far in this book, I have argued that the difficulties faced by the Peruvian human rights movement lie not in the law itself but in the lack of implementation or in the manipulation of existing legal norms. This chapter has taken us a step further in examining some of the limitations inherent to law itself.

In addition, this chapter has asked what limitations the law sets against those who attempt to mobilize it from below. In this sense, it sheds light on the fact that law and legal mechanisms themselves also have inherent limits that complicate the human rights lawyers' counterhegemonic work. I have identified limitations, especially in the insufficient power of human rights discourses and in the lawyer-plaintiff relationship. As the example of Goldberg and the alternative dispute resolution mechanisms illustrate, however, the law also sets limits for powerful actors. This indicates that there is still hope for the legal mobilization from below and adds to the observation of the ambiguity of law I have described in my previous analysis.

Conclusion. The ambiguous forces of law

This book's analysis of the processes of judicialization in Peru's mining conflicts has revealed that everyone is equal before the law but that some are more equal than others. Courtrooms have become central battlegrounds for disputes over transnational mining projects. I have discussed how social movements as well as corporate and state actors actively use legal means to assert their interests in these social conflicts. Legality has provided the language, procedural mechanisms, and normative framework for negotiating conflicts that were previously fought out in the political field.

The examples of the mining conflicts Conga in Cajamarca and Río Blanco in Piura have demonstrated that the Peruvian justice system is "slow and not always just." Legal proceedings concerning human rights violations committed by state actors in connection with the two transnational mining projects illustrated this in an exemplary manner. The case studies that I analyzed in this book have revealed the obstacles and hurdles with which the Peruvian human rights movement is confronted in its attempts to mobilize the law *from below*. The local judicial system is characterized by corruption, the alleged lack of political will on the part of the authorities, practical problems – for example, in obtaining evidence – structural deficiencies, and weak institutions.

I argued that the figure of the public prosecutor plays a decisive role in criminal proceedings against corporate and state actors. As a sort of gatekeeper of the law, prosecutors render human rights litigation difficult or even impossible. Under these circumstances, hardly any court case involving allegations of human rights violations reaches the trial stage. Within criminal proceedings, however, the trial constitutes a decisive phase in which the legal responsibility of defendants would be addressed and negotiated. In many of the lawsuits that I analyzed, adjudication had become a distant goal that could not be achieved. In this way, corporate and state abuses have often remained unpunished. The difficulty in most cases lies not in the law and legal norms themselves but in their implementation and application to specific cases involving powerful actors.

At the same time, criminal proceedings against social movement activists are progressing relatively easily in Peru. In contrast to complaints filed by legal NGOs and social movements, this mobilization *from above* leads to criminal investigations. The resulting legal proceedings often remain open for a long time and in some cases result in trials and adjudication. I traced an emblematic lawsuit against activists and social leaders involved in protests against the Conga mining project in Cajamarca. The criminal proceedings against sixteen activists from Sorochuco and Celendín revealed how this criminalization of social protest works and what it means for individual defendants to "stand before the law" (Ewick and Silbey 1998).

By characterizing three different ways in which law's domination is exercised in these criminalization cases, I described the threat posed by law and legality – both on a political level for social movements and on a personal level for the individual activists. The domination *of* law includes aspects inherent in law and legality, such as its architecture, language, rituals, and hierarchies. The domination *by* law is related to state and governmental authorities' attempts to strengthen legal norms in order to regulate specific parts of the population. In Peru's mining conflicts, the law's code became, by itself, a source of danger for the social movements because their protest activities were subject to heavy penalties. In recent years, the national authorities in Lima repeatedly made use of legislative modifications to prevent or impede social protests against major economic projects in the provinces.

However, I have also shown that it is usually not this form of law's domination that poses the greatest threat to social movements, but it is rather a third form, which I categorized as *manipulation* or *misuse of* law. In the case study described, the criminal offense of kidnapping was used as a pretext for declaring a protest action to be criminal. The defendants and their lawyer, however, claimed that the protest had constituted a legitimate form of political expression. According to their view, it was only due to a misuse of the law on the part of the complainants and the public prosecutor's office that the proceedings reached the trial phase. During the oral hearings, the activists' lawyer managed to restore the rule of law and obtain an acquittal. In doing so, she also mobilized the law and explicitly invoked procedural norms to prove the legal manipulation of the opposing party. The human rights lawyer was thus able to put an end to the abuse of the law by making use of law's mechanisms herself.

Both the example of the legal mobilization *from below* and *from above* point to the room for negotiation that exists in the legal sphere. Litigation is about applying generally established norms to specific cases. The implementation and application of legal texts to concrete cases may lead to indeterminate outcomes. This indeterminacy is part of the nature of law, as various authors have described before. Many of them considered the law's indeterminacy to provide an opportunity for elites to use the law to their advantage (see, for example: Kress 1989, Miéville 2005). In contrast, I agree with Marks (2007) that the law's indeterminacy leaves room for negotiation in order to impose counterhegemonic demands from below as well. Legal NGOs and human rights organizations in Peru consider the law to be a contested field in which it is not always clear from the outset which positions will prevail. Through strategic litigation and by changing the legal opportunity structure of the parties involved, it is, in their view, possible to enforce demands from below and to legally challenge the hegemonic position of economic and political elites. The legal NGOs hope that this way of using the law in a counterhegemonic manner on behalf of marginalized groups of the population could initiate social change. In a nutshell, this is the key expectation that the Peruvian human rights movement places on the law.

In chapters 5 and 6 I discussed different strategies of the legal NGOs for overcoming or circumventing the obstacles in the domestic justice system. In both chapters the collaboration with allies abroad as well as the transnational dimension of the social movements' struggles played a crucial role. On the one hand, the Peruvian human rights NGOs have attempted to influence the domestic judicial authorities by relying on the support of transnational advocacy networks. As I have indicated, this can be a promising approach to prevent legal mobilization *from above*. The international attention paid to a specific lawsuit may protect activist defendants from the misuse of law and from criminalization. In this sense, international NGOs and advocacy networks may support counterhegemonic discourses that challenge the criminalization of social protest. However, these transnational advocacy campaigns are often not effective enough to significantly advance the legal mobilization *from below* and thus to overcome impunity for human rights violations. Moreover, the counterglobalization aimed at by such transnational advocacy campaigns also involves risks for the social movements on the ground as well as for the individual persons concerned, as the case of Máxima Acuña has made clear. This is mainly because legal processes lead to an individualization of broader social conflicts, and individual litigants are strongly exposed in this way.

A similar pattern of risks became apparent in the transnational legal actions against parent companies. In these court cases, too, legal activism entails a certain danger for plaintiffs and for social movements on the ground, for example with regard to out-of-court settlements and financial compensation. Under certain circumstances, however, the strategy of litigation *abroad* may have a positive effect on legal proceedings before domestic courts. The FLA application of behalf of Elmer Campos was a case that demonstrated the potential of addressing foreign courts. Thus, this chapter again demonstrated the importance of considering contextual aspects in order to assess the strategy of legal activism and the emancipatory force of legal means.

Finally, in the last chapter I illustrated that the law also has inherent limitations that confront human rights lawyers with doubts about their strategies. I thereby discussed that even those actors who otherwise rely on and trust so heavily in legality become skeptical about the law under certain circumstances. The human rights lawyers learned that relying on the "right of having rights" (Arendt 1998 [1951], 614) and on human rights discourses in general is often not enough to overcome the hardships faced by local communities in Peru. Especially in view of corporate development projects and CSR programs, the resources and strategies of legal NGOs appear to be insufficient. An additional limitation of law arises from the relationship between plaintiffs and lawyers, as I have argued. This relationship is largely predetermined by law's mechanisms. However, in the everyday practices of legal activism, the characteristics of this relationship may lead to social tensions or disagreements on the ground. In human rights litigation in Peru, there are thus not only differences of power between the parties in dispute, but also between plaintiffs and their lawyers.

The processes of judicialization that I have analyzed in this book demonstrates how legal disputes are characterized by struggles over hegemonic positions and discourses in a society. Law is a contested field in this context. Access to institutional power, financial resources, powerful allies, and political influence are important elements of effective legal mobilization. These elements often decide who "comes out ahead in court" (Galanter 1974). At the same time, however, I have also made clear that the use of law can help to strengthen *both* hegemonic and counterhegemonic positions. This points to the ambiguity of law as both a hegemonic means of regulation and control and a counterhegemonic means of resistance.

On closer inspection of this field, it becomes clear that the liberal principle of equality before the law does not correspond to the patterns and processes I observed in my case studies. Law is a social practice and is thus also subject to the processes of negotiation and power within a society. I contend that the various aspects I addressed in the analyses in this book have pointed to different forces of law. We can observe these various forces of law in (1) the hegemony of law, and (2) in the issue of law as a weapon of the weak. I address these different forces of law in the following.

Law's hegemony

The first aspect of the forces of law that I repeatedly encountered in my case studies was the hegemony of law. Law's hegemony is based, on the one hand, on the domination *of* law, as I characterized it in Chapter 4. Judicial authorities and institutions hold enormous authority within a society. Moreover, they are equipped with the power of the state. Law intimidates, controls, and regulates; it punishes and acquits; and it judges everyone.

On the other hand, law's hegemony is also based on the "force of law" (Bourdieu 1987) to settle disputes and to mediate between opposing parties. That is the functioning of law as a social practice. In this regard, law provides the grounds for negotiations through its "intrinsic procedural nature" (Rodríguez-Garavito 2011b, 273). By setting a central frame of reference that regulates coexistence in a society and that permeates the everyday life of people, law's hegemony becomes effective. However, this notion of hegemony is not the same as what theorists such as the Comaroffs

(2006) have described when claiming that law serves as a *hegemonic means for elites* to maintain their power and to impede political change from below. Rather, in the notion of *law's hegemony*, it is the law itself that holds a hegemonic position in society.

We could observe law's hegemony in the criminalization cases in Cajamarca, for example. The activists from Sorochuco and Celendín took part in the hearings, although they had doubts that the judicial authorities and the complainants' side would respect and comply with the procedural rules of criminal law. The activists agreed to participate in the legal processes, obeyed the justice system, and were not resistant to the law. By participating in the court hearings and by following the judicial mechanisms in the criminal process, the activists expressed their concession with law and legality. In a Gramscian sense, this highlights the fact that the way in which law is hegemonic is not based on the mere exercise of force, but on the consent of the actors involved. It is a rule by consent and not a rule by force in which law regulates and controls the population (see also: Im 1991, 127).

On the other hand, mining companies also accept the hegemony of the law. I illustrated this with the example of Minera Yanacocha and its parent company, Newmont Mining Corporation. It is true that the companies have repeatedly appealed judgments given by the courts, thereby expressing their disagreement with the rulings. Furthermore, corporate actors have recurrently sought to evade litigation. They attempted to keep the issue of their legal responsibility out of the courtrooms, for example when it came to proceedings over police violence in the context of their mining activities. However, all these efforts were made *within* the framework and *in accordance with* the procedural requirements of the law itself. Thus, corporate actors obeyed the justice system as well. In addition, I mentioned that corporations resort to options outside the law, such as out-of-court settlements, when their legal mobilization fails. This does not call into question the hegemony of the law, but rather underlines the force of law and its hegemonic position in society. It demonstrates that law holds the force to regulate powerful actors, too.

With this research I contend that in disputes and social conflicts law serves as a powerful tool for those who can best use its mechanisms and institutions. Epistemologically, this supports the approach of closely examining what happens in the judicialization processes and considering both the *processes* and the *outcomes*, as I suggested in the introduction (see also: Sieder *et al.* 2005, 16). Based on the analysis of the two mining conflicts, I argue that law's hegemony involves both the elites – be they political or economic elites – and civil society actors and marginalized population groups recognizing law as a binding social framework for the resolution of disputes.

It is the law's codes, i.e. the established norms of a society, that define which behavior is permissible and which is not. The fact that both the elites and marginalized groups and most of the population groups in between acknowledge and recognize the law as such a binding framework makes the hegemony of the law effective within a society. It is true that law, in some cases, helps elites maintain their hegemonic position, as the Comaroffs (2006) argued. However, at the same time, law also helps social movements challenge the elites' discourse and position, as my case studies revealed. This is what Merry references when noting that "law constructs power and provides a way to challenge that construction" (1990, 8).

Being in the right and gaining recognition of being right through a legal process gives social movements and marginalized groups a powerful position, too. This is reflected in the expectation that Peru's human rights movement places on the law. "Justice means to know the truth," David of *Fedepaz* told me. Knowing the truth is, first, a central aim for the directly affected people, the "victims" of human rights violations. I argue that "being in the right" and having the law on their side gives moral authority to those affected by human rights violations. In this perception of legality, we can again observe the hegemony of the law. The force of the law is to identify and acknowledge a human rights violation as such. A judgment clearly identifies who is the perpetrator and who is the victim, whose rights have been violated, who is punished, and who receives compensation. To receive public recognition of the suffering someone has experienced constitutes, in the Peruvian context, a central part of obtaining justice.

Second, establishing the truth through legal proceedings is also pivotal for the human rights movement and its political struggles. In the cases of human rights violations that the legal NGOs bring to court, it is, first, a matter of obtaining public recognition for the suffering of the complainants. Second, it is also a matter of getting official acknowledgment of the guilt of the perpetrators, which may result in sanctions and punishment. Third, relying on the law is about officially attributing responsibility, for example, to a mining company or a state institution like the Ministry of the Interior. This is aimed at disclosing the underlying chains of responsibility that link the direct perpetrators to the "intellectual" perpetrators of the abuses. By pointing to these chains of responsibility, the human rights movement seeks to bring about change within state institutions and in the behavior of corporate actors. For Peruvian human rights lawyers, the court cases are not only legal battles, but also political struggles. Taking a case to court therefore does not mean depoliticization, but rather constitutes a political act.

Finally, the fact that the law is such a contested field also points to the notion of the hegemony of law within a society. More specifically, it explains why it is so important for both elites and social movements' actors to gain influence in the legal sphere. In many areas of a society, law holds a decisive defining power. It decides on admissibility and prohibition, on possession and entitlement, on abuse and legal redress. Those who have the law on their side have access to one of the most important state institutions. This also applies to those actors who otherwise have little political or economic influence. Thus, if they succeed in mobilizing its resources in their favor, the law can help social movements bring about social change. At the same time, however, this also means that the failure of social movements in legal struggles can lead to a lack of social change. In other words, it means that elites can use their dominance in the legal sphere to prevent social change. Therefore, whoever has the power of law will prevail in the social struggles at stake.

The emancipatory force of law or law as a weapon of the weak?

Thus, the law can be and is mobilized both *from above* and *from below* to enforce political interests. The discourse in legal anthropological research on law's ambiguity has also been confirmed by the example of social conflicts over mining in Peru. However, with regard to the mobilization of law *from below*, the question remains whether law actually serves as a "weapon of the weak" in the sense of Scott (1985), or whether it is – in the case of Peru's human rights movement – another social group that uses law as a weapon *on behalf of* the weak. This issue also raises important aspects with regard to the ambiguous forces of law.

As previously mentioned, one of the human rights lawyers' fundamental tasks in the legal struggles over transnational mining projects is to build trust in the judicial authorities among people who live on the margins of the state. These groups of the population feel abandoned and forgotten by the state's institutions and authorities, as various authors have described (see, for example: Poole 2004, 36, 38, Yashar 2005, 6, Nuijten and Lorenzo 2009, 101). The experience of police violence and the criminalization of social protest has reinforced the negative attitude that many activists and ordinary citizens in the mining regions hold toward state institutions. Under these conditions, legal NGOs sought to convince the people they represent before the courts that it makes sense to use the law – not only to counter criminalization, but also to demand justice for suffered abuses.

In comparison to the people they represent before court, human rights lawyers form part of a national elite. Most of them belong to the middle class of Lima, have a regular income, and have a good education. Within the legal sphere, they are experts and "repeat players" (Galanter 1974, 114) in litigation. In comparison with the power of the "armies of corporate lawyers" that the mining companies hire to defend their interests, the human rights lawyers may seem relatively "weak." However, compared to the people they represent in court, they have a powerful position. This reveals that the question of who is among the "weak" in the legal processes is relative and highly contextual.

At the same time, human rights activism in Peru is not, however, a privilege of a group of middle-class lawyers from the capital that is brought to the marginalized regions of the country. Rights discourses and the reliance on legal demands form part of the social movements' political mobilization on the ground and provide the activists with an important frame of reference to make demands on the state. The juridification has strengthened their social protest and allowed them to establish networks and to take up larger political discourses. Law and legality provide the language for their resistance and their protest against corporate and state actors' behavior within the social conflicts. Thus, within the social movements a strong "rights consciousness" (Epp 1998, 13–7) was already present before the judicialization of the mining conflicts.

Thus, there is a part of the population that feels forgotten and abandoned by the state but that, on the other hand, claims its rights as citizens of that very same state. In this way, the social movements in Peru analyzed in this research differ, for example, from anarchist or indigenous movements, which question the state per se, its institutions and its influence. While the local population in Peru's mining regions distrusts the state institutions as well, they, at the same time, adhere to the actual idea of the state, in particular to the idea of the state as a guarantor of rights. This points to a phenomenon that Eckert (2006) observed in her research as well. As she wrote, legalism from below creates new relationships "between the governing and the governed" (*ibid.*, 70), thus between the state and its population. By mobilizing the law, the governed make demands on the state and claim to become beneficiaries of its institutions and services. Thereby, they confirm the importance and the power of the state and its institutions within society. If the movements were to reject the state, they would not invoke its legal norms. This explains why state institutions are met with mistrust but why they are nevertheless accepted and respected by the population in Peru's highland regions.

It was in this context that human rights NGOs sought to use the domestic justice system with all its mechanisms and instruments to the benefit of these marginalized population groups. As I mentioned before, it was not these legal NGOs that promoted the *juridification* of social protest. However, these organizations were decisively involved in using rights not only discursively in political struggles, but also as a means in court. Thus, they played a pivotal role in the *judicialization* of social conflicts. In their strategies, human rights lawyers build on the fact that the state plays an important role for the people in the mining regions. Through the mobilization of law, they aimed to restore people's trust in the state. The legal NGOs' aim, in this sense, was not to act against the state, but rather to strengthen its institutions. In the perspective of human rights movements, litigation is intended to restore the rule of law and thus to reaffirm the functioning of the institutions. This in turn should ensure that marginalized population groups can also benefit from the rule of law and that their fundamental rights are guaranteed and respected.

I argue that this is the emancipatory force of law.

Furthermore, the human rights organizations that I have portrayed in this book perceive the strategy of legal mobilization as a way to strengthen marginalized population groups in their negotiating position *vis-à-vis* state or corporate actors. Empowerment processes are part of the legal advocacy trainings they conduct with communities and grassroots organizations. The aim of this strategy is to make plaintiffs aware of the legal mechanisms available to them. Thus, the legal NGOs actually attempt to make the law a weapon of the weak.

In the field, I witnessed how individual complainants could become eloquent users of the law and acquire a great deal of knowledge about legal processes. Thus, they are unexperienced and "one-shotters" (Galanter 1974) in legal proceedings, but they know their rights, and as a result, they have specific expectations of the justice system. According to my observations, the people concerned acquired this legal expertise both by participating in the NGOs' legal capacity trainings and by being involved as litigants in lawsuits on human rights violations. Thus, the judicialization led to an empowerment process among the involved complaints and activists.

However, I had a completely different perception after accompanying the criminalized activists from Sorochuco and Celendín to the court hearings. They had also acquired a certain expertise about their rights, but in the context of law's domination, which the actual proceedings revealed, they became largely powerless. During the trial, the activists depended on their lawyers, who told them when and how to speak, who suggested the legal strategy, and who presented the arguments that eventually led to the acquittal. The criminalized activists were dependent on the expert knowledge required in the legal sphere, which the lawyers have due to their training and experience, and which they themselves lack as ordinary citizens. This central importance of expert knowledge in litigation fundamentally calls into question the idea that the "weak" can use the law as a weapon by themselves when standing before the law.

In addition, further doubts about the notion of law as a weapon of the weak become apparent when looking at the original concept as Scott (1985) used it. In his research, Scott described the way peasants develop strategies of opposition in their everyday life and how they engage in so-called "everyday forms of resistance." In social anthropology and other disciplines, the concept was subsequently used by various authors to categorize legal activism from below in general as a powerful instrument of "the weak" (see, for example: Sieder 2000, Eckert 2006, Jacquot and Vitale 2014, Gloppen 2018).

However, as I demonstrated using the criminalization cases in Cajamarca, judicial proceedings can have a massive impact on the everyday lives and social relations of the defendants. What I found in the field, however, was that the use of legal mechanisms is, for complainants or activist defendants, anything but ordinary or linked to their "everyday lives." Most of my interlocutors had never before been involved in litigation. To enter into the field of the law means for them to – literally and figuratively – leave their everyday life. People directly involved in the court cases constantly stressed about the loss of time due to the court cases. Furthermore, they were unfamiliar with the judicial field, with the legal authorities, and with the processes and practices the legal sphere entails.

In this sense, the knowledge and resource requirements that make access to the legal system possible in the first place prevent "the weak" from using these mechanisms. Only when they have a "support structure" (Epp 1998) that provides them with legal expertise and knowledge, financial resources, and political influence can they successfully participate in court proceedings. Only in this way can they gain the opportunity to "come out ahead in court" (Galanter 1974). In the case of the legal disputes in Peru's mining regions, it was the legal NGOs that provided this support structure. However, to my understanding, once litigants have received this support and thus successfully strengthened their legal opportunity structure they no longer belong to the "weak."

All these aspects point to the fact that the legal sphere is not only a highly contested field, but also an ambiguous field that allows for changing positions. I started this book with the notion of, on the one hand, the activists on the ground, who do not believe in the law because "all judges and prosecutors in Peru are corrupt, and the law only serves the elites." On the other hand, there were the human rights lawyers who enthusiastically spoke of strategic litigation and the use of the law on behalf of marginalized and vulnerable groups of the population. Both positions were contested and have undergone considerable changes on the journey that the judicialization processes took.

I argue that this reveals the ambiguous forces of law.

Bibliography

Books, articles, and (online) reports

Action Solidarité Tiers Monde (ASTM). 2018. *Comprendre le monde. Creer la solidarité.* Luxembourg.

Agamben, G. 2010. *Die souveräne Macht und das nackte Leben.* Deutsche Erstausgabe, Originalausgabe 1995. Frankfurt am Main: Suhrkamp.

Alayza Moncloa, A. 2007. *No pero sí: comunidades y minería: consulta y consentimiento previo, libre e informado en el Perú.* Lima: CooperAcción.

Amancio, N.L. 2015. Chadín II, la megahidroeléctrica de Odebrecht que inundará el Marañón. *Ojo Público (online)*, 13 Aug.

Amancio, N.L. 2016. Perú quiere más minería, más industria, más China. *openDemocracy (online)*, 27 Jul.

Amnesty International. 2016. *Write for Rights 2016: A Human Rights Education Pack.* London: Amnesty International.

Amnesty International. 2017. Perú: Amnistía Internacional llevó cientos de miles de mensajes de solidaridad a Máxima Acuña [online]. Available from: https://www.amnesty.org/es/latest/news/2017/02/peru-amnistia-internacional-llevo-cientos-de-miles-de-mensajes-de-solidaridad-a-maxima-acuna-1/ [Accessed 3 Aug 2018].

Amnesty International. 2018. *Una receta para criminalizar: Personas defensoras del ambiente, el territorio y la tierra en Perú y Paraguay.* London.

Anders, G. and M. Nuijten, eds. 2017. *Corruption and the Secret of Law: A Legal Anthropological Perspective.* Aldershot, UK: Ashgate Publishing.

Andina (online). 2017. Ministra Pérez Tello: El Estado tiene la obligación de defender a los más débiles. *Andina – Agencia peruana de noticias*, 14 Feb.

Arellano-Yanguas, J. 2011a. *¿Minería sin fronteras? Conflicto y desarrollo en regiones mineras del Perú.* Lima: Pontificia Universidad Católica del Perú.

Arellano-Yanguas, J. 2011b. Aggravating the Resource Curse: Decentralisation, Mining and Conflict in Peru. *Journal of Development Studies*, 47(4), pp. 617–38.

Arellano-Yanguas, J. 2014. Religion and Resistance to Extraction in Rural Peru: Is the Catholic Church Following the People? *Latin American Research Review*, 4(49), pp. 61–80.

Arellano-Yanguas, J. 2016. Mining Policies in Humala's Peru: A Patchwork of Improvised Nationalism and Corporate Interests. *In*: P. Haslam and P. Heidrich, eds. *The Political Economy of Natural Resources and Development: From Neoliberalism to Resource Nationalism*. London: Routledge, pp. 174–90.

Arendt, H. 1998. *Elemente und Ursprünge totaler Herrschaft: Antisemitismus, Imperialismus, Totalitarismus*. 6. Auflage, Übersetzung, Originalausgabe 1951. München: Piper.

Asociación por los Derechos Civiles (ADC). 2008. *El litigio estratégico como herramienta para la exigibilidad del derecho a la educación*. Buenos Aires: ADC.

Augenstein, D. 2018. Torture as Tort? Transnational Tort Litigation for Corporate-Related Human Rights Violations and the Human Right to a Remedy. *Human Rights Law Review*, 18(3), pp. 593–612.

Avant, D.D. 2005. *The Market for Force: The Consequences of Privatizing Security*. Cambridge: Cambridge University Press.

Barrig, M. 2008. La persistencia de la memoria. Feminismo y estado en Perú de los noventa. *Debate Feminista*, 37, pp. 213–46.

Bebbington, A. 2008. Social Capital and Development Studies III: Social Capital and the State (seen from Peru). *Progress in Development Studies*, 8(3), pp. 271–9.

Bebbington, A., ed. 2012a. *Industrias extractivas, conflicto social y dinámicas institucionales en la Región Andina*. Lima: Instituto de Estudios Peruanos.

Bebbington, A. 2012b. Social Conflict and Emergent Institutions: Hypotheses from Piura, Peru. *In*: A. Bebbington, ed. *Social Conflict, Economic Development and Extractive Industry: Evidence from South America*. London: Routledge, pp. 67–88.

Bebbington, A. and D.H. Bebbington. 2009. Actores y ambientalismos: Continuidades & cambios de los conflictos socioambientales en el Perú. *In*: J. de Echave, R. Hoetmer, and M. Palacios Panéz, eds. *Minería y territorio en el Perú: Conflictos, resistencias y propuestas en tiempos de globalización*. Lima: Colección: Diálogos y Movimientos, pp. 65–83.

Bebbington, A. and J. Bury. 2009. Institutional Challenges for Mining and Sustainability in Peru. *Proceedings of the National Academy of Sciences*, 106(41), pp. 17296–301.

Bebbington, A., M. Connarty, W. Coxshall, H. O'Shaughnessy, and M. Williams. 2007. *Mining and Development in Peru: With Special Reference to the Río Blanco Project, Piura*. London: Peru Support Group.

Bebbington, A., D. Humphreys Bebbington, and J. Bury. 2010. Federating and Defending: Water, Territory and Extraction in the Andes. *In*: R. Boelens, D. Getches, and A. Guevara-Gil, eds. *Out of the Mainstream: Water Rights, Politics and Identity*. London: Earthscan, pp. 307–27.

Bebbington, A., D. Humphreys Bebbington, J. Bury, J. Lingan, J.P. Muñoz, and M. Scurrah. 2008. Mining and Social Movements: Struggles over Livelihood and Rural Territorial Development in the Andes. *World Development*, 36(12), pp. 2888–905.

Bebbington, A., M. Scurrah, and C. Bielich. 2008. *Mapeo de movimientos sociales en el Perú actual*. Lima: Centro Peruano de Estudios Sociales (CEPES).

Bebbington, A. and M. Williams. 2008. Water and Mining Conflicts in Peru. *Mountain Research and Development*, 28(3/4), pp. 190–5.

Bens, J. and O. Zenker, eds. 2017. *Gerechtigkeitsgefühle: Zur affektiven und emotionalen Legitimität von Normen*. Bielefeld: transcript-Verlag.

Benson, P. and S. Kirsch. 2010. Capitalism and the Politics of Resignation. *Current Anthropology*, 51(4), pp. 459–86.

van den Berge, M.P. 2011. Child Miners in Cajamarca, Peru. *In*: G.K. Lieten, ed. *Hazardous Child Labour in Latin America*. Springer Science & Business Media, pp. 67–79.

Bertha Foundation. n.d. Lawyers: Bertha Justice Initiative. *Bertha Foundation*.

Blackburn, D. 2017. *Removing Barriers to Justice: How a Treaty on Business and Human Rights Could Improve Access to Remedy for Victims*. London / Amsterdam: International Centre for Trade Union Rights (ICTUR) / Stichting Onderzoek Multinationale Ondernemingen (SOMO).

Blanco Galdós, H. 2017. *Nosotros los indios*. 3a edición. Cusco: Centro de Estudios Bartolomé de Las Casas.

Bourdieu, P. 1987. The Force of Law: Toward a Sociology of the Juridical Field. *Hastings Law Journal*, 38(5), pp. 814–53.

Brett, P. 2018. *Human Rights and the Judicialisation of African Politics*. New York: Routledge.

Brinks, D.M. and V. Gauri. 2014. The Law's Majestic Equality? The Distributive Impact of Judicializing Social and Economic Rights. *Perspectives on Politics*, 12(2), pp. 375–93.

Brinks, D.M., V. Gauri, and K. Shen. 2015. Social Rights Constitutionalism: Negotiating the Tension Between the Universal and the Particular. *Annual Review of Law and Social Science*, 11(1), pp. 289–308.

Brown, W. 2015. *Undoing the Demos: Neoliberalism's Stealth Revolution*. New York: Zone Books.

Bury, J. 2004. Livelihoods in Transition: Transnational Gold Mining Operations and Local Change in Cajamarca, Peru. *The Geographical Journal*, 170(1), pp. 78–91.

Bury, J. 2005. Mining Mountains: Neoliberalism, Land Tenure, Livelihoods, and the New Peruvian Mining Industry in Cajamarca. *Environment and Planning A*, 37(2), pp. 221–39.

Bury, J. 2007. Mining Migrants: Transnational Mining and Migration Patterns in the Peruvian Andes. *The Professional Geographer*, 59(3), pp. 378–89.

Bury, J. 2008. Transnational Corporations and Livelihood Transformations in the Peruvian Andes: An Actor-Oriented Political Ecology. *Human Organization*, 67(3), pp. 307–21.

Bury, J. and A. Kolff. 2002. Livelihoods, Mining and Peasant Protests in the Peruvian Andes. *Journal of Latin American Geography*, 1(1), pp. 3–16.

de la Cadena, M. 1998. Silent Racism and Intellectual Superiority in Peru. *Bulletin of Latin American Research*, 17(2), pp. 143–64.

de la Cadena, M. 2000. *Indigenous Mestizos: The Politics of Race and Culture in Cuzco, Peru, 1919–1991*. Durham, N.C: Duke University Press.

de la Cadena, M. 2010. Indigenous Cosmopolitics in the Andes: Conceptual Reflections beyond "Politics". *Cultural Anthropology*, 25(2), pp. 334–70.

Calderón Concha, P. 2010. Para comprender y transformar los conflictos socio ambientales en Perú: El conflicto en torno al Proyecto Minero Río Blanco desde la perspectiva de la teoría de conflictos de Johan Galtung. Tesis doctoral. Instituto de la Paz y los Conflictos, Universidad de Granada.

Canan, P. and G.W. Pring. 1988. Strategic Lawsuits Against Public Participation. *Social Problems*, 35(5), pp. 506–19.

de las Casas, R.P.-P. 2015. ¿Qué juzgado debe ser el competente (en razón de la materia) cuando se involucra a un tercero civilmente responsable? *THĒMIS-Revista de Derecho*, (68), pp. 217–26.

Cassels, J. 1991. The Uncertain Promise of Law: Lessons from Bhopal. *Osgoode Hall Law Journal*, 29(1), pp. 1–50.

Castells, M. 2005. Global Governance and Global Politics. *PS: Political Science & Politics*, (01), pp. 9–16.

Centro de Estudios Legales y Sociales (CELS). 2008. *Litigio estratégico y derechos humanos: La lucha por el derecho*. Buenos Aires: Siglo Veintiuno Editores Argentina.

Chacón Pagán, R.E. 2005. Percepciones y acciones ambientalistas de las campesinas y ronderas de Bambamarca en tiempos de contaminación minera. *In*: F. Eguren, M.I. Remy, and P. Oliart, eds. *Perú: El problema agrario en debate*. Lima: SEPIA/Oxfam, pp. 351–84.

Chatterjee, P. 2004. *The Politics of the Governed: Reflections on Popular Politics in Most of the World*. New York: Columbia University Press.

Chérrez, C., C. Padilla, S. Otten, and M.R. Yumbla. 2011. *Cuando tiemblan los derechos, extractivismo y criminalizacion en América Latina*. Quito: Acción Ecológica; OCMAL.

Chimni, B. 2007. A Just World Under Law: A View From the South. *American University International Law Review*, 22(2), pp. 199–220.

Clarke, K.M. and M. Goodale, eds. 2010. *Mirrors of Justice: Law and Power in the Post-Cold War Era*. New York: Cambridge University Press.

Comaroff, J. and J. Comaroff. 2007. Law and Disorder in the Postcolony. *Social Anthropology*, 15(2), pp. 133–52.

Comaroff, J. and J.L. Comaroff. 2012. *Theory from the South, or, How Euro-America Is Evolving toward Africa*. Boulder: Paradigm Publishers.

Comaroff, J.L. 2012. Foreword. *In*: M. Lazarus-Black and S.F. Hirsch, eds. *Contested States: Law, Hegemony and Resistance*. New York: Routledge, pp. ix–xiii.

Comaroff, J.L. and J. Comaroff. 2006. Law and Disorder in the Postcolony: An Introduction. *In*: J. Comaroff and J. Comaroff, eds. *Law and Disorder in the Postcolony*. Chicago: University of Chicago Press, pp. 1–56.

Comaroff, J.L. and J. Comaroff. 2009. Reflections on the Anthropology of Law, Governance and Sovereignty. *In*: F. von Benda-Beckmann, K. von Benda-Beckmann, and J. Eckert, eds. *Rules of Law and Laws of Ruling: On the Governance of Law*. Farnham: Ashgate, pp. 31–59.

Comisión de la Verdad y Reconciliación (CVR). 2003a. *Informe final. Anexo 2. ¿Cuántos peruanos murieron? Estimación del total de víctimas por el conflicto armado interno entre 1980 y el 2000*. Lima.

Comisión de la Verdad y Reconciliación (CVR). 2003b. *Informe final. Tomo VIII. Tercera parte: Las secuelas de la violencia. Conclusiones generales*. Lima.

Comisión Interamericana de Derechos Humanos (CIDH). 2015. *Criminalización de defensoras y defensores de derechos humanos*. Organización de los Estados Americanos, No. Doc. 49/15.

Comunidad Nativa Awajún de Supayaku, Fundación Ecuménica para el Desarrollo y la Paz (Fedepaz), Grupo de Formación e Intervención para el Desarrollo Sostenible (Grufides), Ingeniería Sin Fronteras (ISF), and Soluciones Prácticas. 2015. *Plan de vida de la Comunidad Nativa Awajún de Supayaku al 2024*. Cajamarca: Grupo de Formación e Intervención para el Desarrollo Sostenible (Grufides).

Concha Takeshita, Y. and A. Navarro Elguera. 2016. Transacciones extrajudiciales: ¿Mecanismo adecuado en una situación de desastre? Análisis en el caso de derrame de mercurio en Choropampa y San Juan. *Revista Pólemos*, 6(10), pp. 155–72.

Conley, J. and W. O'Barr. 1993. Legal Anthropology Comes Home: A Brief History of the Ethnographic Study of Law. *Loyola of Los Angeles Law Review*, 27(1), p. 41.

Consejo de Ministros. 2008. Exposición de motivos, Decreto Legislativo N° 982 [online]. Available from: http://spij.minjus.gob.pe/Graficos/Peru/2007/julio/22/DL-982_22-07-07.pdf.

Coordinadora Nacional de Derechos Humanos (CNDDHH). 2019. *Coordinadora Nacional de Derechos Humanos*. Lima.

Coordinadora Nacional de Derechos Humanos Perú (CNDDHH). 2012. *Informe Anual: 2011–2012 (Julio). Un año del gobierno de Ollanta Humala*. Lima.

Coordinadora Nacional de Derechos Humanos Perú (CNDDHH). 2015. *Informe Anual 2014–2015*. Lima.

Coordinadora Nacional de Derechos Humanos Perú (CNDDHH). 2017. *Informe Anual 2015–2016*. Lima.

Corte Suprema de Justicia, V Pleno Jurisdiccional de las Salas Penales Permanente y Transitorias. 2009. Acuerdo Plenario N° 1–2009/CJ-116 [online]. Available from: https://www.pj.gob.pe/wps/wcm/connect/06089c804075b990b629f699ab657107/ACUERDO_PLENARIO_01-2009-CJ-116_301209.pdf?MOD=AJPERES&CACHEID=06089c804075b990b629f699ab657107 [Accessed 10 Jan 2020].

Cotler, J., R. Berrenechea, M. Glave, R. Grompone, and M.I. Remy. 2009. *Poder y cambio en las regiones*. Lima: Instituto de Estudios Peruanos.

Coxshall, W. 2005. From the Peruvian Reconciliation Commission to Ethnography. *PoLAR: Political and Legal Anthropology Review*, 28(2), pp. 203–22.

Coxshall, W. 2010. "When They Came to Take Our Resources": Mining Conflicts in Peru and Their Complexity. *Social Analysis*, 54(1), pp. 35–51.

Dagnino, E. 2003. Citizenship in Latin America: An Introduction. *Latin American Perspectives*, 30(2), pp. 211–25.

Das, V. 1995. *Critical Events: An Anthropological Perspective on Contemporary India*. Delhi: Oxford University Press.

Das, V. and D. Poole. 2004. State and Its Margins: Comparative Ethnographies. *In*: V. Das and D. Poole, eds. *Anthropology in the Margins of the State*. Santa Fe: School of American Research Press, pp. 3–33.

Defensoría del Pueblo. 2001. *Informe Defensorial N°62: El caso del derrame de mercurio que afectó a las localidades de San Sebastián de Choropampa, Magdalena y San Juan, en la provincia de Cajamarca*. Lima.

Degregori, C.I. 2012. *La década de la antipolítica: Auge y huida de Alberto Fujimori y Vladimiro Montesinos*. Lima: Instituto de Estudios Peruanos.

DEMUS. 2017. Caso Máxima Acuña: Sociedad civil rechaza archivamiento de denuncia por violencia de género en conflictos sociales [online]. *DEMUS – Estudio para la Defensa de los Derechos de la Mujer*. Available from: https://www.demus.org.pe/noticias/caso-maxima-acuna-sociedad-civil-rechaza-archivamiento-de-denuncia-por-violencia-de-genero-en-conflictos-sociales/ [Accessed 22 Apr 2018].

Deva, S. 2012. *Regulating Corporate Human Rights Violations: Humanizing Business*. London: Routledge.

Domingo, P. 2005. Judicialization of Politics: The Changing Political Role of The Judiciary in Mexico. *In*: R. Sieder, L. Schjolden, and A. Angell, eds. *The Judicialization of Politics in Latin America*. New York: Palgrave Macmillan, pp. 21–46.

Drinot, P. 2006. Nation-building, Rascism and Inequality: Institutional Development in Peru in Historical Perspective. *In*: J. Crabtree, ed. *Making Institutions Work in Peru*. London: Institute for the Study of the Americas, pp. 5–23.

Duffy, H. 2018. *Strategic Human Rights Litigation*. Oxford: Hart.

Duque, C. 2014. ¿Por qué un litigio estratégico en Derechos Humanos? *Aportes Andinos*, 35, pp. 9–23.

Durand, F. 2016. *Cuando el poder extractivo captura al Estado: Lobbies, puertas giratorias y paquetazo ambiental en Perú*. Lima: Oxfam.

EarthRights International. 2006. *Transnational Litigation Manual for Human Rights and Environmental Cases in United States Courts: A Resource for Non-Lawyers*. Washington D.C.

EarthRights International. 2018a. Maxima Acuña-Atalaya v. Newmont Mining Corp. [online]. *EarthRights International*. Available from: https://earthrights.org/case/maxima-acuna-atalaya-v-newmont-mining-corp/ [Accessed 2 Aug 2018].

EarthRights International. 2018b. Communities File Lawsuit for Recognition of Rights of the Marañon River in Peru [online]. *EarthRights International*. Available from: https://earthrights.org/media/communities-file-lawsuit-for-recognition-of-rights/ [Accessed 19 May 2020].

de Echave, J. 2008. Mining and Communities in Peru: Constructing a Framework for Decision-Making. *In*: L. North, V. Patroni, and T.D. Clark, eds. *Community Rights and Corporate Responsibility Canadian Mining and Oil Companies in Latin America*. Toronto: Between the Lines, pp. 17–36.

de Echave, J., M. Palacios Panéz, and R. Hoetmer. 2009. Introducción. *In*: J. de Echave, R. Hoetmer, and M. Palacios Panéz, eds. *Minería y territorio en el Perú: Conflictos, resistencias y propuestas en tiempos de globalización*. Lima: Colección Diálogos y Movimientos, pp. 15–31.

Eckert, J. 2006. From Subjects to Citizens: Legalism from Below and the Homogenisation of the Legal Sphere. *The Journal of Legal Pluralism and Unofficial Law*, 38(53–54), pp. 45–75.

Eckert, J. 2012. Rumours of Rights. *In*: J. Eckert, B. Donahoe, C. Strümpell, and Z.Ö. Biner, eds. *Law Against the State: Ethnographic Forays into Law's Transformations*. Cambridge: Cambridge University Press, pp. 147–70.

Eckert, J. 2014. Preventive Laws and the Policing of the Urban Poor. *In*: N. Gooptu and J.P. Parry, eds. *Persistence of Poverty in India*. New Delhi: Social Science Press, pp. 291–314.

Eckert, J. 2016. Tugend, Recht und Moral: Tendenzen der Verantwortungszuschreibung. *Deutsche Zeitschrift für Philosophie*, 64(2), pp. 246–57.

Eckert, J. 2017. Opening Remarks. Presented at the EASA Lawnet Conference Anticipating Law: The Prognostics of Fear and Hope, Institute of Social Anthropology, University of Bern.

Eckert, J. 2021. Entangled Hopes. Towards Relational Coherence. *In*: N. Krisch, ed. *Entangled Legalities beyond the State*. Cambridge: Cambridge University Press, pp. 399–423.

Eckert, J., B. Donahoe, C. Strümpell, and Z.Ö. Biner. 2012a. Introduction: Law's Travels and Transformations. *In*: J. Eckert, B. Donahoe, C. Strümpell, and Z.Ö. Biner, eds. *Law Against the State: Ethnographic Forays into Law's Transformations*. Cambridge: Cambridge University Press, pp. 1–22.

Eckert, J., B. Donahoe, C. Strümpell, and Z.Ö. Biner, eds. 2012b. *Law Against the State: Ethnographic Forays into Law's Transformations*. Cambridge: Cambridge University Press.

Eckert, J.M. 2008. Laws for Enemies. *In*: Eckert, ed. *The Social Life of Anti-terrorism Laws: The War on Terror and the Classifications of the 'Dangerous Other'*. Bielefeld: transcript-Verlag, pp. 7–31.

El Comercio (online). 2014. Cajamarca: Yanacocha ganó juicio por tierras a familia Chaupe. *El Comercio (online)*, 5 Aug.

El Montonero (online). 2016. ¿Grufides y Marco Arana detrás de Máxima Acuña de Chaupe? *El Montonero*, 22 Apr.

Englund, H. 2006. *Prisoners of Freedom: Human Rights and the African Poor*. Berkeley: University of California Press.

Enneking, L. 2014. The Future of Foreign Direct Liability? Exploring the International Relevance of the Dutch Shell Nigeria Case. *Utrecht Law Review*, 10(1), pp. 44–54.

Epp, C.R. 1998. *The Rights Revolution: Lawyers, Activists, and Supreme Courts in Comparative Perspective*. University of Chicago Press.

Ewick, P. and S.S. Silbey. 1998. *The Common Place of Law: Stories from Everyday Life*. Chicago: The University of Chicago Press.

Ezer, T. and P. Patel. 2018. Strategic Litigation to Advance Public Health. *Health and Human Rights*, 20(2), pp. 149–60.

Facing Finance. 2017. Presseerklärung: Schweizer Bergbaukonzern Glencore droht deutscher Menschenrechtsorganisation [online]. *Facing Finance*. Available from: http://www.facing-finance.org/de/2017/05/presseerklarung-schweizer-bergbaukonzern-glencore-droht-deutscher-menschenrechtsorganisation/ [Accessed 21 Oct 2019].

Faulk, K.A. and S. Brunnegger. 2016. Introduction: Making Sense of Justice. *In*: S. Brunnegger and K.A. Faulk, eds. *A Sense of Justice: Legal Knowledge and Lived Experience in Latin America*. Stanford: Stanford University Press, pp. 1–21.

Faundez, J. 2005. Community Justice Institutions and Judicialization: Lessons from Rural Peru. *In*: R. Sieder, L. Schjolden, and A. Angell, eds. *The Judicialization of Politics in Latin America*. New York: Palgrave Macmillan, pp. 188–209.

Felstiner, W.L.F., R.L. Abel, and A. Sarat. 1980. The Emergence and Transformation of Disputes: Naming, Blaming, Claiming . . . *Law & Society Review*, 15(3/4), pp. 631–54.

Femia, J. 1975. Hegemony and Consciousness in the Thought of Antonio Gramsci. *Political Studies*, 23(1), pp. 29–48.

Ferguson, J. 1994. *Anti-Politics Machine: Development, Depoliticization, and Bureaucratic Power in Lesotho*. Minneapolis: University of Minnesota Press.

Ferguson, J. 2015. *Give a Man a Fish: Reflections on the New Politics of Distribution*. Durham: Duke University Press.

Fitzpatrick, P. and A. Hunt. 1987. Introduction. *Journal of Law and Society*, 14(1), pp. 1–3.

Fortun, K. 2001. *Advocacy After Bhopal: Environmentalism, Disaster, New Global Orders*. Chicago: The University of Chicago Press.

Foucault, M. 2004. *Geschichte der Gouvernementalität II: Die Geburt der Biopolitik. Vorlesung am Collège de France, 1978–1979*. Frankfurt am Main: Suhrkamp.

Fowks, J. 2012. Absueltas en Perú 107 personas acusadas por un conflicto minero en 2005. *El País (Online)*, 10 Nov.

Franciscans International and Grupo de Formación e Intervención para el Desarrollo Sostenible (Grufides). 2017. *El derecho a un recurso efectivo: El caso de Máxima Acuña*.

Fraser, N. 2009. *Scales of Justice: Reimagining Political Space in a Globalizing World*. New York: Columbia University Press.

Fumerton, M. 2001. Rondas Campesinas in the Peruvian Civil War: Peasant Self-defence Organisations in Ayacucho. *Bulletin of Latin American Research*, 20(4), pp. 470–97.

Fundación Ecuménica para el Desarrollo y la Paz (Fedepaz). 2009. Nota de Prensa 17–03-09: Sobre caso Majaz [online]. Available from: http://fedepaz.org/index.php?option=com_content&view=article&id=139:casa-matriz-de-minera-majaz-sa-indemniza-a-33-campesinos&catid=29&Itemid=146 [Accessed 12 May 2017].

Fundación Ecuménica para el Desarrollo y la Paz (Fedepaz). 2011. Casa matriz de Minera Majaz S.A. indemniza a 33 campesinos [online]. Available from: http://fedepaz.org/index.php?option=com_content&view=article&id=139:casa-matriz-de-minera-majaz-sa-indemniza-a-33-campesinos&catid=29&Itemid=146 [Accessed 26 Sep 2019].

Fundación Ecuménica para el Desarrollo y la Paz (Fedepaz). 2016. Piura: Justicia para los campesinos que sufrieron tortura en el campamento minero de Río Blanco Copper S.A. [online]. Available from: http://fedepaz.org/index.php?option=com_content&view=article&id=139:casa-matriz-de-minera-majaz-sa-indemniza-a-33-campesinos&catid=29&Itemid=146 [Accessed 17 May 2017].

Fundación Ecuménica para el Desarrollo y la Paz (Fedepaz). 2018a. Primera Demanda de Amparo por Consulta Previa en Minería [online]. Available from: http://fedepaz.org/?option=com_content&view=article&id=346:consulta-previa-ppii-mineria-supayaku-awajun&catid=29&Itemid=146 [Accessed 17 Dec 2018].

Fundación Ecuménica para el Desarrollo y la Paz (Fedepaz). 2018b. 2ª Sala Penal de Apelaciones de Piura ordena que se incorpore al Ministerio del Interior como Tercero Civil Responsable, en el proceso penal por tortura y secuestro agravado en campamento minero Ex Majaz [online]. Available from: http://fedepaz.org/index.php?option=com_content&view=article&id=139:casa-matriz-de-miner

a-majaz-sa-indemniza-a-33-campesinos&catid=29&Itemid=146 [Accessed 10 May 2018].

Galanter, M. 1974. Why the 'Haves' Come out Ahead: Speculations on the Limits of Legal Change. *Law & Society Review*, 9(1), pp. 95–160.

García Pérez, A. 2007a. Receta para acabar con el perro del hortelano. *El Comercio*, 25 Nov.

García Pérez, A. 2007b. El síndrome del perro del hortelano. *El Comercio*, 28 Oct.

García Pérez, A. 2008. El perro del hortelano contra el pobre. *El Comercio*, 2 Mar.

Garrett, B.L. 2014. *Too Big to Jail: How Prosecutors Compromise with Corporations*. Cambridge: Belknap Press of Harvard University.

Gesellschaft für bedrohte Völker (GfbV). 2012. *Gold: Die Rolle der Schweiz in einem schmutzigen Geschäft*. Ostermundigen: Gesellschaft für bedrohte Völker (GfbV).

Gesellschaft für bedrohte Völker (GfbV). 2016. *Tatort Cajamarca: Goldkonzern Yanacocha und Menschenrechtsverletzungen in Peru*. Ostermundigen: Gesellschaft für bedrohte Völker (GfbV).

Gitlitz, J.S. 2013. *Administrando justicia al margen del Estado: las rondas campesinas de Cajamarca*. Lima: Instituto de Estudios Peruanos.

Gloppen, S. 2018. *Conceptualizing Lawfare: A Typology & Theoretical Framework*. Bergen: Centre on Law & Social Transformation, CMI / LawTransform working paper.

Goldman Environmental Foundation. 2020. Nominations [online]. *Goldman Environmental Foundation*. Available from: https://www.goldmanprize.org/nominations/ [Accessed 7 May 2020].

Gómez, E. 2013. Continuidades y rupturas de la minería en el país. *In*: R. Hoetmer, M. Castro, M. Daza, J. de Echave, and C. Ruiz, eds. *Minería y movimientos sociales en el Perú: Instrumentos y propuestas para la defensa de la vida, el agua y los territorios*. Lima: Colección Diálogos y Movimientos, pp. 123–31.

Gonzáles-Ocantos, E.A. 2017. *Shifting Legal Visions: Judicial Change and Human Rights Trials in Latin America*. Cambridge: Cambridge University Press.

González-Ocantos, E. 2016. Evaluations of Human Rights Trials and Trust in Judicial Institutions: Evidence from Fujimori's Trial in Peru. *The International Journal of Human Rights*, 20(4), pp. 445–70.

Goodale, M. 2017. *Anthropology and Law: A Critical Introduction*. New York: New York University Press.

Goodale, M. and K.M. Clarke. 2010. Introduction: Understanding the Multiplicity of Justice. *In*: K.M. Clarke and M. Goodale, eds. *Mirrors of Justice: Law and Power in the Post-Cold War Era*. New York: Cambridge University Press, pp. 1–27.

Gramsci, A. 1992. *Gefängnishefte: Kritische Gesamtausgabe in 10 Bänden, Band 4, Hefte 6–7*. Hamburg: Argument Verlag.

Grieco, K. 2016. Motherhood, Mining and Modernity in the Peruvian Highlands from Corporate Development to Social Mobilization. *In*: Dhawan, Nikita, E.

Fink, J. Leinius, and R. Mageza-Barthel, eds. *Negotiating Normativity*. Cham: Springer International Publishing, pp. 131–46.

Grieco, K. and C. Salazar-Soler. 2013. Les enjeux techniques et politiques dans la gestion et le contrôle de l'eau: Le cas du projet Minas Conga au nord du Pérou. *Autrepart*, (65), pp. 151–68.

Haller, D. and C. Shore, eds. 2005. *Corruption: Anthropological Perspectives*. London; Ann Arbor: Pluto Press.

Hannerz, U. 2003. Being There… and There… and There! Reflections on Multi-site Ethnography. *Ethnography*, 4(2), pp. 201–16.

Harvey, P. and H. Knox. 2015. *Roads: An Anthropology of Infrastructure and Expertise*. Ithaca: Cornell University Press.

Herrera, H.P. 2013. Los pasivos mineros ambientales y los conflictos sociales en Hualgayoc. *Investigaciones Sociales*, 17(30), pp. 265–77.

Hetherington, K. 2011. *Guerrilla Auditors: The Politics of Transparency in Neoliberal Paraguay*. Durham: Duke University Press.

heute journal. 2017. Ein Rohstoffkonzern am Pranger, Zweites Deutsches Fernsehen (ZDF). May 30.

Hill, D. 2015a. Brazilian Firm's Mega-Dam Plans in Peru Spark Major Social Conflict. *Mongabay Environmental News (online)*, 11 May.

Hill, D. 2015b. Peru's Mega-Dam Projects Threaten Amazon River Source and Ecosystem Collapse. *Mongabay Environmental News (online)*, 28 Apr.

Hill, D. 2016. Hitler Rojas – The Peruvian Farmer Killed for Opposing a Mega-Dam? *The Guardian (online)*, 25 Jan.

Hirsch, S.F. and M. Lazarus-Black. 2012. Introduction: Performance and Paradox. Exporing Law's Role in Hegemony and Resistance. *In*: M. Lazarus-Black and S.F. Hirsch, eds. *Contested States: Law, Hegemony and Resistance*. New York: Routledge, pp. 1–31.

Hoetmer, R. 2010. «Esta democracia, ya no es democracia…»: Reflexiones a propósito de la consulta vecinal sobre la minería en la frontera norte del Perú. *YUYAYKUSUN*, (3), pp. 183–208.

Hoetmer, R. 2013. Minería, movimientos sociales y las disputas del futuro: Claves de lectura y pisas de reflexión-acción. *In*: R. Hoetmer, M. Castro, M. Daza, J. de Echave, and C. Ruiz, eds. *Minería y movimientos sociales en el Perú: Instrumentos y propuestas para la defensa de la vida, el agua y los territorios*. Lima: Colección Diálogos y Movimientos, pp. 265–80.

Hoetmer, R., M. Castro, J. de Echave, and C. Ruiz. 2013. Introducción. *In*: R. Hoetmer, M. Castro, M. Daza, J. de Echave, and C. Ruiz, eds. *Minería y movimientos sociales en el Perú. Instrumentos y propuestas para la defensa de la vida, el agua y los territorios*. Lima: Colección: Diálogos y Movimientos, pp. 19–28.

Hoffman, B. 2017. Zooming Out, Then Zooming In: Using International Law to Advance Justice. *Columbia Human Rights Law Review*, 48(2), pp. 56–68.

Hönke, J. and T.A. Börzel. 2012. *Security and Human Rights: Mining Companies between International Commitment and Corporate Practice*. Nomos: Baden-Baden.

Huarcaya, S.M. 2015. Performativity, Performance, and Indigenous Activism in Ecuador and the Andes. *Comparative Studies in Society and History*, 57(3), pp. 806–37.

Huarcaya, S.M. 2019. Plurinationality, Indigeneity, Neoliberalism, and Social Movements. *In*: L.J. Seligmann and K.S. Fine-Dare, eds. *The Andean World*. London: Routledge, pp. 571–86.

Hull, M.S. 2003. The File: Agency, Authority, and Autography in an Islamabad Bureaucracy. *Language & Communication*, 23(3), pp. 287–314.

Hull, M.S. 2012. *Government of Paper: The Materiality of Bureaucracy in Urban Pakistan*. Berkeley: University of California Press.

Huneeus, A., J. Couso, and R. Sieder. 2010. Cultures of Legality: Judicialization and Political Activism in Contemporary Latin America. *In*: J. Couso, A. Huneeus, and R. Sieder, eds. *Cultures of Legality: Judicialization and Political Activism in Latin America*. Cambridge: Cambridge University Press, pp. 3–22.

Hunt, A. 1986. The Theory of Critical Legal Studies. *Oxford Journal of Legal Studies*, 6(1), pp. 1–45.

Hunt, A. 1990. Rights and Social Movements: Counter-Hegemonic Strategies. *Journal of Law and Society*, 17(3), pp. 309–28.

Hurtado Poma, J.R. 2009. *¿Qué se discute en la audiencia de control de acusación?* Lima: Instituto de Ciencia Procesal Penal.

Im, H.B. 1991. Hegemony and Counter-Hegemony in Gramsci. *Asian Perspective*, 15(1), pp. 123–56.

Instituto de Defensa Legal (IDL). 2013. Con licencia para matar: Análisis de la autógrafa que modifica elartículo 20 inciso 11 del Código Penal para exonerar de responsabilidad penal a policías y militares que causen lesiones o muerte, en cumplimiento de sus funciones [online]. Available from: http://www.justiciaviva.org.pe/webpanel/doc_trabajo/doc20062013-165854.pdf [Accessed 11 Apr 2014].

Instituto de Defensa Legal (IDL). 2019. Peligra ecosistema del río Marañón por proyecto Chadín 2 [online]. *Instituto de defensa Legal*. Available from: https://idl.org.pe/peligra-ecosistema-del-rio-maranon-por-proyecto-chadin-2/ [Accessed 19 May 2020].

Instituto Nacional de Estadística e Informática (INEI). 2018a. *Perú: Perfil sociodemográfico. Informe Nacional. Censos Nacionales 2017: XII de Población, VII de Vividenda y III de Comunidades Indígenas*. Lima.

Instituto Nacional de Estadística e Informática (INEI). 2018b. *I Censo de Comunidades Campesinas 2017: Resultados definitivos*. Lima.

Instituto Nacional de Estadística e Informática (INEI). 2020. Nota de prensa: INEI presentó el Mapa de Pobreza Monetaria 2018 [online]. Available from: http://m.

inei.gob.pe/media/MenuRecursivo/noticias/np028-2020.pdf [Accessed 30 Mar 2020].

International Finance Corporation. n.d. IFC finaliza su participación en el Proyecto Minero de Yanacocha en el Perú [online]. Available from: https://www.ifc.org/wps/wcm/connect/Industry_EXT_Content/IFC_External_Corporate_Site/OGM+Home/Priorities/Mining/Yanacocha-Gold-Mine_Spanish [Accessed 26 Jun 2018].

Jacquot, S. and T. Vitale. 2014. Law as Weapon of the Weak? A Comparative Analysis of Legal Mobilization by Roma and Women's Groups at the European Level. *Journal of European Public Policy*, 21(4), pp. 587–604.

Jahncke, J. 2011. Human Rights Abuses by Corporations: The Case of Río Blanco Copper in Peru. *Aportes DPLF*, 4(15), pp. 50–2.

Jaskoski, M. 2012. Public Security Forces with Private Funding: Local Army Entrepreneurship in Peru and Ecuador. *Latin American Research Review*, 47(2), pp. 79–99.

Jaskoski, M. 2014. Environmental Licensing and Conflict in Peru's Mining Sector: A Path-Dependent Analysis. *World Development*, 64, pp. 873–83.

Kafka, F. 2009. *The Trial*. Translation; German original edition 1925. Oxford; New York: OUP Oxford.

Kaleck, W. 2008. Der Kampf um transnationale Gerechtigkeit. Neue Chancen für die Menschenrechtsbewegung? *Kritische Justiz*, 41(3), pp. 284–9.

Kaleck, W. and M. Saage-Maaß. 2010. Corporate Accountability for Human Rights Violations Amounting to International Crimes: The Status Quo and its Challenges. *Journal of International Criminal Justice*, 8(3), pp. 699–724.

Kamphuis, C. 2011. La extracción de recursos mineros por empresas extranjeras y la privatización del poder coercitivo: Un estudio de caso sobre la empresa de seguridad Forza. *Apuntes: Revista de Ciencias Sociales*, 38(68), pp. 63–108.

Kamphuis, C. 2012a. Foreign Investment and the Privatization of Coercion: A Case Study of the Forza Security Company in Peru. *Brooklyn Journal of International Law*, 37(2), pp. 529–78.

Kamphuis, C. 2012b. Foreign Mining, Law and the Privatization of Property: A Case Study from Peru. *Journal of Human Rights and the Environment*, 3(2), pp. 217–53.

Karp, D.J. 2020. What Is the Responsibility to Respect Human Rights? Reconsidering the 'Respect, Protect, and Fulfill' Framework. *International Theory*, 12(1), pp. 83–108.

Keck, M.E. and K. Sikkink. 1998. *Activists beyond Borders: Advocacy Networks in International Politics*. Ithaca: Cornell University Press.

Kelman, M. 1987. *A Guide to Critical Legal Studies*. Cambridge: Harvard University Press.

Kirsch, S. 1997. Is Ok Tedi a Precedent? Implications of the Settlement. *In*: G. Banks and C. Ballard, eds. *The Ok Tedi Settlement: Issues, Outcomes and Implications*. Canberra: National Centre for Development Studies and Resource Management in Asia-Pacific Project, pp. 118–1140.

Kirsch, S. 2006. *Reverse Anthropology: Indigenous Analysis of Social and Environmental Relations in New Guinea*. Stanford: Stanford University Press.

Kirsch, S. 2007. Indigenous Movements and the Risks of Counterglobalization: Tracking the Campaign against Papua New Guinea's Ok Tedi Mine. *American Ethnologist*, 34(2), pp. 303–21.

Kirsch, S. 2014. *Mining Capitalism: The Relationship Between Corporations and Their Critics*. Oakland: University of California Press.

Kirsch, S. 2016. Virtuous Language in Industry and the Academic. *In*: C.S. Dolan and D. Rajak, eds. *The Anthropology of Corporate Social Responsibility*. Oxford: Berghahn, pp. 48–66.

Kirsch, S. 2018. *Engaged Anthropology: Politics beyond the Text*. Oakland: University of California Press.

Kremnitzer, M. 2010. A Possible Case for Imposing Criminal Liability on Corporations in International Criminal Law. *Journal of International Criminal Justice*, 8(3), pp. 909–18.

Kress, K. 1989. Legal Indeterminacy. *California Law Review*, 77(2), pp. 283–337.

Kristenson, O. 2009. Pastor in the Shadow of Violence: Gustavo Gutiérrez as a Public Pastoral Theologian in Peru in the 1980s and 1990s. Uppsala University.

La Ley (online). 2018. Crean la Junta Nacional de Justicia que reemplazará al CNM. *La Ley – El Ángulo Legal de la Noticia*, 19 Sep.

La Ley (online). 2019. Ley de Reforma Constitucional: Estas son las funciones de la Junta Nacional de Justicia. *La Ley – El Ángulo Legal de la Noticia*, 10 Jan.

Langdon, S. 2000. *Peru's Yanacocha Gold Mine: The IFC's Midas Touch?* Washington D.C. / Geneva: Center for International Environmental Law.

Laplante, L.J. and K. Theidon. 2007. Truth with Consequences: Justice and Reparations in Post-Truth Commission Peru. *Human Rights Quarterly*, 29, pp. 228–50.

Laplante, L.J. and K. Theidon. 2010. Commissioning Truth, Constructing Silences: The Peruvian Truth Commission and the Other Truths of 'Terrorists'. *In*: K.M. Clarke and M. Goodale, eds. *Mirrors of Justice: Law and Power in the Post-Cold War Era*. New York: Cambridge University Press, pp. 291–315.

Leigh Day. 2018. *Pushing the Boundaries, Taking a Stand*. London: Leigh Day.

Leigh Day & Co. 2011. Peruvian Torture Claimants Compensated by UK Mining Company [online]. Available from: https://www.leighday.co.uk/News/2011/July-2011/Peruvian-torture-claimants-compensated-by-UK-minin [Accessed 24 Sep 2019].

Li, F. 2009. Documenting Accountability: Environmental Impact Assessment in a Peruvian Mining Project. *PoLAR: Political and Legal Anthropology Review*, 32(2), pp. 218–36.

Li, F. 2013. Relating Divergent Worlds: Mines, Aquifers and Sacred Mountains in Peru. *Anthropologica*, 55(2), pp. 399–411.

Li, F. 2015. *Unearthing Conflict: Corporate Mining, Activism, and Expertise in Peru*. Duke University Press.

Li, F. 2017a. Illness, Compensation, and Claims for Justice: Lessons from the Choropampa Mercury Spill. *In*: S.N. Grovogui and L. Leonard, eds. *Governance in the Extractive Industries: Power, Cultural Politics and Regulation*. London: Routledge, pp. 176–94.

Li, F. 2017b. *Desenterrando el conflicto: Empresas mineras, activistas y expertos en el Perú*. Lima: Instituto de Estudios Peruanos.

Li, F. and A.P. Paredes Peñafiel. 2019. Stories of Resistance: Translating Nature, Indigeneity, and Place in Mining Activism. *In*: C. Vindal Ødegaard and J.J. Rivera Andía, eds. *Indigenous Life Projects and Extractivism: Ethnographies from South America*. Cham: Springer International Publishing, pp. 219–43.

Lindt, A. 2015. '¡Conga no va – ni hoy ni nunca!' – Soziale Konflikte und transnationale Bergbauprojekte in Peru: Die soziale Bewegung der Stadt Cajamarca und ihre Forderung nach Staatsbürgerrechten. unpublished M.A. thesis. University of Bern.

Lindt, A. 2020. Transnational Human Rights Litigation: A Means of Obtaining Effective Remedy Abroad? *Journal of Legal Anthropology*, 4(2), pp. 57–77.

Lindt, A. 2023. The Dark Side of Judicialization: Criminalizing Mining Protests in Peru. *Latin American Research Review*, 58(2), pp. 368–82.

Lo Lau, J. 2016. La polémica envuelve un megaproyecto en el río Marañón. *RPP Noticias (online)*, 18 Sep.

Machacuay, M. 2017. Máxima Acuña denuncia al Estado peruano ante la CIDH por falta de protección. *La República (online)*, 27 Nov.

Maquet, P. 2013. 'Este Estado no es garante de derechos públicos sino de derechos privados'. Entrevista con Marco Arana Zegarra. *In*: R. Hoetmer, M. Castro, M. Daza, J. de Echave, and C. Ruiz, eds. *Minería y movimientos sociales en el Perú: Instrumentos y propuestas para la defensa de la vida, el agua y los territorios*. Lima: Colección Diálogos y Movimientos, pp. 339–55.

Marcus, G.E. 1995. Ethnography in/of the World System: The Emergence of Multi-Sited Ethnography. *Annual Review of Anthropology*, 24(1), pp. 95–117.

Marks, S. 2007. International Judicial Activism and the Commodity-Form Theory of International Law. *European Journal of International Law*, 18, pp. 199–211.

Martinez-Alier, J. 2002. *The Environmentalism of the Poor: A Study of Ecological Conflicts and Valuation*. Cheltenham: Edward Elgar.

Mattei, U. and L. Nader. 2008. *Plunder: When the Rule of Law is Illegal*. Malden: Blackwell.

McCann, M.W. 1994. *Rights at Work: Pay Equity Reform and the Politics of Legal Mobilization*. Chicago: University of Chicago Press.

Meeran, R. 2011. Tort Litigation Against Multinational Corporations for Violation of Human Rights: An Overview of the Position Outside the United States. *City University of Hong Kong Law Review*, 3(1), pp. 1–41.

Meeran, R. 2012. Legal Accountability of Multinationals: The Current State of Play in the UK. *International Union Rights*, 19(4), pp. 18–20.

Meeran, R. 2013. Access to Remedy: The United Kingdom Experience of MNC Tort Litigation for Human Rights Violations. *In*: S. Deva and D. Bilchitz, eds. *Human Rights Obligations of Business: Beyond the Corporate Responsibility to Respect?* Cambridge: Cambridge University Press, pp. 378–402.

Mehta, S. 2015. Stand with the Woman Who Stood Up to Mining Industry Bullying [online]. *Earthworks*. Available from: https://earthworks.org/blog/stand_with_maxima_acuna_de_chaupe/ [Accessed 7 May 2020].

Merino, R. 2017. El Derecho como campo de crítica y poder: La política de la teoría legal desde América Latina. *Derecho y Sociedad*, 48, pp. 225–54.

Merry, S.E. 1990. *Getting Justice and Getting Even: Legal Consciousness among Working-Class Americans*. Chicago: University of Chicago Press.

Merry, S.E. 2006a. Anthropology and International Law. *Annual Review of Anthropology*, 35(1), pp. 99–116.

Merry, S.E. 2006b. Transnational Human Rights and Local Activism: Mapping the Middle. *American Anthropologist*, 108(1), pp. 38–51.

Merry, S.E. 2017. Foreword. *In*: M. Goodale, ed. *Anthropology and Law: A Critical Introduction*. New York: New York University Press, pp. ix–xii.

Merry, S.E. and M.C. Canfield. 2001. Law: Anthropological Aspects. *In*: N.J. Smelser and P.B. Baltes, eds. *International Encyclopedia of the Social & Behavioral Sciences*. Oxford: Pergamon, pp. 535–41.

Mertz, E. 2007. *The Language of Law School: Learning to 'Think Like a Lawyer'*. Oxford: Oxford University Press.

Michel, V. 2017. The Role of Prosecutorial Independence and Prosecutorial Accountability in Domestic Human Rights Trials. *Journal of Human Rights*, 16(2), pp. 193–219.

Miéville, C. 2005. *Between Equal Rights: A Marxist Theory of International Law*. Leiden: Brill.

Minera Yanacocha. 2015a. Una vez más, Yanacocha realiza pacíficamente defensa posesoria en Tragadero Grande [online]. Available from: http://www.yanacocha.com/una-vez-mas-yanacocha-realiza-pacificamente-defensa-posesoria-en-tragadero-grande/ [Accessed 30 Aug 2018].

Minera Yanacocha. 2015b. Nueva defensa posesoria pacífica en terrenos de Yanacocha [online]. Available from: http://www.yanacocha.com/nueva-defensa-posesoria-pacifica-en-terrenos-de-yanacocha/ [Accessed 30 Aug 2018].

Minera Yanacocha. 2016. Yanacocha ejerció defensa posesoria pacífica [online]. Available from: http://www.yanacocha.com/yanacocha-ejercio-defensa-posesoria-pacifica/ [Accessed 30 Aug 2018].

Ministerio de Energía y Minas (MINEM). 2020. Perú: País Minero [online]. Available from: http://mineria.minem.gob.pe/institucional/peru-pais-minero/ [Accessed 24 Feb 2020].

Ministerio de Justicia y Derechos Humanos. 2016. *Decreto Legislativo N$ 957: Código Procesal Penal. Cuarta Edición Oficial*. Lima: Ministerio de Justicia y Derechos Humanos.

Ministerio del Interior. 2020. Convenios interinstitucionales vigentes [online]. Available from: https://www.mininter.gob.pe/content/convenios-interinstitucionales-vigentes [Accessed 18 Mar 2020].

Moore, S.F. 2001. Certainties Undone: Fifty Turbulent Years of Legal Anthropology, 1949–1999. *The Journal of the Royal Anthropological Institute*, 7(1), pp. 95–116.

Moyn, S. 2010. *The Last Utopia: Human Rights in History*. Cambridge: The Belknap Press of Harvard University Press.

Moyn, S. 2018. *Not Enough: Human Rights in an Unequal World*. Cambridge, Massachusetts: The Belknap Press of Harvard University Press.

Mugler, J. 2019. *Measuring Justice: Quantitative Accountability and the National Prosecuting Authority in South Africa*. Cambridge: Cambridge University Press.

Mukherjee, A. 2019. *The Legal Right to Housing in India*. Cambridge: Cambridge University Press.

Müller-Hoff, C. 2011. Strategic Human Rights Litigation: Can It Be Used Effectively against Transnational Corporations? *Aportes DPLF*, 4(15), pp. 24–6.

Mutua, M.W. 2001. Savages, Victims, and Saviors: The Metaphor of Human Rights. *Harvard International Law Journal*, 42(1), pp. 201–45.

Nader, L. 1999. The Globalization of Law: ADR as "Soft" Technology. *Proceedings of the ASIL Annual Meeting*, 93, pp. 304–11.

Nader, L. 2002. *The Life of the Law: Anthropological Projects*. Berkeley: University of California Press.

Nash, K. 2012. Human Rights, Movements and Law: On Not Researching Legitimacy. *Sociology*, 46(5), pp. 797–812.

Newmont Corporation. 2022. Newmont to Acquire Remaining Stake in Yanacocha [online]. Available from: https://www.newmont.com/investors/news-release/news-details/2022/Newmont-to-Acquire-Remaining-Stake-in-Yanacocha/default.aspx [Accessed 11 Aug 2023].

Newmont Mining Corporation. 2015. An Update on the Habeas Corpus Filing by the Chaupe Family [online]. Available from: https://www.newmont.com/investors/news-release/news-details/2015/An-Update-on-the-Habeas-Corpus-Filing-by-the-Chaupe-Family/default.aspx [Accessed 5 May 2020].

Newmont Mining Corporation. 2016. Form 10-K: Annual Report Pursuant to the United States Securities and Exchange Commission [online]. Available from: http://d1lge852tjjqow.cloudfront.net/CIK-0001164727/050eb34a-9eba-4984-a379-7684d1ab4d2e.pdf?noexit=true [Accessed 15 Nov 2016].

Newmont Mining Corporation. 2018. Newmont Welcomes Sumitomo as Valued Partner at Yanacocha [online]. Available from: https://www.newmont.com/newsroom/newsroom-details/2018/Newmont-Welcomes-Sumitomo-as-Valued-Partner-at-Yanacocha/default.aspx [Accessed 26 Jun 2018].

Nuijten, M. and D. Lorenzo. 2009. Ritual and Rule in the Periphery: State Violence and Local Governance in a Peruvian Comunidad. *In*: F. von Benda-Beckmann, K. von Benda-Beckmann, and J. Eckert, eds. *Rules of Law and Laws of Ruling: On the Governance of Law*. Aldershot, Burlington: Ashgate, pp. 101–23.

Observatorio de Conflictos Mineros en el Perú. 2017. Audiencia de Máxima Acuña se posterga por falta de votos en deliberación [online]. Available from: /?q=alertas/12/04/2017/audiencia-de-m-xima-acu-se-posterga-por-falta-de-votos-en-deliberaci-n [Accessed 24 Apr 2017].

O'Donnell, G. 2005. Afterword. *In*: R. Sieder, L. Schjolden, and A. Angell, eds. *The Judicialization of Politics in Latin America*. New York: Palgrave Macmillan, pp. 293–8.

Ordoñez, R. 2017. Cajamarca: Buscan que Minera Yanacocha indemnice a ciudadano herido de bala en protestas contra proyecto Conga el año 2011. *NoticiasSer.pe (online)*, 15 Nov.

Oré Guardia, A. and G. Loza Avalos. 2005. La Estructura del Proceso Común en el Nuevo Código Procesal Penal Peruano. *Derecho & Sociedad*, 25, pp. 163–177.

Panorama Cajamarquino. 2014a. Revocan sentencia contra familia Chaupe. *Panorama Cajamarquino*, 18 Dec, p. 4.

Panorama Cajamarquino. 2014b. Absuelven a familia Chaupe. *Panorama Cajamarquino*, 18 Dec, p. 1.

Paredes, M. 2008a. El caso Tambogrande. *In*: M. Scurrah, ed. *Defendiendo derechos y promoviendo cambios: El Estado, las empresas extractivas y las comunidades locales en el Perú*. Lima: Instituto de Estudios Peruanos; Oxfam América, pp. 269–300.

Paredes, M. 2008b. *Weak Indigenous Politics in Peru*. Oxford: Centre for Research on Inequality, Human Security and Ethnicity, Queen Elizabeth House, University of Oxford.

Paredes Peñafiel, A.P. 2016. Desenhos, relações e desenvolvimento: conflitos em torno da mineração na região andina de Cajamarca, Peru. Tese submetida ao Programa de Pós-Graduação. Universidade Federal do Rio Grande do Sul, Porto Alegre.

Paredes Peñafiel, A.P. and F. Li. 2017. Nourishing Relations: Controversy over the Conga Mining Project in Northern Peru. *Ethnos*, pp. 1–20.

Passuni, S. and A. Chirinos. 2013. Ordenamiento territorial. *In*: R. Hoetmer, M. Castro, M. Daza, J. de Echave, and C. Ruiz, eds. *Minería y movimientos sociales en el Pe-*

rú: Instrumentos y propuestas para la defensa de la vida, el agua y los territorios. Lima: Colección Diálogos y Movimientos, pp. 479–90.

Pinker, A. 2015. Papering Over the Gaps: Documents, Infrastructure, and Political Experimentation in Highland Peru. *The Cambridge Journal of Anthropology*, 33(1), pp. 97–112.

Pistor, K. 2019. *The Code of Capital: How the Law Creates Wealth and Inequality*. Princeton, Oxford: Princeton University Press.

Pitts, C. 2011. Voluntary Principles on Security and Human Rights. *In*: T. Hale and D. Held, eds. *Handbook of Transnational Governance: Institutions and Innovations*. Cambridge: Polity Press, pp. 357–63.

Poole, D. 2001. La ley y la posibilidad de la diferencia: La antropología jurídica peruana entre la justicia y la ley. *In*: C.I. Degregori, P. Sendon, and P. Sandoval, eds. *No hay país más diverso: compendio de antropología peruana*. Lima: Instituto de Estudios Peruanos, pp. 200–46.

Poole, D. 2004. Between Threat and Guarantee: Justice and Community in the Margins of the Peruvian State. *In*: V. Das and D. Poole, eds. *Anthropology in the Margins of the State*. Santa Fe: School of American Research Press, pp. 35–65.

Prado, E. 2009. En Majaz sí se torturó el año 2005. *La República (online)*, 9 Jan.

Prado, E. 2018. Comunidades de Cajamarca interponen acción de amparo contra el proyecto Chadín II. *La República (online)*, 17 May.

Pring, G.W. and P. Canan. 1996. *Slapps: Getting Sued for Speaking Out*. Philadelphia: Temple University Press.

de la Puente, L. 2014. Conga ante la Comisión Interamericana de Derechos Humanos. *Gestión (online)*, 15 May.

Quispe Mamani, M. and M. Barboza López. 2019. La defensa del río Marañon frente al formalismo procesal en los procesos de amparo [online]. *Instituto de Defensa Legal (IDL)*. Available from: https://idl.org.pe/la-defensa-del-rio-maranon-frente-al-formalismo-procesal-en-los-procesos-de-amparo/ [Accessed 10 May 2019].

Rajagopal, B. 2003. *International Law from Below: Development, Social Movements and Third World Resistance*. Cambridge: Cambridge University Press.

RESOLVE. 2016. *Tragadero Grande – Land, Human Rights, and International Standards in the Conflict Between the Chaupe Family and Minera Yanacocha: Report of the Independent Fact Finding Mission*. Washington D.C.

Rodríguez-Garavito, C.A. 2005. Nike's Law: The Anti-Sweatshop Movement, Transnational Corporations, and the Struggle Over International Labor Rights in the Americas. *In*: B. de S. Santos and C.A. Rodríguez-Garavito, eds. *Law and Globalization from Below: Towards a Cosmopolitan Legality*. Cambridge: Cambridge University Press, pp. 64–91.

Rodríguez-Garavito, C.A. 2011a. Beyond the Courtroom: The Impact of Judicial Activism on Socioeconomic Rights in Latin America. *Texas Law Review*, 89(7), pp. 1669–98.

Rodríguez-Garavito, C.A. 2011b. Ethnicity.gov: Global Governance, Indigenous Peoples, and the Right to Prior Consultation in Social Minefields. *Indiana Journal of Global Legal Studies*, 18(1), pp. 263–305.

Rodríguez-Garavito, C.A. 2013. Más allá de la jurisprudencia: El impacto de los fallos sobre derechos sociales. *In*: M. Langford, ed. *Teoría y jurisprudencia de los derechos sociales tendencias emergentes en el derecho internacional y comparado*. Bogotá: Siglo del Hombre Editores Universidad de los Andes, pp. 897–916.

Rodríguez-Garavito, C.A. 2019. Empowered Participatory Jurisprudence: Experimentation, Deliberation and Norms in Socioeconomic Rights Adjudication. *In*: K. Young, ed. *The Future of Economic and Social Rights*. Cambridge: Cambridge University Press, pp. 233–58.

Rodríguez-Garavito, C.A. and L.C. Arenas. 2005. Indigenous Rights, Transnational Activism, and Legal Mobilization: The Struggle of the U'wa People in Colombia. *In*: B. de S. Santos and C.A. Rodríguez-Garavito, eds. *Law and Globalization from Below: Towards a Cosmopolitan Legality*. Cambridge: Cambridge University Press, pp. 241–66.

Rojas, P. 2009. Marco Arana Zegarra: Defensor ambiental y constructor del poder popular en el Perú. *Ecología Política*, (38), pp. 112–7.

Romero, C. 2017. Corte Suprema absuelve a Máxima Acuña ante denuncia de Yanacocha. *La República (online)*, 4 May.

Root, R.K. 2009. Through the Window of Opportunity: The Transitional Justice Network in Peru. *Human Rights Quarterly*, 31(2), pp. 452–73.

Rosenberg, G.N. 1991. *The Hollow Hope: Can Courts Bring About Social Change?* Chicago: University of Chicago Press.

Rubin, J. 2008. Adjudicating the Salvadoran Civil War: Expectations of the Law in Romagoza. *PoLAR: Political and Legal Anthropology Review*, 31(2), pp. 264–85.

Saage-Maaß, M. and S. Rau. 2016. Transnationale juristische Kämpfe gegen Menschenrechtsverletzungen durch Unternehmen. *Forschungsjournal Soziale Bewegungen*, 28(4), pp. 106–18.

Salazar, M. 2012. *Las comunidades que mueven el país: El estado de las comunidades rurales en el Perú*. Lima: Instituto del Bien Común.

Sanca Vega, I.N. 2017. La paz de los guerreros: Una experiencia de transformación de conflicto socioambiental en territorios del pueblo awajún de Cajamarca – Peru. Tesis doctoral. Instituto Interuniversitario de Desarrollo Social y Paz, Universitat Jaume I, Castellón de la Plana.

Sánchez, P. and O. Vargas. 2019. Artefactos para la creación de poder y conocimiento: el caso de las disputas por la minería en Cajamarca. *Latin American and Latinx Visual Culture*, 1(4), pp. 113–9.

Santiago, C. 2017. Conga no va carajo! Unpublished Doctoral Thesis. Columbia University.

Santos, B. de S. 2002. *Toward a New Legal Common Sense: Law, Globalization, and Emancipation*. London: Butterworths LexisNexis.

Santos, B. de S. 2005. Beyond Neoliberal Governance: The World Social Forum as Subaltern Cosmopolitan Politics and Legality. *In*: B. de S. Santos and C.A. Rodríguez-Garavito, eds. *Law and Globalization from Below: Towards a Cosmopolitan Legality*. Cambridge: Cambridge University Press, pp. 29–63.

Santos, B. de S. 2015. *If God Were a Human Rights Activist*. Stanford, California: Stanford University Press.

Santos, B. de S. and C.A. Rodríguez-Garavito. 2005. Law, Politics, and the Subaltern in Counter-Hegemonic Globalization. *In*: B. de S. Santos and C.A. Rodríguez-Garavito, eds. *Law and Globalization from Below: Towards a Cosmopolitan Legality*. Cambridge: Cambridge University Press, pp. 1–26.

Sawyer, S. and E.T. Gomez. 2012. Transnational Governmentality in the Context of Resource Extraction. *In*: S. Sawyer and E.T. Gomez, eds. *The Politics of Resource Extraction: Indigenous Peoples, Multinational Corporations, and the State*. New York: Palgrave Macmillan United Nations Research Institute for Social Development, pp. 1–8.

Sawyer, S.M. 2004. *Crude Chronicles: Indigenous Politics, Multinational Oil, and Neoliberalism in Ecuador*. Durham: Duke University Press.

Scheingold, S.A. 2004. *The Politics of Rights: Lawyers, Public Policy, and Political Change*. 2nd edition, first published 1974. Ann Arbor: University of Michigan Press.

Schrempf-Stirling, J. and F. Wettstein. 2017. Beyond Guilty Verdicts: Human Rights Litigation and its Impact on Corporations' Human Rights Policies. *Journal of Business Ethics*, 145(3), pp. 545–62.

Scott, C. 2001. Translating Torture into Transnational Tort: Conceptual Divides in the Debate on Corporate Accountability for Human Rights Harms. *In*: C. Scott, ed. *Torture as Tort: Comparative Perspectives on the Development on Transnational Human Rights Litigation*. Oxford: Hart Publishing, pp. 45–63.

Scott, J.C. 1985. *Weapons of the Weak: Everyday Forms of Peasant Resistance*. New Haven: Yale University Press.

Servindi – Servicios de Comunicación Intercultural. 2013. Comunidad de Supayacu interpone demanda para detener exploración de empresa Águila Dorada. *Servindi – Servicios de Comunicación Intercultural (online)*, 8 Nov.

Servindi – Servicios de Comunicación Intercultural. 2016. Mineras pagan 100 soles diarios a policías por reprimir protestas. *Servindi – Servicios de Comunicación Intercultural (online)*, 27 Oct.

Shamir, R. 2004. Between Self-Regulation and the Alien Tort Claims Act: On the Contested Concept of Corporate Social Responsibility. *Law & Society Review*, 38(4), pp. 635–64.

Shaw, R. 2007. Memory Frictions: Localizing the Truth and Reconciliation Commission in Sierra Leone. *International Journal of Transitional Justice*, 1(2), pp. 183–207.

Shaw, R. 2010. The Production of 'Foregiveness': God, Justice, and State Failure in Post-War Sierra Leone. *In*: K.M. Clarke and M. Goodale, eds. *Mirrors of Justice: Law and Power in the Post-Cold War Era*. New York: Cambridge University Press, pp. 208–26.

Sieder, R. 2000. 'Paz, progreso, justicia y honradez': Law and Citizenship in Alta Verapaz during the Regime of Jorge Ubico. *Bulletin of Latin American Research*, 19(3), pp. 283–302.

Sieder, R. 2010a. La antropología frente a los derechos humanos y los derechos indígenas. *In*: A. Estevez and D. Vazquez, eds. *Los derechos humanos en las ciencias sociales: Una perspectiva multidisciplinaria*. México, D.F: Flacso Mexico/UNAM/CISAN, pp. 191–219.

Sieder, R. 2010b. Legal Cultures in the (Un)Rule of Law: Indigenous Rights and Juridification in Guatemala. *In*: J. Couso, A. Huneeus, and R. Sieder, eds. *Cultures of Legality: Judicialization and Political Activism in Latin America*. Cambridge: Cambridge University Press, pp. 161–81.

Sieder, R., ed. 2017. *Exigiendo justicia y seguridad: mujeres indígenas y pluralidades legales en América Latina*. México, D.F.: CIESAS.

Sieder, R. and A. Barrera. 2017. Women and Legal Pluralism: Lessons from Indigenous Governance Systems in the Andes. *Journal of Latin American Studies*, 49(3), pp. 633–58.

Sieder, R., L. Schjolden, and A. Angell. 2005. Introduction. *In*: R. Sieder, L. Schjolden, and A. Angell, eds. *The Judicialization of Politics in Latin America*. New York: Palgrave Macmillan, pp. 1–20.

Sikkink, K. 2011. *The Justice Cascade: How Human Rights Prosecutions Are Changing World Politics*. New York: W.W. Norton & Co.

Silva Santisteban, R. 2013. Porque son perros: Protestas, discursos autoritarios e industrias extractivas. El caso Conga. *In*: R. Hoetmer, M. Castro, M. Daza, J. de Echave, and C. Ruiz, eds. *Minería y movimientos sociales en el Perú: Instrumentos y propuestas para la defensa de la vida, el agua y los territorios*. Lima: Colección Diálogos y Movimientos, pp. 435–56.

Silva Santisteban, R. 2016. Perros y antimineros: Discursos extractivistas y prácticas represivas en el Perú. *Tabula Rasa*, 24, pp. 79–104.

Silva Santisteban, R. 2017. *Mujeres y conflictos ecoterritoriales: Impactos, estrategias, resistencias*. Lima: Entrepueblos; AIETI – Asociación de Investigación y Especialización sobre Temas Iberoamericanos; Demus – Estudio para la Defensa de los Derechos de la Mujer; CMP Flora Tristán; Coordinadora Nacional de Derechos Humanos (CNDDHH).

Simons, P. and A. Macklin. 2014. *The Governance Gap: Extractive Industries, Human Rights, and the Home State Advantage*. London: Routledge.

Sisniegas Rodríguez, A. 2016. Choropampa: El precio de Conga. *Revista Pólemos*, 6(10), pp. 24–33.

Sistema de Información sobre Comunidades Campesinas del Perú (SICCAM). 2016. *Directorio de Comunidades Campesinas del Perú*. Lima: Instituto del Bien Común; Centro Peruano de Estudios Sociales (CEPES).

Skinner, G., R. McCorquodale, and O. De Schutter. 2013. *The Third Pillar: Access to Judicial Remedies for Human Rights Violations by Transnational Business*. The International Corporate Accountability Roundtable (ICAR) / CORE / The European Coalition for Corporate Justice (ECCJ).

Skinner, G.L. 2014. Beyond Kiobel: Providing Access to Judicial Remedies for Violations of International Human Rights Norms by Transnational Business in a New (Post-Kiobel) World. *Columbia Human Rights Law Review*, 46(158), pp. 158–265.

Skrabut, K. 2019. Documents, Law, and the State in the Andes. *In*: L.J. Seligmann and K.S. Fine-Dare, eds. *The Andean World*. London: Routledge, pp. 524–38.

Smulovitz, C. 2005. Petitioning and Creating Rights: Judicialization in Argentina. *In*: R. Sieder, L. Schjolden, and A. Angell, eds. *The Judicialization of Politics in Latin America*. New York: Palgrave Macmillan, pp. 161–85.

Smulovitz, C. 2006. Judicialization of Protest in Argentina: The Case of Corralito. *In*: E. Peruzzotti and C. Smulovitz, eds. *Enforcing the Rule of Law: Social Accountability in the New Latin American Democracies*. Pittsburgh: Pittsburgh University Press, pp. 55–74.

Smulovitz, C. 2010. Judicialization in Argentina: Legal Culture or Opportunities and Support Structures? *In*: J. Couso, A. Huneeus, and R. Sieder, eds. *Cultures of Legality: Judicialization and Political Activism in Latin America*. Cambridge: Cambridge University Press, pp. 234–53.

Sosa, M. and M. Zwarteveen. 2012. Exploring the Politics of Water Grabbing: The Case of Large Mining Operations in the Peruvian Andes. *Water Alternatives*, 5(2), pp. 360–75.

Special Rapporteur on the Situation of Human Rights Defenders. 2016. *Situation of Human Rights Defenders*. United Nations General Assembly, No. A/71/281.

Starn, O. 1993. Presentación. *In*: O. Starn, ed. *Hablan los ronderos: La búsqueda por la paz en los Andes*. Lima: Instituto de Estudios Peruanos, pp. 5–8.

Sullivan, L. 2014. Getting to the Bottom of Extractive Capitalism: A Case Study of Open Pit Mining in Cajamarca, Peru. *Policy & Practice: A Development Education Review*, 19, pp. 124–43.

Sulmont, D. 2011. Race, Ethnicity and Politics in Three Peruvian Localities: An Analysis of the 2005 CRISE Perceptions Survey in Peru. *Latin American and Caribbean Ethnic Studies*, 6(1), pp. 47–78.

Sydow, J. 2016. Global Concepts in Local Contexts: CSR as 'Anti-Politics Machine' in the Extractive Sector in Ghana and Peru. *In*: C.S. Dolan and D. Rajak, eds. *The Anthropology of Corporate Social Responsibility*. Oxford: Berghahn, pp. 217–42.

Szablowski, D. 2008. Regulating Corporate and Community Engagement in a Large Mining Project. *In*: L. North, V. Patroni, and T.D. Clark, eds. *Community Rights and Corporate Responsibility Canadian Mining and Oil Companies in Latin America*. Toronto: Between the Lines, pp. 37–59.

Taylor, M.B., R.C. Thompson, and A. Ramasastry. 2010. *Overcoming Obstacles to Justice: Improving Access to Judicial Remedies for Business Involvement in Grave Human Rights Abuses*. Oslo: Fafo / Amnesty International.

Tello, S. 2013. 'El conflicto Conga cuestiona seriamente el modelo de desarrollo de nuestro país'. Entrevista con Milton Sánchez Cubas. *In*: R. Hoetmer, M. Castro, M. Daza, J. de Echave, and C. Ruiz, eds. *Minería y movimientos sociales en el Perú: Instrumentos y propuestas para la defensa de la vida, el agua y los territorios*. Lima: Colección Diálogos y Movimientos, pp. 371–87.

Terre des Hommes France. 2020. Pérou : Gestion durable et pacifique des territoires. *Terre des Hommes*.

Theidon, K.S. 2013. *Intimate Enemies: Violence and Reconciliation in Peru*. Philadelphia: University of Pennsylvania Press.

Thorp, R. and M. Paredes. 2010. *Ethnicity and the Persistence of Inequality: The Case of Peru*. Basingstoke: Palgrave Macmillan.

Toledo Orozco, Z. and M. Veiga. 2018. Locals' Attitudes Toward Artisanal and Large-Scale Mining: A Case Study of Tambogrande, Peru. *The Extractive Industries and Society*, 5(2), pp. 327–34.

Torres Pachas, D. and S. Conza Salcedo. 2016. La actuación de la fiscalía distratal de Cajamarca en el caso 'Choropampa'. *Revista Pólemos*, 6(10), pp. 148–54.

Torsello, D. and B. Venard. 2016. The Anthropology of Corruption. *Journal of Management Inquiry*, 25(1), pp. 34–54.

Trubek, D.M. 1984. Where the Action Is: Critical Legal Studies and Empiricism. *Stanford Law Review*, 36(1/2), pp. 575–622.

Uceda, R. 2015. El pantanoso caso Chaupe. *La República (online)*, 24 Feb.

United Nations Human Rights Council. 2014. *Elaboration of an International Legally Binding Instrument on Transnational Corporations and Other Business Enterprises with Respect to Human Rights*. A/HRC/RES/26/9.

United Nations Working Group on Business and Human Rights. 2017. Statement at the end of visit to Peru by the United Nations Working Group on Business and Human Rights [online]. Available from: https://www.ohchr.org/EN/NewsEvents/Pages/DisplayNews.aspx?NewsID=21888&LangID=E [Accessed 23 Oct 2019].

Urteaga-Crovetto, P. 2012. The Broker State and the 'Inevitability' of Progress: The Camisea Project and Indigenous Peoples in Peru. *In*: S. Sawyer and E.T. Gomez, eds. *The Politics of Resource Extraction: Indigenous Peoples, Multinational Corporations, and the State*. New York: Palgrave Macmillan United Nations Research Institute for Social Development, pp. 103–28.

Van Cott, D.L. 2005. *From Movements to Parties in Latin America: The Evolution of Ethnic Politics*. Cambridge: University Press.

Vásquez, M. 2013. La criminalización de la protesta como estrategia de desarticulación del movimiento social en el Perú. *In*: R. Hoetmer, M. Castro, M. Daza, J. de Echave, and C. Ruiz, eds. *Minería y movimientos sociales en el Perú: Instrumentos y propuestas para la defensa de la vida, el agua y los territorios*. Lima: Colección Diálogos y Movimientos, pp. 415–34.

Vásquez, M. 2015. Las luchas ambientales y sus diversas herramientas en el Perú: el caso Conga. *In*: R. Ana, V. Glass, and D. Santini, eds. *Senderos de la justicia: Instrumentos de litigio y defensa de comunidades afectadas por la minería*. São Paulo: Fundación Rosa Luxemburgo; Justiça Global; Justiça nos Trilhos, pp. 88–94.

Vásquez, M. 2016. *El oro no brilla para todos: El impacto de las actividades de Minera Yanacocha S.R.L. sobre los derechos humanos en Cajamarca*. Cajamarca: Grufides.

Vásquez, M. 2018. Y el fiscal se fue de vacaciones. *NoticiasSer.pe (Online)*, 15 Aug.

Velazco Rondón, D.L. and R.M. Quedena Zambrano. 2015. *La criminalización de la protesta social y el caso Majaz*. Lima: Fundación Ecuménica para el Desarrollo y la Paz (Fedepaz) / Oxfam.

Wayka.pe (online). 2020. CIDH pide a Gobierno peruano responder por demanda de Máxima Acuña. *Wayka.pe*, 5 Mar.

Weber, M. 2014. *Politik als Beruf*. Nachdruck, Erstauflage 1919. Berlin: Dearbooks Verlag.

Welker, M.A. 2014. *Enacting the Corporation: An American Mining Firm in Post-authoritarian Indonesia*. Berkeley: University of California Press.

Wilson, B.M. 2005. Changing Dynamics: The Political Impact of Costa Rica's Constitutional Court. *In*: R. Sieder, L. Schjolden, and A. Angell, eds. *The Judicialization of Politics in Latin America*. New York: Palgrave Macmillan, pp. 47–65.

Wilson, R. 2001. *The Politics of Truth and Reconciliation in South Africa: Legitimizing the Post-Apartheid State*. Cambridge: Cambridge University Press.

Wirtz, M.A., ed. 2014. Bumerang-Effekt. *In*: *Dorsch – Lexikon der Psychologie*. Bern: Hogrefe Verlag, p. 312.

Working Group on the Issue of Human Rights and Transnational Corporations and Other Business Enterprises. 2018. *Report of the Working Group on the Issue of Human Rights and Transnational Corporations and Other Business Enterprises on its Mission to Peru: Advanced Edited Version*. United Nations Human Rights Council (UNHRC), No. A/HRC/38/48/Add.2.

Yashar, D.J. 2005. *Contesting Citizenship in Latin America: The Rise of Indigenous Movements and the Postliberal Challenge*. Cambridge: Cambridge University Press.

Youngers, C.A. 2000. Human Rights and Politics in Peru Today. Presented at the XXII International Congress of the Latin American Studies Association, Miami.

Youngers, C.A. 2003. *Violencia política y sociedad civil en el Perú*. Lima: Instituto de Estudios Peruanos.

Youngers, C.A. 2006. Promoting Human Rights: NGOs and the State in Peru. *In*: J. Crabtree, ed. *Making Institutions Work in Peru*. London: Institute for the Study of the Americas, pp. 158–84.

Youngers, C.A. 2007. En busca de la verdad y la justicia: La Coordinadora Nacional de Derechos Humanos del Perú. *In*: A. Pérotin-Dumon, ed. *Historizar el pasado vivo en América Latina*. Santiago de Chile: Centro de Ética, Universidad Alberto Hurtado, pp. 1–49.

Youngers, C.A. and S.C. Peacock. 2002. *Peru's Coordinadora Nacional de Derechos Humanos: A Case Study of Coalition Building*. Washington D.C.: Washington Office on Latin America (WOLA).

Zerk, J.A. 2006. *Multinationals and Corporate Social Responsibility: Limitations and Opportunities in International Law*. Cambridge: Cambridge University Press.

Zerk, J.A. 2014. *Corporate Liability for Gross Human Rights Abuses: Towards a Fairer and More Effective System of Domestic Law Remedies*. UNHCHR.

U.S. court documents

U.S. Court of Appeals for the Third Circuit. 2019. Opinion. Case 18–2042, Document 003113189403.

U.S. Court of Appeals for the Third Circuit. 2020. Not precedential opinion. Case 20–1765, Document 47.

U.S. District Court for the District of Colorado. 2014a. Application of Elmer Eduardo Campos-Álvarez for Discovery Pursuant to 28 U.S.C. § 1782. Case 1:14-cv-00208-REB, Document 1.

U.S. District Court for the District of Colorado. 2014b. Declaration of María del Mar Pérez Aguilera. Case 1:14-cv-00208-REB, Document 1–2.

U.S. District Court for the District of Colorado. 2014c. Motion for Leave to Serve Limited Discovery and Request for Scheduling Conference. Case 1:14-cv-00208-REB, Document 13.

U.S. District Court for the District of Colorado. 2014d. Respondents' Response to Applicant's Application for Order to Show Case. Case 1:14-cv-00208-REB, Document 18.

U.S. District Court for the District of Colorado. 2014e. Respondents' Reply in Support of Their Motion for Leave to Serve Limited Discovery and for Scheduling Conference. Case 1:14-cv-00208-REB, Document 17.

U.S. District Court for the District of Colorado. 2014f. Applicant's Reply in Support of Applications for an Order to Show Cause and for Discovery Pursuant to 28 U.S.C. § 1782. Case 1:14-cv-00208-REB, Document 20.

U.S. District Court for the District of Colorado. 2014g. Opposition of Elmer Eduardo Campos-Álvarez to Respondents' Motion to Conduct Discovery. Case 1:14-cv-00208-REB, Document 16.

U.S. District Court for the District of Colorado. 2014h. Motion to Expedite Consideration of Elmer Eduardo Campos-Álvarez's Application for Discovery Pursuant to 28 U.S.C. § 1782. Case 1:14-cv-00208-REB, Document 21.

U.S. District Court for the District of Colorado. 2015a. Order Concerning Application for Discovery under 28 U.S.C. § 1782. Case 1:14-cv-00208-REB, Document 22.

U.S. District Court for the District of Colorado. 2015b. Respondents' Motion for Protective Order. Case 1:14-cv-00208-REB, Document 29.

U.S. District Court for the District of Colorado. 2016a. Protective Order. Case 1:14-cv-00208-REB, Document 40.

U.S. District Court for the District of Colorado. 2016b. Order Concerning Application for Discovery under 28 U.S.C. § 1782. Case 1:14-cv-00208-REB, Document 41.

U.S. District Court for the District of Colorado. 2017. Emergency Motion of Applicant Elmer Eduardo Campos-Álvarez for an Order Requiring Respondents to Certify the Authenticity of the Documents They Produced. Case 1:14-cv-00208-REB, Document 43.

U.S. District Court for the District of Colorado. 2018. Order Concerning Certification of Authenticity. Case 1:14-cv-00208-REB, Document 49.

U.S. District Court for the District of Delaware. 2017. Complaint for Damages and Equitable Relief, Case 1:17-cv-01315-GAM, Document 1.

U.S. District Court for the District of Delaware. 2018a. Order, Case 1:17-cv-01315-GAM, Document 93.

U.S. District Court for the District of Delaware. 2018b. Memorandum, Case 1:17-cv-01315-GAM, Document 92.

U.S. District Court for the District of Delaware. 2020a. Memorandum Opinion, Case 1:17-cv-01315-GAM, Document 127.

U.S. District Court for the District of Delaware. 2020b. Notice of Appeal to U.S. Court of Appeals, Third Circuit. Case 1:17-cv-01315-GAM, Document 129.